More Hoosier Cooking

*M*ore

Hoosier

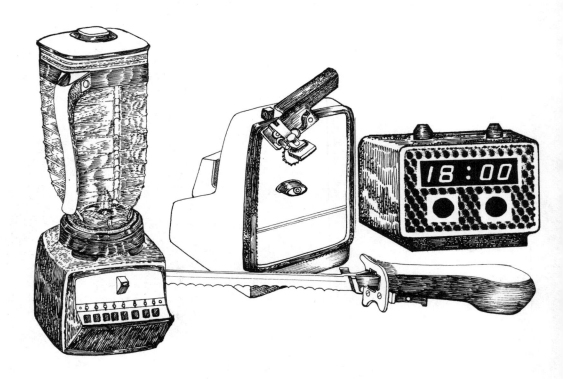

Illustrated by Rudy Pozzatti

Cooking

Edited by
Elaine Lumbra

Indiana University Press

Bloomington and Indianapolis

First Paperback Edition 1994

Copyright © 1982 by Indiana University Press

Manufactured in the United States of America

Library of Congress Cataloging in Publication Data
Main entry under title:
More Hoosier cooking.
Includes index
1. Cookery, American—Indiana.   I. Lumbra, Elaine.
TX715.M8295 1982   641.59772   82-47959
ISBN 0-253-15430-8   AACR2
ISBN 0-253-20917-X (pbk.)

2 3 4 5 6 99 98 97 96 95 94

Contents

Preface

Today's busy, time and energy conscious homemakers are creating a demand for more convenience foods and more labor-saving kitchen equipment. Many recipes included in this book illustrate how technological progress continually alters the methods required for food preparation. Current food trends also show great concern for improved nutrition and a more healthful lifestyle. Food additives, nutrition labeling, protein substitutes, whole-grain foods, and weight control are important issues.

Food habits, however, change slowly. Many traditional recipes are included for those among us who feel more comfortable with the tried and true. In spite of all our technological advances, the secret ingredient in most successful cooking is still Love. New cooks are well advised to relax, to be willing to make mistakes, and to make food preparation a creative, joyful experience.

The several thousand Indiana Extension Homemakers who offered to share their current favorite recipes for *More Hoosier Cooking* give ample evidence of the basic generosity and willingness to help others that is a tradition in Hoosier kitchens. It is sincerely regretted that it was not possible to print all recipes submitted.

Extension Homemakers and their friends represent the very "grass roots" of Hoosier cooking. Recipes printed in the pages that follow bear the endorsement of the homemaker submitting the recipe. Read the recipes shared, adapt them according to your own needs, and most of all Enjoy.

Bloomington, Indiana   ELAINE LUMBRA

Food Processors and Blenders

The food processor makes extraordinary cooking possible for us all; it chops, slices, dices, grinds (either raw or cooked meats), and grates. With the processor you can make your own mayonnaise in a minute. It's great for making a foolproof pie crust, and many models even mix and knead bread. Most processors will not grind coffee beans or grains. It won't beat egg whites or whip cream but it does a great job at mincing herbs.

Many of the most dedicated food processor cooks do not have special processor recipes for sharing. They simply admit to using their processor constantly; chopping, shredding, and slicing ingredients for casseroles, mincing onions, garlic, and green peppers for dips, grinding meats for Chinese egg rolls, chopping accompaniments for curries, etc.

Leave your processor out and in a position to be easily used. The biggest problem for the novice will be over-processing. Use a quick on/off method of processing, and practice until preparing foods with the processor becomes second nature to you.

Plan counter space for your blender too. It is still your best appliance choice if you have large amounts of food to puree. Blenders also do a top-notch job at blending drink mixtures and thin batters.

Appetizers, Beverages, and Soups

COTTAGE CHEESE DIP

1 C. small-curd
cottage cheese
1 C. mayonnaise
1 small onion,
grated

1 T. Worcester-
shire sauce
1 t. garlic salt
1 t. celery seed

Blend all ingredients in blender until smooth.

Jean LaRowe
DeKalb County

HUNGARIAN CHEESE DIP

8 oz. pkg. cream
cheese
1 stick salted
butter
3 T. sour cream
1 medium onion
1 t. anchovy
paste

1 T. prepared
mustard
1 T. paprika
1 t. caraway seed
½ t. salt
1 T. capers
(optional)

Mince onion first in food processor. Add all other ingredients, except capers, and process until well-blended. Stir in capers. Serve on crackers or small slices of heavy rye bread.

Jean Sinor
Monroe County

FRESH VEGETABLE DIP

8 oz. pkg. cream
cheese
½ C. mayonnaise
2 T. chopped
onion
1 t. parsley flakes

¼ t. garlic salt
1 T. horseradish
sauce
pinch of Italian
seasoning or
oregano

Mix all ingredients in blender thoroughly and refrigerate overnight.

Anne Harris
Madison County

MOCK SOUR CREAM

1 C. low-fat
creamed cot-
tage cheese

¼ C. buttermilk

Blend both ingredients in blender at high speed, scraping down sides often, until mixture is smooth and creamy. Use on fresh fruits and baked potatoes, or in any recipe that doesn't call for baking.

Variations:

Pimiento Dip: 1 T. chili sauce, 1 T. chopped pimiento, and ¼ t. salt.

12 calories per T.

Garlic Dip: ¹⁄₁₆ t. garlic powder, 1 t. salt, and 1 T. dried parsley flakes.

11 calories per T.

Onion Dip: 1 T. dry onion flakes and 1 envelope or 1 t. instant beef broth.

12 calories per T.

Roquefort Dip: 2 T. crumbled Roquefort cheese, ½ t. salt, and ½ t. Worcestershire sauce.

15 calories per T.

Nancy Sinders
Clay County

SPINACH NUGGETS

2 10-oz. pkg. fro-
zen spinach,
cooked and
drained
4 oz. Parmesan
cheese, cut in
½" pieces

6 eggs
¾ C. butter,
softened
2 C. packaged
stuffing mix
salt and pepper

Insert steel blade in food processor. Process cheese until finely grated; set aside. Insert plastic blade. Pour in eggs and mix well. Add butter, cheese, and spinach and process to combine. Sprinkle stuffing mix over mixture and process, turning on/off, until crumbs disappear. Season with salt and pepper. Roll into walnut-sized balls. Freeze. Bake frozen on a cookie sheet for 10 min. at 350°.

Eloise Gerig
Allen County

FRUIT DRINK

2 C. frozen strawberries	2–3 C. reconstituted frozen orange juice
1 banana	

Blend fruits and juice until smooth in blender. Serves 4. Other fruits may be used if desired.

Know Your Neighbor E.H. Club
Decatur County

TROPICAL FRUIT PUNCH

5 bananas, pureed in blender	2 t. lemon juice
1 12-oz. can frozen orange juice concentrate	½–2 C. sugar, dissolved in 3 C. water (boil together 3 min.)
1 45-oz. can pineapple juice	4 C. ginger ale
	4 C. lemon soda

Combine all ingredients except ginger ale and lemon soda in large punch bowl and chill. Add carbonated beverages just before serving.

Mary Slipher
Hendricks County

Variation: Combine all ingredients except carbonated beverage; cover and freeze. Remove from freezer 1–2 hr. before serving. Just before serving, spoon partially thawed mixture into punch bowl; gently stir in 2–4 qt. ginger ale (no lemon soda).

Terry Ramsey
Hancock County

PEACH DELIGHT PUNCH

5 fresh peaches, blended in blender	1 6-oz. can frozen orange juice concentrate
4 C. pineapple juice	1 C. hot water
	6 C. water
1 3-oz. pkg. peach gelatin	1 C. sugar
	1 qt. 7-Up

Dissolve gelatin in hot water. Stir together all ingredients except 7-Up; chill. Add 7-Up just before serving.

Mildred Schermerhorn
Noble County

FRESH FRUIT SPARKLE

Into a blender jar, squeeze the juice from 2 oranges, 1 grapefruit, and ½ lemon. Add 1 C. cracked ice and ¼ C. sugar. Blend on medium speed until well-blended. Fill glass ¾ full with blended fruit mixture. Fill glass the rest of the way with your favorite lemon-lime carbonated beverage. Stir to mix and serve. Makes 2 12-oz. glasses.

Joe Huse
Boone County

STRAWBERRY ROMANOFF SWIZZLE

2 C. frozen whole unsweetened strawberries, partially thawed	1 12-oz. can low-calorie lemon-lime carbonated beverage, chilled
2 12-oz. cans low-calorie strawberry carbonated beverage, chilled	2 C. orange juice

In blender, puree orange juice and berries. Pour into a large pitcher. Pour carbonated beverages down side of pitcher. Stir gently. Serve over ice in tall glasses.

Note: For individuals not on a diet, use carbonated beverages with sugar.

Sonja Widmer
Hancock County

MILK SHAKE

1 C. frozen cantaloupe or 1 C. frozen unsweetened strawberries or ½ C. frozen unsweetened pineapple or any unsweetened frozen fruit of your choice

⅓ C. nonfat dry milk
⅔ C. water
Artificial sweetener to taste (I use 2 pkg.)
1 t. vanilla extract or flavor of your choice

Combine all ingredients in blender. Blend until thick. Serve in glass, with a straw. Serves 1.

Audrey Gehlbach
Harrison County

PEANUT BUTTER SHAKE

½ C. cold milk
2 T. nonfat milk
1 T. peanut butter

1 medium banana or ½ C. peaches or ½ C. apricots

Combine all ingredients in blender. Blend 30–60 sec., or until smooth. Serve in tall glass.

Mrs. Joe Martens
LaGrange County

STRAWBERRY DAIQUIRI

1 6-oz. can frozen lemonade
1 6-oz. can light rum

1 pint of strawberries
Ice cubes (4-6)

Put all ingredients, except ice, into blender, cover, and blend. Remove cover and add ice; continue to process until ice is liquefied, or slushy. Pour into cocktail glasses.

Sybil E. Tjardes
Monroe County

HOOSIER SOUR

1 small can frozen limeade (or lemonade)

1 empty limeade can of bourbon
1 beer (12 oz.)

Put frozen limeade in blender; add bourbon. Whip until blended. Add beer and stir by hand.

Georgia Spilly
Monroe County

WHISKEY SOUR

1 12-oz. can frozen orange juice
1 12-oz. can frozen lemonade

2 12-oz. cans water
1 12-oz. can whiskey

Blend all ingredients in blender. Serve over crushed ice. Garnish with orange slice or cherry. Makes 15 5-oz. servings.

Linda Hess
Perry County

BETTY'S V 6 JUICE

½ bushel tomatoes, washed
1 lb. carrots
3 medium onions
5 stalks celery

2 large green peppers
1 medium head cabbage
salt to taste

Cook all vegetables together until tender. Add salt. Put 2–3 C. of mixture at a time into blender or food processor and blend/process until liquefied. Pour into hot pint jars. Place in pressure cooker and process at 10 lbs. pressure for 35 min.

Betty Ratliff
Hendricks County

CREAM OF BROCCOLI SOUP

1 bunch of fresh broccoli (about 1½ lb.)	2 13¾-oz. cans chicken broth
½ C. chopped onion	½ t. salt dash cayenne pepper
2 T. butter or margarine	1 C. light cream
1 potato, pared and diced (1 C.)	⅛ t. nutmeg

Cook broccoli in boiling salted water 5 min.; drain well. Sauté onion in melted butter in saucepan until soft but not brown (5 min.); add potato, chicken broth, salt, and cayenne. Heat mixture to boiling; lower heat and simmer 15 min. Add broccoli, reserving a few flowerettes for garnish; simmer 5 min. longer, or until vegetables are tender. Pour mixture half at a time into container of electric blender; cover and blend until smooth. Return mixture to saucepan; add cream and nutmeg. Heat to boiling (if soup is too thick, add more cream or milk). Taste and add more salt if needed. Garnish with flowerettes. Serves 6.

Can be frozen. Add cream when thawed.

Winifred Nilson
LaPorte County

CREAM OF LETTUCE SOUP

1 large head iceberg lettuce	1 C. evaporated milk or light cream
4 C. chicken broth	salt to taste
¼ C. butter	⅛ t. nutmeg

Wash and chop lettuce; combine with broth. Place in covered saucepan; simmer 15 min. Process in blender or food processor until grainy, but not pureed. Return mixture to pan; add butter and milk. Heat to a simmer; add nutmeg. Serve with a dollop of sour cream, if desired. Serves 6.

Nancy Hardy
Monroe County

GAZPACHO

4 C. tomato juice	1 garlic bud, minced
1 small green pepper, minced	¾ t. seasoned salt
½ large cucumber, minced	¼ t. ground pepper
½ onion, minced	1 large tomato, finely diced
2 canned green chilies (veins removed), chopped (optional)	2 T. chopped green onion tops
1½ t. Worcestershire sauce	2 lemons, cut in wedges

Put 2 C. tomato juice and all other ingredients, except diced tomato, green onion tops, and lemon wedges into a blender; blend well. Slowly add the remaining tomato juice to the blender. Pour the mixture into a large bowl and add diced tomato. Garnish with chopped onion. Serve cold with lemon wedges.

Mary Bryant
Harrison County

Salads and Salad Dressings

OVERNIGHT CABBAGE SLAW

½ medium cabbage, cut in wedges	1 small sweet or red onion, halved	½ medium green pepper	⅔ C. vinegar
		2 carrots, peeled	⅓ C. vegetable oil

¼ C. sugar   ¼ t. pepper
1 t. salt

Put slicing disc in food processor; slice cabbage, onion, and pepper; remove to separate bowl. Position shredding disc; shred carrots. Add to cabbage mixture. Position mixing blade in bowl. Add vinegar, oil, sugar, salt, and pepper. Process until well-mixed, about 10 sec. Pour vinegar mixture over vegetables; stir to combine. Cover; refrigerate at least 8 hr. before serving. At serving time stir; drain. Serves 6.

Janice Sebasty
St. Joseph County

CREAMY PINEAPPLE SALAD

1 20-oz can   ½ t. salt
   crushed pineap-   1 C. unsweetened
   ple, drained   pineapple juice
½ C. pineapple   1 C. orange juice
   juice (add water   rind of ½ lemon
   if necessary)   3 T. lemon juice
2 envelopes un-   1 8-oz. pkg.
   flavored gelatin   cream cheese,
½ C. sugar   cubed

Heat ½ C. pineapple juice to boiling. Put juice and gelatin into blender. Cover and run on low until gelatin is dissolved. Add remaining ingredients, except pineapple, and blend until smooth. Pour into a 9x13″ pan and chill for 30 min., or until consistency of unbeaten eggs. Stir in pineapple and pour into a 2 qt. mold. Chill until set.

Loretta Johnson
Benton County

FROZEN SALAD OR DESSERT

1 large or 2 small   1 8-oz. bottle
   cans frozen or-   7-Up
   ange juice   1 C. sugar
   concentrate   3 small bananas

2 20-oz. cans   ple with juice
   crushed pineap-

Pour all ingredients in the blender and blend until liquefied. Pour into 9x13″ dish. Garnish by sticking in strawberries or mint. When frozen and ready to serve, cut into cubes and serve in sherbet dishes. Serves 8.

Nancy Hannum
Hancock County

BLUE CHEESE DRESSING

1 C. low-fat cot-   1 T. lemon juice
   tage cheese   1 oz. crumbled
3 T. skim milk   blue cheese

Place cottage cheese, milk, and lemon juice in blender; blend at medium speed until smooth. Fold in blue cheese. Refrigerate in covered jar.

Ruthella Creek
Wells County

BLENDER HOLLANDAISE SAUCE

3 egg yolks   dash cayenne
2 T. lemon juice   ¼ C. melted but-
¼ t. salt   ter or margarine

In blender container, combine egg yolks, lemon juice, salt, and cayenne. Cover, turn motor on and off; remove cover. Turn motor to high speed; gradually add butter in steady stream. Turn off motor. Serve immediately. Makes 1 C.

Sheila Whitehead
Clay County

PROCESSOR MAYONNAISE

1 egg   ½ t. dry mustard
⅓ C. vegetable   ½ t. salt
   oil   ⅔ C. vegetable
2 T. vinegar   oil
1 t. sugar

Position knife blade in dry bowl of food

processor. Recipe will not work if bowl is not dry. Add all ingredients, except ⅔ C. vegetable oil. Process 5 sec.; add remaining vegetable oil in a steady stream through food chute while processor is running. After all oil is added, process only until mixture is thick and smooth, about 10 sec.

THOUSAND ISLAND DRESSING

1 recipe Processor Mayonnaise	1 hard cooked egg, quartered
¼ C. chili sauce	¼ green pepper, cut in thirds
1 medium sweet or dill pickle, quartered	1 t. instant minced onion
¼ t. paprika	

Position knife blade in processor bowl. Prepare mayonnaise as directed; add remaining ingredients and process until finely chopped but not smooth, about 15 sec. Stop to scrape down sides of bowl once while processing.

GREEN GODDESS DRESSING

1 recipe Processor Mayonnaise	½ C. dairy sour cream

1 t. dry parsley flakes	1 T. lemon juice
1 t. instant minced onion	Dash pepper
⅛ t. garlic powder	3 drops green food coloring, optional

Position knife blade in the dry processor bowl. Prepare mayonnaise as directed; add remaining ingredients and process until finely chopped, but not smooth, about 10 sec.

Marilyn Baker
Lawrence County

SALAD OIL DRESSING

2 C. vegetable oil	1 t. celery seed
1–2 small onions, cut up	⅔ C. cider vinegar
¼–1 C. sugar	1 t. salt
2 t. dry mustard	

Put ingredients into blender container in the order given, mixing on high speed after each addition. Refrigerate.

Linda Love
Hancock County

Main Dishes & Miscellaneous

CHEESY BEEF BURROS

½ lb. lean ground beef	1 4-oz. can green chili peppers, rinsed and seeded
3 oz. Neufchâtel cheese	
¼ C. finely chopped onion	1 t. sugar (optional)
¼ t. salt	1 t. coriander, crushed
5 7" flour or corn tortillas	½ t. salt
1 16-oz. can tomatoes	3 C. shredded lettuce
1 t. cornstarch	½ C. plain yogurt

Brown beef; drain. Combine beef with cheese, onion, and salt. Spoon onto tortillas; roll up. Place seam side down in a 12x7¼x2" baking dish. Cover with foil, bake at 350° for 30 min. Combine tomatoes, chili peppers, sugar, corn starch, coriander, and salt in blender or food processor. Cover. Process until smooth. Heat mixture to boiling, stirring occasionally. Reduce heat; simmer 2 min. To serve: divide lettuce on five plates, top with hot beef mixture. Spoon on tomato sauce and top with yogurt. Serves 5.

Shirley J. Campbell
Brown County

CREAMED CHICKEN ON TOAST

10 oz. pkg. fro-
  zen cauliflower
½ C. celery,
  minced
1 t. onion flakes
1 C. water
1 chicken bouil-
  lon cube

6 oz. cooked
  chicken, diced
2 T. red or green
  peppers,
  chopped
2 T. green onion
  tops
2½ T. dry milk
  powder

Cook cauliflower, celery, onion flakes, and chicken bouillon cube in water until soft. Puree entire contents of pan in blender; return to saucepan. Add remaining ingredients, stirring milk powder in last. Heat and serve on toast. Serves 2.

Mary Ann Schoenemann
Huntington County

TURKEY AND DRESSING CASSEROLE

1¼ lb. loaf white
  bread
1 medium onion
2 stalks celery
2 eggs
1 t. poultry
  seasoning
½ t. sage

1 t. salt
¼ t. pepper
1 T. parsley flakes
3 chicken bouil-
  lon cubes
1 C. water
3 C. turkey pieces
  or cubes

In blender, make crumbs out of bread; set crumbs aside. Chop onion and celery in blender; add to bread crumbs. Dissolve bouillon cubes in hot water in saucepan; pour into blender, and add eggs and seasonings. Mix until well blended; mix with crumbs. Dice leftover turkey and stir into bread crumb mixture. If mixture is too dry, add more water; pour into a greased 9x13" pan. Cover pan and bake at 375° for about 1 hr. Serve with poultry gravy. Freezes well.

JoAnn Folke
Dearborn County

EGG ROLLS

medium head
  cabbage
2 onions
4 oz. can water
  chestnuts,
  drained
8 oz. can mush-
  rooms, drained
1 lb. hamburger

14 oz. can bean
  sprouts, drained
egg roll wrappers
2 T. peanut
  butter
soy sauce
½ t. garlic salt,
  optional
vegetable oil

Chop cabbage, onions, chestnuts, and mushrooms in food processor; set aside. Brown hamburger with ¼ cup of soy sauce. Drain hamburger and add chopped vegetables. Add 2 T. oil, garlic salt, and ½ C. soy sauce to mixture. Add sprouts. Stir mixture over medium heat until cabbage is soft. Drain off most of juice. Add peanut butter and mix well. On each egg roll wrapper put 2 heaping tablespoonfuls of mixture and roll according to egg roll pkg. instructions. Fry in 2" of hot oil until golden brown. Drain on several layers of paper toweling. Serve with Chinese style mustard and sweet-sour sauce. Makes approx. 20 egg rolls.

Caroline Cutshall
Monroe County

BASIC SWEET-AND-SOUR SAUCE

2 T. cornstarch
⅓ C. Japanese
  vinegar
1 t. thick soy
  (optional)

¾ C. sugar
1 t. sherry
⅓ C. water
2 T. soy sauce
  (optional)

Mix all ingredients in saucepan. Bring to a boil stirring constantly. Cool.

HOT MUSTARD SAUCE

enough sherry to
  make a smooth
  paste

¼ C. dry mustard

Note: Use both, or either sauce, as a dip for wontons, egg rolls, tempura, etc.

Edna Marshall
Madison County

RUSSIAN VEGETABLE PIE

Pastry:

1¼ C. flour	1 onion, chopped
1 t. sugar	at least ⅛ t. each:
1 t. salt	basil, marjoram
4 oz. softened	tarragon,
cream cheese	crushed
1 T. butter	salt and pepper to
Filling:	taste
1 small head cab-	3 T. butter
bage (about 3	4 oz. softened
C.), shredded	cream cheese
½ lb. mush-	4–5 hard-cooked
rooms, sliced	eggs
	dill weed

Make a pastry by sifting together the dry ingredients, cutting in the butter and working it together with the cream cheese (in a food processor, using a steel blade, process until it forms a ball). Roll out ⅔ of pastry and line a 9″ pie plate or casserole. Roll out remaining pastry, making a circle large enough to cover the dish. Chill while assembling filling. Shred cabbage, slice mushrooms, and chop onion, using food processor. Melt 2 T. butter, sauté onion and cabbage 3–4 min., stirring constantly. Add marjoram, tarragon, and basil and some salt and fresh-ground pepper. Continue to cook until cabbage is wilted and onion is soft. Either push mixture aside or remove from pan; add last T. butter and sauté mushrooms 5–6 min., stirring constantly. Spread the softened cream cheese in bottom of pie shell. Slice the eggs and arrange in a layer over the cheese. Sprinkle with a little chopped dill; cover with cabbage-onion mixture. Make final layer of sautéed mush-

rooms and cover with circle of pastry. Seal and flute. Slash top. Bake at 400° for 15 min., then at 350° for 20–25 min. Serve hot or cold.

Eleanor Arnold
Rush County

BLENDER BRANCAKES

2 eggs	2 C. Bran Chex
1½ C. milk	cereal
2 T. vegetable oil	1 C. pancake mix

Process eggs, milk, oil, and cereal in blender to mix; add pancake mix. Process to combine (do not overmix). Scrape sides of container if necessary. Let stand 5 min. Stir. Bake on hot (400°), lightly greased griddle, using a scant ¼ C. batter for each pancake. Cook until edges are set. Turn. Cook until browned. Makes 15 pancakes.

Joe Huse
Boone County

CRANBERRY BLENDER RELISH

1 envelope unfla-	1 medium apple,
vored gelatin	cored and cut
1 C. cold water	in eighths
2 C. fresh or fro-	¾ C. sugar
zen cranberries	¼ C. chopped
1 naval orange,	walnuts or
seeded and cut	pecans
in eighths	

Soften gelatin in cold water in saucepan for 5 min.; heat over low heat until gelatin is dissolved. Place cranberries and gelatin mixture in blender jar; cover and blend until smooth. Add orange, apple, and sugar; cover and blend until orange is finely chopped. Fold in nuts. Pour into bowl; cover and refrigerate. Garnish with orange slices.

Maxine Brechbill
DeKalb County

Desserts

PIE CRUST

1½ C. flour	½ t. salt
1 stick margarine	4–5 T. cold water

Sift flour and salt into food processor. Process at medium speed 3 sec. to mix. Cut margarine in ½″ chunks and place in processor. Process at medium high speed until consistency of coarse corn meal, 5–8 sec. Measure water and pour through chute while processor runs on medium to high until dough balls up. Roll out on floured pastry board. Makes a 2-crust pie.

Dorothy Beck
Greene County

BLENDER CUSTARD PIE

4 eggs	½ C. biscuit mix
2 C. milk	1 t. vanilla
½ C. sugar	dash of salt
3 T. margarine	

Put all ingredients in blender container and mix for 30 sec. to 1 min. Pour into 9″ or 10″ buttered pie pan. Sprinkle with cinnamon, nutmeg, or coconut. Bake at 350° for 40–45 min.

Patricia Ann Wilkinson
LaGrange County

PECAN TARTLETS

Crust:	2 medium eggs
¼ lb. butter	1½ C. dark
3 oz. cream	brown sugar
cheese	2 T. butter,
1 C. flour	melted
Filling:	¼ t. vanilla
½ C. pecans	

Combine crust ingredients in work bowl of food processor. Blend with steel processing blade until a ball forms. Divide dough into 24 small balls; press into 2″ tart tins. Chop

pecans in processor with steel blade; remove from work bowl and set aside. Combine remaining filling ingredients in bowl and blend until smooth; mix in pecans. Spoon mixture into prepared shells. Bake at 350° for 30 min.

Charlotte Zietlow
Monroe County

PINEAPPLE CHEESECAKE

graham cracker	1 envelope plain
pie shell	gelatin
1 C. unsweetened	8 oz. cream
crushed pineap-	cheese, cubed
ple, drained,	1 C. vanilla
juice reserved	yogurt
2 T. water	cinnamon

Spread pineapple into pie shell. Put 2 T. water in blender; sprinkle gelatin over water to soften. Add sufficient water to pineapple juice to make 1 C.; heat to boiling. Add boiling juice mixture to gelatin; cover and blend on high speed until gelatin is completely dissolved. Add cream cheese to blender; cover and blend smooth. Add yogurt; cover and blend smooth. Spoon into pie shell and sprinkle with cinnamon. Refrigerate. Serves 8.

Ellen Hummel
Marshall County

ORANGE-PINEAPPLE ICE CREAM

1 small can fro-	2 qt. milk
zen concentrate	(approximately)
orange juice,	6 whole eggs
thawed	1 large can evap-
1 15¼-oz. can	orated milk
crushed pineap-	2½ C. sugar
ple, drained	

Put pineapple and orange juice into blender

and blend to mix; set aside. Beat eggs with electric mixer until thick and creamy; gradually add sugar and evaporated milk while beating at medium speed. Slowly mix in pineapple mixture; add 1 qt. milk. Pour into freezer can and add milk to within 3" of top of freezer can. Freeze in electric freezer following directions. Serves 12–14.

Mrs. Marvin McNeely
Scott County

BANANA SMOOTHIES

Layer whole very ripe bananas in a large freezer container. Sprinkle a small amount of lemon juice on each layer to retard browning; freeze. Remove one frozen banana for each serving desired; place in food processor with steel mixing blade. Add a small amount of fluid milk and a small amount of powdered milk; process until smooth.

Note: This is an excellent way to make use of the very ripe bananas one often finds on sale.

Judy Lannan
Monroe County

CHOCOLATE REFRIGERATOR DESSERT

½ C. hot milk
2 C. miniature
  marshmallows
4 1-oz. chocolate
  almond candy
  bars
22 graham
  crackers
2 T. confection-
  ers' sugar
6 T. butter,
  melted
1 C. whipping
  cream,
  whipped

Put milk, marshmallows, and candy bars (each bar broken into 4 pieces) into container of blender; cover and run on high until smooth. Pour into a bowl and refrigerate while preparing crumbs and whipped cream. Break 4 graham crackers into blender container; cover and run on low until finely crumbed. Empty crumbs into a bowl. Repeat process. Mix confectioners' sugar and crumbs; stir in melted butter. Pat ⅔ of crumb mixture into an 8x8x2" pan. Fold whipped cream into chilled chocolate mixture; pour into crumb-lined pan. Sprinkle remaining crumbs over top. Chill 4 hr.

Carla Hoffman
Martin County

Microwave Ovens

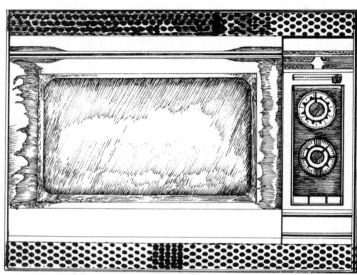

With your microwave oven you can produce in minutes what traditionally would have taken hours; microwaving is the speediest cooking method yet developed. You actually can cook a cut-up chicken in 15 minutes. Microwaved foods may be more nutritious for two reasons: the speed of the cooking process means fewer nutrients are "cooked away," and because little or no water is added there is less chance of "boiling the food value out."

Microwave cooking does require learning new food preparation and cooking methods. While your oven will defrost foods quickly, is great for "warm-ups," and will heat your water for instant coffee, it will also cook a whole meal with a minimum of time and energy. Since cooking time will vary depending on your oven, watch food closely when first trying a recipe. When in doubt, undercook and check the product. Add small amounts of cooking time until food is done to your taste.

Microwave ovens are available with a multitude of features: from variable power settings to browning dishes to computer-type controls. Choose an oven with the features that best fit your family's needs.

Microwave energy is safe. It is a form of non-ionizing energy like radio waves and infrared light. All microwave appliances are designed and manufactured according to strict government and industry standards. All ovens have a series of locks and switches designed to make them operate safely and properly. Read and follow the directions that come with your oven.

Microwave Cookings Hints and Helps

- Yeast dough recipes require special formulation for baking in the microwave oven.
- In making yeast dough products, much time can be saved by allowing the dough to double in bulk (or rise) in your microwave. To do this, place dough in well-greased microproof bowl; turn to coat dough with fat. Set bowl in shallow dish of hot water; cover loosely with waxed paper. Microwave at 50%, 30%, or 10% power for 1 min. and let stand 15 min. Rotate dish of water one-quarter turn. Use the lower setting if your oven has an uneven pattern. Turn dough over in bowl if surface appears to be drying. Repeat microwaving, standing, and rotating cycle until dough is light and doubled in size. Punch down dough and shape as directed in your recipe.
- Quick breads rise higher and bake much faster in a microwave oven than they do in conventional ovens. Muffins are microwaved on HIGH. Dense heavy batters like banana bread are microwaved on MEDIUM so they can rise slowly and not overcook on the edges before the center is done; change the power level to HIGH for the last few minutes of cooking time.
- If a sugar substitute is used, the lack of sugar in the recipe increases the microwave cooking time 1–2 minutes.
- Spray cake pans with spray-on vegetable shortening; line bottom of dish with waxed paper. Respray dish and waxed paper; cake will drop out and paper will peel off easily.
- Microwaving simplifies candy making. Chocolate melts smoothly in the microwave oven without danger of scorching. Remember you cannot use a conventional candy thermometer while microwaving.
- To test custards, use a metal knife, not a plastic one. The plastic will not come out clean and you could overcook your custard.
- When cooking puddings, stir the pudding mixture about two-thirds of the way through the total cooking time. If stirred at this time, the pudding will be smooth and creamy.
- Soups can be microwaved on HIGH. When you dilute soups with milk, microwave on MEDIUM to prevent overboiling.
- A microwave oven is great for making white sauces. It practically eliminates the danger of scorching and requires much less stirring than "top of the stove cooking."
- For grilled chicken, precook on HIGH for 6 minutes per pound of chicken; grill until brown, about 12–15 minutes.
- Many people honestly prefer their fish microwaved. Be careful not to overcook fish or seafood. Fish is done as soon as it flakes and loses its translucent appearance.
- Bacon from the refrigerator can be separated quickly by cooking it in the microwave oven for about 15 seconds, or until edges just begin to separate.
- To soften tortillas, microwave on HIGH 4 at a time between moist paper towels for 10–20 seconds.
- To dry herbs in the microwave oven, place up to ½ cup of leaves between paper towels and heat for about 2 minutes, or until dry and crumbly. Exact time will depend on the herb.
- Read oven direction booklet before using aluminum foil. Use aluminum foil shiny side out or shiny side in—it makes no difference.

DRYING FLOWERS IN THE MICROWAVE OVEN

fresh flowers

scissors or garden clippers

silica gel (buy at craft or florist shop)

florist wire and tape

toothpick or knitting needle

soft paint brush

clear plastic spray (optional)

shoe box or glass container

Best flower choices for drying: zinnias, asters, pansies, daisies, carnations, roses, marigolds, and daffodils. Magnolias, geraniums, gladiola, and iris do not work as well. When in doubt, experiment with one blossom. Cut flowers when temperatures are cool and dry, leaving 1 or 2″ stems; store in refrigerator.

To dry flowers, trim stems to within ½″ of flower. Use custard cups to dry individual flowers, or dry 3 or 4 in a shoe box or casserole dish. Place blossoms on a 2″ layer of silica gel, leaving ¾″ between each blossom. Fill all spaces around each petal with the silica gel, using toothpick to lift petals. Continue to add silica gel until each flower is completely covered.

Place a microproof cup filled with water in a corner of the oven. Microwave flower(s) on HIGH for 1–2 min. for easy to dry flowers; 2–5 min. for difficult to dry. Remove container from oven and let stand for 20–30 min. Remove blossom(s) and place on cake rack to dry. After drying, brush lightly with soft brush to remove silica gel. Attach florist wire and wrap with tape. Finish with artificial leaves, or experiment with drying fresh leaves, using same procedure as with flowers.

Cool silica gel before reusing. When crystals turn pink, heat in oven for a few minutes until blue color returns. If desired, spray flowers with clear plastic spray.

Appetizers, Breads, Soups and Salads

TANGY CHEESE DIP

1 8 oz. pkg. cream cheese

1 5-oz. jar sharp American cheese spread

1 5-oz. jar pimiento cheese spread

⅓ C. beer

2 T. snipped green onion tops

¾ t. prepared horseradish

½ t. dry mustard

In a 1½ qt. casserole, combine cheeses. Microwave covered on HIGH, just until softened, about 1 min. Gradually beat in, by hand, the beer, onion, horseradish, and mustard until smooth. Microwave covered on MEDIUM, until heated throughout, about 3½–4 min., stirring after each minute. Stir before serving. Serve warm with crackers and vegetables. Makes 2¼ C.

Teresa Daniel
Monroe County

CRANBERRY-GLAZED FANTAIL FRANKS

1 8-oz. can whole berry or jellied cranberry sauce

1 T. lemon juice

1½ T. prepared mustard

1 lb. frankfurters

Set power select at HIGH. In square baking dish, combine cranberry sauce, mustard, and lemon juice. Heat 2–3 min., stirring once. Meanwhile, cut frankfurters into chunks. Stir into glaze mixture. Heat 5–6 min., stirring once. Serve with toothpicks.

Janean DePlanty
Starke County

STUFFED MUSHROOMS

8 oz. cleaned, destemmed fresh mushroom caps	1 T. parsley
	1 small onion, finely chopped
Stuffing:	⅓ C. seasoned bread crumbs
mushroom stems, finely chopped	¼ t. salt
	⅛ t. garlic
2 T. butter	powder

Place stems in small bowl with onion and butter; cover with plastic wrap. Microwave on HIGH for 1½-2½ min. Stir in remaining ingredients. Mound in mushroom caps. Arrange caps on paper-towel-lined plate with larger caps to outside. Microwave 1½-3 min. on HIGH, until heated, rotating plate once or twice.

Variations:

Ham and Cheese: chopped mushroom stems and 3 oz. cream cheese, softened 15–30 sec. on HIGH. Stir in ½ C. finely chopped ham and ¼ C. finely chopped almonds. Follow remaining directions as in basic recipe.

Cheese and Walnut: chopped mushroom stems, 3 oz. bleu cheese (crumbled), ½ C. chopped walnuts, and ¼ C. seasoned bread crumbs. Microwave stems. Stir in cheese. Add walnuts and bread crumbs, reserving 2–3 T. of each. Stuff mushrooms, garnish with reserved nuts and crumbs. Finish microwaving as in basic recipe.

Martha Daniel
Monroe County

MICROWAVE CORN BREAD

1 C. yellow cornmeal	1 t. salt
1 C. flour	1 egg
¼ C. sugar	1 C. milk
4 t. baking powder	¼ C. shortening, soft

Sift together dry ingredients. Combine egg, milk, and shortening; add to dry ingredients. Place a straight-sided 2″ diameter juice glass upright in the center of a greased 8″ round glass cake dish. (The juice glass helps the center cook more evenly. Do not use a plastic juice glass, as it could warp when heated). Pour in batter. Microwave on HIGH 6–7 min., or until batter is no longer moist around the juice glass and a toothpick inserted comes out clean. Rotate dish ½ turn after half the cooking time.

Charlotte Hight
Madison County

MICROWAVE MUSH

1 C. yellow cornmeal	1 t. salt
	4 C. boiling
½ C. cold water	water

Bring 4 C. water covered to a boil—microwave on HIGH 6 min. Stir together cornmeal, cold water, and salt, and pour mixture (by spoonfuls) into boiling water. Cook uncovered on MEDIUM-HIGH for 2 min. and on MEDIUM for 4 min., stirring frequently. Let stand covered 3 min.; then pour into bread pan. Refrigerate. Next day may be sliced, fried, and topped with syrup or honey.

MICROWAVE SYRUP

6 C. white sugar	3 C. water
¾ C. brown sugar	1½ t. maple flavoring

In large mixing bowl, combine sugars and water. Cook covered on HIGH for 9 min.

and on MEDIUM for 8 min. Add maple flavoring, cover, and let stand until cool. Ladle into plastic containers. Store in refrigerator.

Judy Ross
Ohio County

PUMPKIN GEMS

⅓ C. shortening	1⅓ C. flour
1⅓ C. sugar	¾ t. salt
2 eggs	¼ t. cinnamon
1 C. cooked	½ t. nutmeg
pumpkin	1 t. vanilla
1 t. baking	⅓ C. water
powder	

Beat together first 4 ingredients. Sift together the dry ingredients and stir into pumpkin mixture. Stir in vanilla and water. Place paper baking cups in custard cups or microwave muffin cups and fill cups ½ full with batter. Microwave on HIGH 2½-4½ min. per 6 muffins.

Note: Since muffins do not brown, use colorful batters like Pumpkin Gems, or add a topping such as cinnamon and sugar to give plain muffins a tasty-looking top.

Mrs. Everett Rhamy
Huntington County

ONE POT MEAT SOUP

3 carrots, bias cut	1 C. milk
1 medium onion,	2 C. cubed
sliced	cooked turkey
1 C. sliced un-	¾ t. salt
peeled	½ t. celery seed
cucumber	¼ t. leaf thyme
½ C. flour	⅛ t. pepper

2 C. water	key or chicken
1 10¾-oz. can	broth for con-
condensed	densed chicken
chicken broth	broth and
(Substitute	water)
homemade tur-	

Combine carrots, onion, and cucumber in 2½ qt. glass casserole. Cover with glass lid or plastic wrap. Microwave on HIGH for 5 min. Blend flour with milk in small mixing bowl. Stir into vegetables along with remaining ingredients. Recover and continue cooking on HIGH for 8 min. Stir; recover, and continue cooking on HIGH for 7–8 min., or until vegetables are tender-crisp. Serves 4–5.

Marge George
Greene County

POTATO SOUP

2 medium pota-	¼ t. salt
toes, cubed	1 C. milk
1 small onion,	1 T. butter
chopped	⅛ t. pepper
1 C. water	

In a 2½ qt. glass dish, place potatoes, water, salt, and onion. Microwave on HIGH for 9–10 min. Add milk, butter, and pepper. Heat on MEDIUM for 2–3 min.

Loretta Roberts
Parke County

GERMAN POTATO SALAD

4 medium	1 T. flour
potatoes	1 t. or 1 cube
6 slices bacon	beef bouillon
¼–½ C. chopped	1 t. salt
onion or	¼ t. allspice
6 green onions,	dash pepper
sliced	¼ C. vinegar
2 T. sugar	½ C. water

Wash and dry potatoes. Prick skins and cook approximately 10 min. on HIGH. Turn potatoes over and rearrange them halfway through cooking time. In glass casserole, place 1 layer paper toweling. Cut bacon in pieces and place in a single layer on toweling. Cook about 2½–4 min. on HIGH, or until crisp. Remove towel and bacon, leaving drippings in bowl. Add onion to drippings and cook uncovered at HIGH 1 min. Stir in sugar, flour, bouillon, salt, allspice, and pepper. Blend in vinegar and water.

Cook uncovered on HIGH 3 min., or until mixture boils and thickens, stirring twice. While mixture cooks, peel potatoes and slice. Add to hot mixture and toss lightly to coat potatoes. Crumble bacon over top, or mix in if you prefer, and serve warm. Salad can be prepared several hours ahead and reheated, covered, in microwave oven. Serves 4.

Note: To reheat, always cover main dishes.

Naomi Lizenby
Pulaski County

Main Dishes

BEEF STEW

2 lb. stew meat, cut in 1″ cubes	½ t. salt
1 1½-oz. pkg. brown gravy mix with mushrooms	3 medium carrots, cut in small chunks
3 stalks celery, cut in pieces	2 medium potatoes, peeled and cut in eighths
1 medium onion, cut in chunks	1 C. tomato, cut up

Put beef in 3 qt. casserole. Sprinkle with salt. Combine gravy mix with 1 C. water and stir well; pour over meat. Cook covered on MEDIUM, or until meat is almost tender. Add celery, carrots, potatoes, onion, and tomato and stir lightly so that the vegetables are covered with gravy. Add more water for a thinner gravy and a little additional salt for vegetables, if desired. Cook covered on MEDIUM for about 20 min., or until vegetables and meat are tender. Remove and let stand 5 min.

Mrs. Donald Jessup
Ripley County

DRIED BEEF GRAVY

2 T. butter	½ t. salt
2 T. flour	1 C. milk

Place butter in 1 qt. casserole. Melt at HIGH 30–50 sec. Stir in flour and salt; blend smooth. Add milk and blend. Microwave on HIGH 4–6 min., stirring every minute, until thick and bubbly. Add dried beef and cook on HIGH 45 sec. Serve over bread, toast, or mashed potatoes. Serves 2.

Mrs. Treva Geiger
Wells County

BEEFBURGER STROGANOFF

1 lb. ground beef chuck	1 can cream of mushroom soup
½ C. onion, finely chopped	3 T. flour
¼–½ t. garlic powder	1 t. salt
1 8-oz. can mushrooms, undrained	¼ t. pepper
	¼ C. chopped green mangoes (optional)

¼ C. red pi-
  miento
  (optional)

1 C. dairy sour
  cream (8 oz.)
1½ t. bottled
  brown sauce

Into 2 qt. casserole, crumble beef. Add on-ions, garlic powder, soup, flour, mangoes, pimientoes, salt, and pepper; mix thoroughly. Cover with plastic wrap. Microwave on HIGH for 15–18 min., stirring after first 8 min. Stir casserole thoroughly after cooking, then stir in sour cream and brown sauce. Serve over cooked rice or chow mein noodles. Serves 6.

Jeanette Thompson
Wabash County

HAMBURGER AND POTATO CASSEROLE

1 lb. ground beef
5 medium pota-
  toes, peeled
  and thinly
  sliced
½ t. salt

1 10½-oz. can
  vegetable beef
  soup
1 3-oz. can
  French-fried
  onion rings

Crumble hamburger in 12x8″ baking dish. Microwave at HIGH 4–6 min., or until meat loses most of its pink color; break up and drain. Stir in potatoes, soup, and salt; cover with waxed paper. Microwave at HIGH 14–18 min., or until potatoes are tender and liquid is absorbed. Stir after half the cooking time. Stir mixture and sprinkle onion rings over top. Microwave uncovered at HIGH 1½–3 min., or until heated through. Serves 4–6.

Mary Jane Reuter
Lawrence County

LASAGNE

¼ lb. lasagne
  noodles

½ lb. lean
  ground beef

¼ C. chopped
  onion
1 clove garlic,
  pressed
1 T. olive oil
2 8-oz. cans to-
  mato sauce
½ t. salt
¼ t. pepper
¾ t. oregano

2 T. chopped
  parsley
8 oz. thinly sliced
  mozzarella
  cheese
8 oz. ricotta or
  cottage cheese
¼ C. Parmesan
  cheese

Place 4 C. boiling salted water in a 3 qt. ovenware casserole dish; add noodles. Cover with wax paper. Cook noodles in microwave on HIGH for 10 min.; let set 10 min. Rinse with warm water; drain. Combine ground beef, onion, garlic, and oil in a 2 qt. ovenware casserole; cover. Microwave on HIGH 5–6 min., or until meat is no longer pink. Stir occasionally to break up meat. Add tomato sauce, salt, pepper, oregano, and parsley. Continue cooking until hot throughout, about 5–6 min. Layer noodles, meat sauce, mozzarella, and cottage cheese in an 11¾x7½x1¾″ glass baking dish. Sprinkle with Parmesan cheese. Cover with waxed paper. Microwave 8–10 min. on MEDIUM, or until cheese melts and center is hot. Serves 4.

Charlotte Hight
Madison County

EXTRA GOOD MEATBALLS

3 lb. hamburger
1 C. milk
2 C. quick oats
1 T. onion or 1½
  t. onion
  powder
2 eggs
1 T. Worces-
  tershire sauce
1 t. chili powder

½ t. garlic salt
Sauce:
1½ C. brown
  sugar
2 C. catsup
1 T. dry mustard
1 T. chili powder
1 T. salt
1 T. garlic salt

Mix ingredients to make small (1½") meatballs. Blend sauce ingredients together. Place meatballs in 9 × 13" pan. Microwave 4–5 min. on HIGH; drain. Rearrange, bringing balls from the outside of dish to the center. Pour sauce over meatballs and microwave on HIGH for 6–8 min.

Virginia Bosstick
Dearborn County

STROGANOFF MEATBALLS

24 basic frozen meatballs, uncooked	¼ t. dried thyme, crushed
1 3-oz. pkg. cream cheese, cut in cubes	⅛ t. garlic powder
1 can cream of mushroom soup	½ C. dairy sour cream
¾ C. milk	hot cooked rice or hot cooked noodles
2 T. catsup	snipped parsley

Place frozen meatballs on a 12x7½x2" baking dish in single layer. Microwave on HIGH until thawed, about 4 min., rearranging balls after each minute. Microwave on HIGH for about 6 min., or until done. Drain off excess fat. In a 2 qt. casserole, soften cream cheese at HIGH; thoroughly blend in milk. Stir in catsup, thyme, and garlic powder. Microwave covered until cheese melts and mixture is smooth, about 8 min. Add meat balls, microwave covered on MEDIUM until bubbly, about 5 min., stirring twice. Stir sour cream into casserole, microwave covered just until hot (1 min.). Serve over hot cooked rice or noodles. Sprinkle with snipped parsley. Serves 4–6.

Olive Ferguson
Spencer County

BASIC MEAT LOAF

1½ lb. ground chuck	1 C. milk
¾ C. chopped onion	1 t. salt
½ C. fine dry bread crumbs	¼ t. pepper
1 egg	⅛ t. paprika
	2 T. catsup (to spread on top)

Mix all ingredients well and put into ring mold. Brush with catsup. Cook 15–20 min. on HIGH. Serves 6.

Beverly Givens
Madison County

LITTLE MEAT LOAVES

1 egg	1 T. instant minced onion
¾ C. evaporated milk	1½ lb. ground beef
1 C. soft white bread crumbs	Glaze:
1½ t. salt	⅓ C. marmalade
pepper	1 t. vinegar
½ t. Italian seasoning or poultry seasoning	½ t. bottled browning sauce

Mix together well all meat loaf ingredients. Shape mix into four individual loaves. Place loaves in shallow 2 qt. baking dish. Microwave for 10 min. on HIGH, turning dish 180° at 3 min. intervals. Carefully turn loaves over half way through cooking time. Mix together glaze ingredients; brush or spoon over tops and sides of loaves. Microwave on HIGH for 2 min., turning dish twice (if necessary). Let stand 5 min.

Maxine Hite
Noble County

MEATZA PIE

1 lb. ground beef	⅛ t. basil
⅔ C. evaporated milk	¼ t. salt
½ C. bread crumbs	⅛ t. pepper
1 t. instant minced onion	1 4-oz. can mushrooms, drained
½ t. garlic salt	½ C. shredded mozzarella cheese
1 6 oz. can tomato paste	grated Parmesan cheese
⅛ t. oregano	

Mix beef, milk, bread crumbs, onion, and garlic salt. Shape into pie pan as crust. Combine tomato paste and seasonings and spread over meat. Spread mushrooms over tomato mix. Cover with waxed paper. Microwave on HIGH 8 min. Sprinkle with mozzarella cheese; dust with Parmesan cheese. Microwave on HIGH 1–2 min. to melt cheeses. Serves 4–6.

Wilhelmene J. Wallis
Gibson County

CRUSTLESS PASTIE CASSEROLE

1 lb. lean ground beef	½ C. finely grated rutabaga
4 C. potatoes, sliced thin	½ C. chopped onion
½ C. finely grated carrot	¼ C. water
	salt and pepper

In 2½ qt. microproof casserole make several layers of beef, potatoes, carrots, rutabaga, and onion. Sprinkle each layer with salt and papper. Pour water over the top layer. Cover and cook on HIGH for 20–30 min., or until done. Rotate dish 2 times during cooking.

Patricia Marshall
Morgan County

SALISBURY STEAK

1½ lbs. ground beef	1 egg, slightly beaten
1 can golden mushroom soup	¼ C. chopped onion
½ C. bread crumbs	dash of pepper
	⅓ C. water

Combine ground beef, ¼ C. soup, bread crumbs, egg, onion, and pepper. Shape into 6 patties. Using 2 qt. utility dish, microwave on HIGH 10 min. Turn patties and drain fat halfway through cooking time. Blend remaining soup with water; pour over meat. Microwave on HIGH 4 min. Turn dish halfway through cooking time.

Sue Childes
Monroe County

SPECIALTY CASSEROLE

1 lb. lean ground beef	1 can cream of mushroom soup
½ C. chopped onion	1 12-oz. can whole kernel corn, drained
1 8-oz. pkg. cream cheese, cubed	1 2-oz. jar pimiento, drained and chopped
1 t. salt	
dash of pepper	

In a 2 qt. casserole dish, brown meat and onions uncovered on HIGH 5 min. Stir occasionally to break up meat chunks; drain. Blend cream cheese and soup in a small bowl; heat uncovered on HIGH 5 min. Stir twice. Mix all ingredients together and microwave on HIGH 10 min. Serves 4.

Susan Elkins
Monroe County

FRIED CHICKEN

1 C. dried bread crumbs	¼ t. pepper
1½ t. paprika	1 egg white
1 t. salt	1 T. water
¼ t. finely crumbled bay leaf	1 3-lb. broiler-fryer chicken, cut up
¼ t. garlic powder	¼ C. butter or margarine

On sheet of waxed paper combine bread crumbs, paprika, salt, bay leaf, garlic powder, and pepper. In pie plate mix egg white with the water. Dip each piece of chicken into the egg white; then coat evenly with bread crumb mixture. Place in 12x8″ glass baking dish with larger pieces on the outside, smaller in the center. In 1 C. glass cup, melt butter on HIGH for 45 sec., or until melted; pour over chicken and cook uncovered on HIGH 5 min. Cover chicken with waxed paper and cook 10 min.; rotate dish a quarter turn after 5 min. Let stand covered 10 min. before serving. The paprika is what gives the chicken that "fried" look. Serves 4.

Meta Katter
Dubois County

SWEET-AND-SOUR CHICKEN

1 20-oz. can pineapple chunks in natural juice	¼ C. soy sauce
½ C. light brown sugar	1¼ C. green pepper strips
½ t. ginger	1 C. sliced onion
½ C. cider vinegar	2 C. cubed, cooked chicken or turkey
¼ C. cornstarch	1 C. sliced carrots

Drain pineapple, reserving juice. Add enough water to juice to make 2½ C. Combine brown sugar, cornstarch and ginger in 3 qt. glass casserole. Gradually stir in 2½ C. reserved liquid, vinegar, and soy sauce. Microwave on HIGH 10 min., or until mixture boils and thickens, stirring every 2 min. Add pineapple, green pepper, onion, carrots and chicken. Cover with lid or waxed paper. Microwave on HIGH 20 min., or until vegetables are tender-crisp, stirring every 5 min. Serve with rice. Serves 5–6.

Mrs. John Hensel
Hamilton County

KASEY'S TIPSY CHICKEN

1 whole broiler-fryer chicken	⅛ t. salt
¼ C. butter	2 T. sherry
½ t. chopped fresh parsley	¾ t. onion salt
¼ t. garlic powder	¼ t. celery salt
	⅛ t. pepper
	¼ t. poultry seasoning

Place butter in 8 oz. measuring cup. Microwave on HIGH 1½ min., or until melted. Add parsley, garlic powder, salt, and sherry. Microwave on MEDIUM 30 sec. to blend flavors; set aside for basting. Mix together onion salt, celery salt, pepper and poultry seasoning and sprinkle mixture on inside and outside of chicken. Place chicken, breast side down, on roasting rack in large shallow microwave baking dish. Microwave on HIGH 5 min. Spoon basting mixture on chicken. Microwave on HIGH 5 min. longer, or until fork can be inserted in chicken with ease. Remove chicken from oven; cover with foil and let stand about 5 min. before serving. Serve with pan juices. Serves 4.

Elizabeth Laws
Hendricks County

BAKED CHICKEN SALAD

3 eggs, hard-cooked	¼ C. chopped onion

2 C. cubed,
cooked chicken
1 can cream of
chicken soup
1 C. slivered
almonds
1 C. diced celery
1 T. lemon juice

2 t. chopped pi-
miento,
optional
½ t. salt
¼ t. pepper
1 can shoestring
potatoes,
divided

Chop eggs coarsely; set aside. Combine celery and onion in 1½ qt. casserole; cover. Microwave on HIGH 3–4 min., or until vegetables are tender. Stir in remaining ingredients, except half of shoestring potatoes. Microwave on HIGH uncovered 3 min.; stir. Sprinkle with remaining potatoes; microwave on HIGH 2–3 min., or until heated through. Serves 4–6.

Mary Jane Reuter
Lawrence County

CHICKEN BREASTS ROCKEFELLER

2 whole chicken
breasts, halved,
boned,
skinned, and
flattened
½ t. seasoned salt
1 10-oz. pkg. fro-
zen, chopped
spinach,
thawed and
well drained
½ C. minced
green onions

⅛ t. paprika
1 C. shredded
sharp Cheddar
cheese
1 can cream of
chicken soup
2 T. light cream
1 T. Worces-
tershire sauce
2 T. toasted, but-
tered bread
crumbs

Sprinkle seasoned salt and paprika on chicken. In bowl, mix spinach and green onions. Place 1 T. spinach mixture on each chicken breast half. Place 1 T. of cheese on top of spinach mixture. Roll chicken jelly-roll fashion, and secure with wooden picks. In large shallow glass baking dish, mix together soup, cream, Worcestershire, re-

maining cheese, and spinach mixture. Microwave on HIGH 2 min.; stir until cheese is melted. Place chicken rolls in soup mixture. Spoon soup mixture over chicken; top with crumbs. Sprinkle paprika on top and cover with waxed paper. Microwave on HIGH about 20 min., turning dish every 5 min., or until fork can be inserted with ease. Let stand covered 5 min.

Dianna Crouse
Union County

BUTTER HERB BAKED FISH

½ C. butter
¼ C. grated Par-
mesan cheese
½ t. each: sweet
basil, oregano
¼ t. garlic
powder

⅔ C. saltine
crackers,
crushed
1 lb. sole, perch,
or any white
fish fillets

In 13x9″ pan, melt butter in microwave oven. Combine cracker crumbs, Parmesan cheese, basil, oregano and garlic powder. Dip fish in butter, then in crumb mixture. Arrange fillets in baking pan and microwave on HIGH 5–7 min., or until fish is tender and flakes with a fork. Allow to stand 5 min. before serving.

Edith DeAmicis
Monroe County

TUNA NOODLE CASSEROLE (1)

1 7¾-oz. can
tuna
1 can cream of
mushroom
soup
2 C. wide noo-
dles, cooked
and drained

crushed potato
chips
1 medium onion,
chopped
1 C. milk
black pepper
2 T. butter

Place noodles in buttered casserole dish.

Combine soup, milk, and onion; mix with noodles. Sprinkle liberally with black pepper. Dot with butter. Top with crushed potato chips. Cover with vented Saran Wrap. Microwave on MEDIUM 10 min.

Kaye Hudson
Monroe County

TUNA NOODLE CASSEROLE (2)

1 C. water	1 4-oz. can mush-
1½ C. uncooked	room stems and
noodles	pieces, drained
1 6½-oz. can	1 17-oz. can
flaked tuna,	green beans,
drained	drained
1 can cream of	½ C. coarsely
mushroom	crushed potato
soup	chips

Pour water into 2 qt. casserole. Cover with glass lid or plastic wrap. Microwave on HIGH for 3–5 min., or until water comes to a boil. Stir in noodles. Recover and cook on DEFROST for 11–12 min. or until noodles are tender. Drain noodles and stir in remaining ingredients except potato chips; recover. Microwave on REHEAT for 8–10 min. or until hot. Let stand covered 5 min. Sprinkle potato chips on top and serve. Serves 6–8.

Marge George
Greene County

LAMB STEW

1 lb. lamb, cut in	⅛ t. pepper
1″ cubes	1 clove garlic,
1 ⅝-oz. pkg.	minced
brown gravy	½ t. Worces-
mix	tershire sauce
2 T. flour	¼ C. wine
1 t. salt	(optional)

3 medium car-	2 potatoes,
rots, peeled and	peeled and cut
cut in chunks	in cubes
2 stalks celery,	1 onion, chopped
cut in pieces	

In a 3 qt. microproof casserole, combine lamb and gravy mix. Cook uncovered on HIGH for 5 min., stirring once during cooking time. Add remaining ingedients and 1 C. water. Stir well. Cover and cook on MEDIUM-HIGH for 20–25 min., or until meat and vegetables are tender. Stir once during cooking time. Let stand 3–4 min. before serving. Serves 3–4.

Janet Dawson
Dearborn County

LIVER AND ONIONS

1 lb. liver	6 slices bacon
¼ C. flour	1 C. onion,
1 t. salt	chopped
dash of pepper	

Coat liver with mixture of flour, salt, and pepper. Place bacon and onion in 2 qt. casserole. Microwave covered on HIGH for 8–10 min. Remove bacon and onion. Add liver to bacon grease. Cook on HIGH for 8 min. Turn liver over once halfway through cooking time. Put onion and bacon on top of liver. Microwave on HIGH for 1 min. Serves 4–6.

Georgia Potter
Ohio County

MANDARIN ORANGE PORK

1 lb. boneless	1 t. grated fresh
pork	gingerroot
1 T. cooking oil	½ t. grated or-
2 t. cornstarch	ange peel
2 T. soy sauce	½ C. orange
	juice

1 6-oz. pkg. fro- 1 11-oz. can man-
zen pea pods,   darin oranges,
thawed   drained

Cut pork into very thin strips. For easier cutting, partially freeze meat; allow to thaw completely before cooking. Pre-heat browning dish on HIGH for 5 min. Add oil and pork strips. Cook uncovered on HIGH for 3 min., stirring twice. Blend together cornstarch, soy sauce, gingerroot, orange peel, and juice; pour over pork. Cook on HIGH for 2–3 min. until thickened and bubbly, stirring after each min. Stir in pea pods. Cook covered on HIGH for 1 min. Serves 4.

Ruth Augustine
Monroe County

CENTER CUT HAM WITH APRICOTS

1 16-oz. can   ¼ C. brown
apricots   sugar
3–3¼ lb. center   2 T. vinegar
cut ham slice,   ¼ t. nutmeg
2″ thick   2 T. butter or
2 T. cornstarch   margarine

Drain apricots, reserving juice. Trim fat from ham slice. Score edges. Place in 2 qt. glass baking dish. Combine apricot juice, brown sugar, cornstarch, vinegar, and nutmeg. Pour over ham. Top with apricots. Dot with butter. Microwave at MEDIUM-HIGH for 20–25 min., or until ham is hot and sauce is thickened, turning once. Let stand for 5 min. before serving. Serves 6–8.

Joyce McClain
Hendricks County

SAUSAGE STRATA

1 lb. sausage   2 C. grated Ched-
3 slices bread,   dar cheese
cubed   ½ t. dry mustard

4 eggs   1 T. chopped
2 C. milk   chives

Microwave sausage in 1 qt. casserole on HIGH for 5–6 min., or until no longer pink; drain. Layer bread cubes, sausage, and cheese in greased dish, ending with bread cubes. Beat together eggs, milk, and mustard. Pour over bread cubes. Cover and refrigerate 4 hr. Microwave on HIGH for 12–15 min., or until knife inserted in center comes out clean.

Anne Burris
Whitley County

SMOKED SAUSAGE LASAGNE

6 oz. lasagne noo-   3 C. spaghetti
dles, cooked,   sauce
drained   16 oz. pkg. sliced
1½ C. ricotta   mozzarella
cheese   cheese
1 lb. smoked sau-   ⅓ C. Parmesan
sage links,   cheese
thinly sliced   salt to taste
1 T. oregano

Place ½ C. sauce in the bottom of a 2 qt. oblong glass baking dish. Alternate layers of noodles, ricotta cheese, spaghetti sauce, smoked sausage, and cheese. Sprinkle top with oregano, Parmesan cheese, and salt. Cover with fitted casserole lid or plastic wrap. Microwave on HIGH for 10–12 min., or until heated through. Allow to stand 5–10 min. before serving. Serves 6.

Carolyn Stant
Hancock County

PIZZA ROLL-UPS

1 12-oz. pkg.   1 8-oz. can to-
bulk pork   mato sauce
sausage   2 C. shredded
½ C. chopped   mozzarella
green pepper   cheese, divided

1 4-oz. can mushroom stems and pieces, drained
½ t. oregano leaves

6 flour tortillas
1 can tomato soup
1 T. dry onion soup mix

Crumble sausage into 1½ qt. glass casserole; stir in green pepper. Cover with glass lid. Microwave for about 5 min. on HIGH, or until meat is browned; drain. Stir in tomato sauce, 1 C. mozzarella cheese, mushrooms, and oregano. To soften tortillas, microwave 15 sec. on HIGH. Spoon about ¼ C. sausage mixture along center of each tortilla and roll up jelly-roll fashion; place in 2 qt. (12x7″) glass baking dish. Combine soup and dry soup mix; pour over tortillas. Sprinkle with remaining 1 C. cheese. Microwave for 14–16 min. on MEDIUM-HIGH, or until hot. Serves 4–6.

Margaret Fouts
DeKalb County

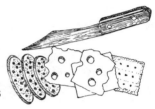

Cheeses, Pastas, and Quiches

BIRDELLA'S MICROWAVE ENCHILADAS

1 lb. ricotta (or cottage cheese)
1 egg
½ C. chopped chilies
1 C. grated Monterey Jack cheese

½ C. green onion (chopped)
8 medium-sized tortillas
1 10-oz. can enchilada sauce
1 C. grated Cheddar cheese

Mix the first five ingredients together to make filling. Soften tortillas between paper towels in microwave 15 sec. on HIGH to make pliable. Spoon ⅛th filling in tortilla, fold envelope style. Put ⅓ of sauce in shallow baking dish and place enchiladas in dish. Cover with remaining sauce and cook 8 min. on HIGH. Remove from oven; add Cheddar cheese and microwave 1½ min. more. Place waxed paper over top to prevent spatters. Serves 8.

Shirley J. Campbell
Monroe County

SUMMER LASAGNE

1 C. (8 oz.) tomato sauce
1 medium onion, chopped
¼ t. salt, optional
⅛ t. pepper
¼ t. basil leaves
¼ t. oregano leaves
1 C. ricotta cheese
1 t. parsley flakes

½ C. shredded mozzarella cheese
3 medium zucchini (about 9″ long), peeled and sliced lengthwise into strips
1 large tomato, sliced
2 T. grated Parmesan cheese

Combine tomato sauce, onion, basil, salt, pepper, and oregano; set aside. In separate bowl combine ricotta, mozzarella, and parsley. Set aside. Arrange zucchini strips in 8x8″ baking dish; cover with wax paper. Microwave on HIGH 6—8 min., or until fork tender, rearranging after half the time. Drain and place zucchini on paper towels to absorb excess moisture; cool slightly. Layer

4–6 zucchini strips in the bottom of baking dish. Reserve 6 strips for second layer. Spread ricotta mixture over zucchini. Layer with sliced tomatoes. Spread half of tomato sauce mixture over tomatoes; top with zucchini slices. Pour remaining sauce over zucchini and sprinkle with Parmesan. Reduce power to MEDIUM. Microwave uncovered 20–25 min., or until zucchini is tender and mixture is hot in center. Let stand 5 min. before serving. Serves 6.

Ina Jean Moore
Noble County

QUICK MACARONI & CHEESE

1 C. uncooked elbow macaroni	2 T. flour
	1 t. salt
1 C. water	1 C. cubed
1 C. milk	Velveeta
2 T. margarine	1 t. dry onion

Combine above ingredients, except cheese, in 2½ qt. casserole or mixing bowl. Cover; microwave on HIGH 4½ min. Stir. Cook 4½ min., or more, until macaroni is tender. Add cheese; stir and cover. Allow to set about 5 min.; stir and serve. Serves 4–6.

Ruth Anna Cates
Delaware County

FAST MUFFIN PIZZA

1 14-oz. pkg. English muffins	Pizza Garnishes:
	green pepper, sliced
1¼ C. chili sauce	
¾ C. mozzarella cheese, shredded	pepperoni, sliced
	green onion, bias cut
Italian seasoning	mushrooms, sliced
	olives, sliced

Split muffins in half (toast if desired). Top each half with 1½ T. chili sauce, 1 T. cheese, sprinkle of Italian seasoning, and any 2 of the pizza garnishes. Arrange 2 pizzas on paper towel in oven. Microwave for 2–2½ min. on MEDIUM-HIGH until cheese melts.

Mary Bryant
Harrison County

QUICHE

Crust:

1 C. all purpose flour	1 egg
	1 13½-oz. can evaporated milk
⅓ C. lard	
½ t. salt	¼ t. salt
½ t. lemon juice	1 C. shredded Cheddar cheese
¼ t. Worcestershire sauce	
	1 3-oz. can French-fried onion rings
1 T., plus 1¼ t., ice water	

Filling:
½ C. mayonnaise

Mix salt and flour. Cut lard into flour mixture. Mix liquids and add all at once to flour mixture. Blend with fork. Roll and place in deep 9″ microproof pie dish. Prick and microwave 2–4 min. on HIGH. Beat together mayonnaise, egg, and salt. Stir in evaporated milk. Stir in cheese and onion rings. Pour into pie shell. Sprinkle top with nutmeg. Microwave on MEDIUM-HIGH for 14–16 min., rotating every 5 min.
Note: HIGH setting may be used, but set for 12–14 min. and watch carefully. Allow quiche to stand for 5 min. before serving.

Beverley Turner
Montgomery County

CHEESY SPINACH QUICHE

2 C. chopped fresh spinach, firmly packed	⅔ C. chopped onion
	6 T. butter

6 eggs
¼ C. flour
1 t. dry mustard
1 t. lemon juice
½ t. salt
½ t. baking
  powder

1 C. chopped
  ham
1 C. grated Swiss
  cheese, firmly
  packed
1 C. grated Ched-
  dar cheese,
  firmly packed

In glass dish, combine spinach, onion, and butter; microwave on HIGH 2½ min. Set aside. Beat eggs; add and beat well flour, mustard, lemon juice, salt, and baking powder. Gently fold in ham, cheeses, and spinach mixture. Pour mixture into 10½" quiche pan, cover with plastic wrap and microwave on HIGH for 3 min. Remove plastic wrap and gently push outside edges of quiche to center of dish. Microwave on MEDIUM-HIGH for 10 min., rotating dish twice. Let stand 5 min. Serves 6.

Note: This quiche makes its own "crust."

Marjorie W. Klinck
Brown County

HAM & CHEESE QUICHE

9" pastry shell,
  baked
½ C. grated
  Cheddar cheese
½ C. grated
  Swiss cheese
2 C. half and half
1 T. chopped
  chives
2 t. minced onion

½ t. curry
  powder
¼ t. salt
dash hot pepper
  sauce
4 eggs, slightly
  beaten
½ C. finely
  chopped ham

Fill cooled shell with cheese; set aside. Mix together cream, chives, onion, curry powder, salt, and hot pepper sauce in 4 C. measure or 1 qt. casserole. Microwave on HIGH for 2–2½ mins., or until steaming. Stir small amount of hot cream mixture into eggs; then stir egg mixture into remaining hot cream. Pour gently into shell. Sprinkle with ham. Microwave on MEDIUM-HIGH for 12–14 mins., or until knife inserted in center comes out clean. Turn dish a half turn, halfway through cooking time. Allow to stand 10 mins. before cutting, or until center is set.

Virginia Staples
Posey County

MINI MUSHROOM QUICHE

pastry for 2 crust
  pie
1 medium onion,
  diced
2 C. fresh mush-
  rooms, sliced
2 T. butter

3 T. flour
½ C. milk
2 eggs, beaten
¼ C. evaporated
  milk
dash salt and
  pepper

Line microwave muffin pan with pastry to make individual shells; set aside. Combine onion, mushrooms, and butter. Microwave on HIGH 2–3 mins. Add flour, mixing well. Stir in milk and microwave 2 min. on MEDIUM. Add eggs and evaporated milk slowly. Add salt and pepper; spoon into pastry shells. Microwave 5 mins. on MEDIUM-HIGH, or until knife comes out clean. Rotate every 2 mins.

Vera Nicholson
Monroe County

QUICK QUICHE

Place one frozen pie cust in glass pie plate. Microwave on HIGH 30 sec.–1 min. to soften; press firmly into pie plate. Prick crust with fork and brush with 2 T. Worcestershire sauce. Microwave on HIGH 4 min., rotating plate ½ turn after 2 min. Sprinkle 1 C. shredded cheese over bottom of crust. Beat 4 eggs and mix with 1 C. milk; pour over cheese. Take 1 can French-fried onions and cut through the onions, in the can, to chop medium fine; sprinkle and press down lightly over top of quiche. Microwave on MEDIUM 11–13 min., rotating pan ½ turn every 4 min.

Variation: Before topping with onions add any one of the following: ½ C. chopped ham, tuna, turkey, chicken, or 6 slices crisp crumbled bacon.

Loretta Roberts
Parke County

Vegetables

BAKED BEANS

2 slices of bacon, cooked	1 16-oz. can pork and beans
1½ t. instant onion or ¼ C. finely chopped onion	1 16-oz. can red kidney beans, drained
1 16-oz. can lima beans, drained	¼ C. brown sugar
	¼ C. ketchup

Combine the beans in a 2 qt. baking dish; add onion, brown sugar, and ketchup and mix well. Crumble crisp bacon and sprinkle on top of beans. Microwave on HIGH for 15 min.

Loretta Byrne
Harrison County

BROCCOLI SPECIAL

2 10-oz. pkg. frozen broccoli, cooked and drained	1½ C. sour cream
	1 t. vinegar
	½ t. poppy seeds
2 T. butter	½ t. paprika
2 T. minced onion	⅛ t. salt
	dash pepper
2 T. sugar (optional)	⅓ C. chopped cashews

In a 1 qt. sauce dish, melt butter on HIGH and sauté onion for 2 min. Add sour cream, sugar, vinegar, poppy seeds, paprika, salt, and pepper. Heat sauce on HIGH for 2 min.,

stirring twice during cooking time. Pour over broccoli. Garnish with cashews. Serves 6–8.

Teresa Daniel
Monroe County

DELICIOUS BROCCOLI

1 pkg. frozen broccoli, cooked and drained	1 C. grated American cheese
	⅓ C. evaporated milk
1 can mushroom soup	1 can onion rings

Place broccoli in a small buttered casserole dish and sprinkle with cheese. Dilute soup with evaporated milk and pour over top of broccoli and cheese. Microwave 6 min. on PREHEAT. Remove from oven and sprinkle with onion rings. Return to oven and microwave on HIGH 2½ min.

Ruth Newby
Howard County

BRUSSELS SPROUTS

2 10-oz. pkg. frozen Brussels sprouts	⅛ t. salt
	¼ C. milk
¼ C. water	1½ C. shredded sharp American cheese
2 T. butter or margarine	
2 T. flour	1 hard-cooked egg, chopped

In a ½ qt. casserole, place Brussels sprouts and water. Microwave covered until tender, 10–12 min., stirring every 4 min. Drain; halve sprouts. Return to casserole. In a 2 C. glass measure, microwave the butter 30–40 sec. Blend in flour and salt; add milk all at once, stirring well. Microwave uncovered 1 min., stir; microwave until thickened and bubbly, 2–3 min., stirring every 30 sec. Add cheese; stir until melted. Pour over Brussels sprouts. Microwave covered until heated through, about 1 min. more. Sprinkle chopped egg atop casserole. *Note:* This recipe has all microcooking on HIGH. Serves 6.

Olive Ferguson
Spencer County

SWEET-SOUR RED CABBAGE

1 medium red cabbage shredded	½ C. apple cider vinegar
2 peeled tart apples, chopped	3 T. butter or margarine
1 C. boiling water	3 T. sugar
	½ t. salt
	1 stick cinnamon

Combine ingredients in 2½ qt. covered casserole. Microwave on HIGH 10–12 min., until cabbage is barely tender. Stir every 3–4 min.

Martha Daniel
Monroe County

CARROT & CAULIFLOWER BAKE

1 lb. fresh carrots	2 T. grated Parmesan cheese
3 T. margarine	
¼ t. nutmeg	1 medium head cauliflower
1 t. salt	

Cut carrots into 2x¼″ strips. Place in 12x7″ baking dish. Separate cauliflower into flowerets and layer over carrots. Dot with mar-

garine and sprinkle with nutmeg. Cover with plastic wrap; vent at end of dish. Microwave on HIGH 12 min., or until vegetables are crisp-tender. Sprinkle with salt and mix carefully. Before serving, sprinkle Parmesan cheese evenly over top.

Nancy Wagner
Fountain County

CHEESY MUSTARD CAULIFLOWER

1 medium head cauliflower	1 t. prepared mustard
½ C. mayonnaise	½ C. shredded Cheddar cheese
2 t. diced onion	

Place whole, cleaned cauliflower in 1½ qt. casserole with 2 T. water. Cover and microwave 7–8 min. on HIGH or until nearly tender. Mix mayonnaise, onion, mustard, and cheese. Place cauliflower on serving plate. Spread sauce on top and halfway down sides of cauliflower. Microwave uncovered for 1 min. on HIGH. Serves 6–8.

Mrs. Herman Small
Dubois County

CREAMY POTATOES

4 C. thinly sliced, pared potatoes	½ C. water
¼ C. chopped onion	1 can cream of mushroom soup
¼ t. salt	¼ C. milk

Place potatoes, onion, salt, and water in 2 qt. casserole. Microwave covered on HIGH for 10–12 min., or until barely tender. Stir gently after 5 min. Drain well. Combine soup and milk. Add to potatoes. Cook uncovered on HIGH for 8–10 min., or until mixture bubbles, stirring twice. Serves 6.

Donna K. Prather
Clark County

CREAMY CHEESE POTATOES

2 T. butter	¼ t. pepper
4 C. peeled, sliced potatoes	¾ C. evaporated milk or light cream
2 T. chopped onion (optional)	½–1 C. shredded Cheddar cheese
¼ C. water	paprika (optional)
1 t. salt	

Place butter in a 2 qt. glass casserole; microwave on HIGH for 1 min. Add potatoes, onion, water, salt, and pepper. Microwave on HIGH for 8–10 min. Pour milk over potato mixture; sprinkle with cheese and paprika. Microwave on MEDIUM-HIGH for 2–3 min., or until cheese melts. Let stand 2 min. before serving. Serves 6.

Sherry Hendricks
Marshall County

HASH BROWNS AND CHEESE POTATOES

½ C. butter or margarine	2 C. grated Cheddar cheese
2 lb. bag hash brown potatoes	1 can cream of chicken soup
1 C. chopped onion	1 C. dairy sour cream
¾ t. salt	paprika

To partially thaw potatoes, cut a small slit in the bag and place on DEFROST for 3 min. In a 3 qt. glass casserole, melt butter 30–40 sec. on HIGH. Add potatoes, onions, 1 C. cheese, sour cream, salt, and soup. Cook loosely covered with waxed paper on HIGH for 20 min., stirring once. Uncover casserole; sprinkle the remaining 1 C. cheese and paprika over top and cook 3 min. longer, or until cheese melts.

Lorna McIlwain
Grant County

SPINACH CASSEROLE

Mix together:

2 10-oz. pkg. frozen chopped spinach, defrosted and drained	1½ C. cubed Velveeta
	3 eggs, beaten
	¼ C. margarine, cut in pieces
2 C. cottage cheese	1 t. salt
	2½ T. flour

Microwave on LOW 10–12 min., then on HIGH 4–5 min.

Rosie Kenworthy
Howard County

CHEESED ZUCCHINI

2 medium zucchini, sliced ¼" thick lengthwise	cheese slices and bacon slices oregano, garlic powder, salt, and pepper as desired
3 ripe tomatoes, sliced	
2 medium onions, sliced	

In a greased casserole, place alternate layers of zucchini, tomatoes, and onions. Sprinkle each layer with the spices. Next put a layer of cheese slices, not touching the sides. Cover top completely with layer of bacon slices; overlap slices by half. Microwave uncovered on HIGH 20 min., or until bacon is done.

Eleanor Biddle
White County

ZUCCHINI BAKE

1½ lb. zucchini, cut into ½" cubes	3 T. butter
	4 eggs, beaten
1 C. grated sharp Cheddar cheese (4 oz.)	1 can French-fried onion rings

In a 2 qt. glass casserole, combine zucchini and butter. Cover and cook for 5 min. on HIGH, rotating after 5 min. Top zucchini with onion rings and cook uncovered on DEFROST for 2 min.

Beverly Givens
Madison County

Desserts, Snacks, and Candy

MAKE YOUR OWN SWEETENED CONDENSED MILK

½ C. cold water   1¼ C. nonfat dry
¾ C. sugar   milk powder

Measure water in 2 C. glass measure; stir in milk powder until smooth. Microwave on HIGH for 45–60 sec., or until milk is steaming hot. Stir in sugar until dissolved. Allow to cool before using. Use as a substitute in recipes for 1 14-oz. can sweetened condensed milk. Makes 1⅓ C.

Ruth Augustine
Monroe County

BAKED APPLES

6 medium cook-   ½ C. raisins
  ing apples,   ½ t. cinnamon
  cored   ½ C. dry sherry
½ C. brown   or apple juice
  sugar

Cut off the top third of each apple. Place bottom of apple in 2 qt. 8x8″ glass dish. Fill center with raisins. Combine sugar and cinnamon and sprinkle over raisins. Place top of apple over sugar mixture. Pour sherry or apple juice over apple and cover with waxed paper. Place in microwave for 10–12 min. on HIGH, or until tender. Let stand covered 3 min. Serves 6.

Jay County Extension Homemakers

CINNAMON APPLES

4 apples, peeled,   ¼ t. cinnamon
  cored, and   6 oz. strawberry
  halved   or cherry car-
3 t. brown sugar   bonated drink

Arrange apples in microwave dish. Sprinkle cinnamon and sugar over apples and add carbonated liquid. Cover dish. Microwave on HIGH 1 min. per apple. Turn dish and microwave 1 min. more per apple. Serves 4.

Mattie Shafer
St. Joseph County

APPLE CRISP

6 C. peeled and   ¾ C. brown
  sliced apples   sugar
½ C. flour   1 t. cinnamon
½–¾ C. quick   4–6 T. margarine
  oats   or butter

Place apple slices in 2 qt. 8x8″ glass baking dish. Combine flour, oats, sugar, and cinnamon. Cut in butter until crumbly. Sprinkle evenly over apples. Microwave on HIGH for 14–16 min., or until apples are tender. Rotate dish ½ turn after 8 min. of cooking time. Serves 4–6.

Margaret McCammon   *Treva Geiger*
Dearborn County   *Wells County*

Variation: Use other fruits, but reduce brown sugar. Suggestions are: 2 16-oz. cans apricots, drained; 1 can cherry pie filling; or 1 29–oz. can sliced peaches, drained.

Amelia Stedman
Putnam County

HOT FUDGE SUNDAE CAKE

1 C. flour	2 T. salad oil
¾ C. sugar	1 t. vanilla
2 T. cocoa	½–1 C. nuts,
2 t. baking	chopped
powder	1 C. brown sugar
¼ t. salt	¼ C. cocoa
½ C. milk	1¾ C. water

Measure the water into 2 C. glass measure; place in microwave oven on HIGH to boil, about 4 min. In ungreased 9x9x2" microwave pan, stir together flour, sugar, 2 T. cocoa, baking powder, and salt. Mix in milk, oil, and vanilla. Stir in nuts. Spread batter in pan. Sprinkle with brown sugar and ¼ C. cocoa. Pour boiling water over cake. Microwave uncovered on HIGH 4½–5½ min., or until cake is no longer doughy. Let stand a few min.

Mrs. Ken Houin
Marshall County

BEV'S MICROWAVE CARAMEL FROSTING

½ C. margarine	3¼ C. powdered
1 C. brown sugar	sugar
¼ C. milk	

In large glass mixing bowl, microwave margarine on HIGH until melted. Add brown sugar and stir to blend. Microwave on HIGH until mixture comes to a boil. Remove from oven and cool to lukewarm. Add milk and stir until thoroughly mixed and cooled. Add powdered sugar and stir until of spreading consistency. Frosts 2 layers or a 9x13" cake.

Bev McClure
Union County

BUTTERSCOTCH CRUNCH CHEESECAKE

1 12-oz. pkg.	6 T. butter
butterscotch	2 C. graham
bits	cracker crumbs

2 C. chopped	½ C. sugar
pecans	4 eggs
2 8-oz. pkg.	¼ C. flour
cream cheese,	2 T. lemon juice
softened	

In a large glass mixing bowl, place bits and butter. Microwave on MEDIUM 3–4 min. With a fork, mix in crumbs and nuts. Press half this mixture into a large round dish (10–11½"). Microwave on HIGH 2–2½ min. Cream sugar and cream cheese with mixer until smooth. Add eggs, one at a time, beating after each addition. Blend in flour and lemon juice. Pour over crust. Sprinkle with remaining crumbs. Microwave on HIGH 4½ min. chill before serving.

Sue Childes
Monroe County

MY ORDINARY COFFEE CAKE

3 T. cooking oil	Topping:
½ C. sugar	⅓ C. brown
1 egg	sugar
1 C. flour	1 t. cinnamon
1¼ t. baking	2 T. butter or
powder	margarine
¼ t. salt	chopped walnuts
⅓ C. milk	to sprinkle on
½ t. vanilla	top (optional)

Mix oil, sugar, and egg together until creamy; add dry ingredients and milk and stir to form batter. Stir in vanilla. Spread batter evenly in an 8" round or square glass dish. Mix brown sugar and cinnamon together and sprinkle over batter. Sprinkle with chopped nuts. Dot top with butter. Microwave 3½–4 min. on HIGH. *Note:* You may want to line bottom of dish with a waxed paper circle. Do not grease the pan.

Donna P. Thomas
Elkhart County

CHOCOLATE MARSHMALLOW PIE

2 T. margarine	⅛ t. salt
3 T. cocoa	2¾ C. milk
1 t. vanilla	2 C. marsh-
⅔ C. sugar	mallows
4 T. cornstarch	1 baked pie crust

In a 4 qt. Pyrex mixing bowl, melt margarine on HIGH 1 min. Add cocoa and vanilla; mix well. Add sugar, cornstarch, and salt; mix well. Blend milk into cocoa-sugar mixture and microwave on HIGH 6–8 min., stirring every 2 min. Add marshmallows and microwave 1 min. cool and pour into pie crust. Top with whipped cream or chopped nuts.

Loretta Roberts
Parke County

BREAD PUDDING

1 3-oz. pkg.	1 t. cinnamon
French vanilla	½ C. raisins
pudding mix	1½ C. day-old
2 C. milk	bread cubes

In a deep 1 qt. microwave casserole, combine all ingredients. Microwave uncovered on HIGH 3 min. Stir. Microwave 3 min., stirring every min. until mixture boils. Serve either hot or cold. Serves 4.

Joyce L. Broady
Clark County

MICROWAVE CHOCOLATE PUDDING

⅔ C. sugar	¼ t. salt
¼ C. cocoa	2½ C. milk
3 T. cornstarch	2 T. butter
1 t. vanilla	

Combine sugar, cocoa, cornstarch, and salt in medium-sized glass mixing bowl; gradually stir in milk. Microwave on HIGH for 5 min., stirring once during cooking time.

Continue to microwave on HIGH until mixture is cooked and thickened, about 1–2 min. Stir in butter and vanilla. Chill. Serves 4–5.

Meta Katter
Dubois County

EASY RICE PUDDING

1 small pkg. va-	2 C. milk
nilla pudding	½ C. raisins
and pie filling	½ C. quick rice
mix	

In a 4 C. glass measure, combine all ingredients. Microwave on HIGH uncovered for 6 min., or until mixture boils. Stir occasionally during last half of cooking time. Serve warm or cool.

Jean Wrightsman
Monroe County

RASPBERRY JAM CRUMBLE BARS

¾ C. butter or	1½ C. quick oats
margarine	1 t. salt
1 C. dark brown	½ t. baking soda
sugar	¾ C. raspberry
1¾ C. flour	jam

Lightly grease an 8″ microwave baking dish. Cream butter and sugar together until fluffy. Stir in flour, salt, baking soda, and oats. Continue stirring until well-blended. Press ½ mixture into bottom of baking dish. Heat uncovered on MEDIUM-HIGH for 5 min. Spread jam evenly over baked mixture. Crumble remaining oat mixture over jam and press lightly. Heat uncovered on MEDIUM-HIGH additional 7 min. Test for doneness with a wooden pick. Cool and cut into bars.

Grace Spohr
Noble County

STRAWBERRY CRUNCH

½ C. butter or margarine
1 C. flour
¼ C. brown sugar
½ C. chopped walnuts
1 3-oz. pkg. strawberry flavored gelatin

1⅔ C. water
1 pint (2 C.) fresh strawberries, halved
1 4-oz. carton frozen whipped topping, thawed

Microwave butter on HIGH in 8″ glass baking dish 1–1½ min., or until melted. Mix in flour, brown sugar, and walnuts until thoroughly blended. Microwave on HIGH uncovered 5–6 min., or until mixture has a dry appearance and is lightly toasted, stirring 2 or 3 times. Set aside ½ C. crumbs. Press remaining crumbs with fork into bottom of dish. Microwave water on HIGH in 4 C. glass measure 4–4½ min., or until boiling. Stir in gelatin until dissolved. Refrigerate until slightly thickened. Set aside ½ C. gelatin. Stir strawberries into remaining gelatin. Pour mixture into crust. Fold the remaining ½ C. gelatin into the whipped topping. Spoon onto strawberries. Sprinkle with reserved crumbs. Refrigerate 3 hr. Cut into squares. Serves 9.

Marilyn Smendzuik
Greene County

SUPER S'MORES

2 graham cracker squares
⅓ milk chocolate bar

1 large marshmallow

Place 1 graham cracker square on a paper napkin. Top with a piece of chocolate bar and a marshmallow. Microwave on HIGH just until marshmallow puffs, about 15–25

sec. It will scorch if cooked too long. Top with second cracker. Let S'More stand 1 min. so heat from the marshmallow can melt chocolate.

Margaret McCammon
Dearborn County

MICROWAVE CARAMEL CORN

Put in 1 qt. measuring cup:
1 C. brown sugar
½ C. margarine

¼ C. white corn syrup
½ t. salt
½ t. baking soda

Microwave on HIGH and boil 2–4 min. Stir once or twice during cooking. Pop 3 poppers of corn (about 12 C.). Spray non-stick shortening in large grocery sack. Put popped corn in bag and pour caramel mixture over it. Put in microwave on HIGH for 1½ min. Remove from oven and shake unopened bag. Microwave again 1½ min.; shake; microwave 45 sec.; shake; microwave 30 sec.; shake. Pour out on cookie sheet or large cake pan to cool.

Sue Ward
Benton County

GRANOLA

3 C. uncooked oatmeal
1 C. untoasted wheat germ
1 C. unsweetened coconut
2 T. cinammon

2 T. brown sugar
¼ C. powdered milk
⅓ C. honey
⅓ C. oil
1 t. vanilla

Mix all the dry ingredients together in a large, shallow glass dish. Combine the honey, oil, and vanilla and heat in the microwave at HIGH for 30 seconds. Drizzle this warm liquid over the dry ingredients, coating thoroughly, using your hands to stir. Microwave at HIGH 10–15 min. Cool completely before removing from dish, and store in an airtight container. *Variation:* Seeds, nuts, raisins, or dates, when desired, should be added after the mixture has cooled.

Mary Ann Lienhart-Cross
Elkhart County

MICROWAVE PARTY MIX

2 C. Corn Chex	¼ lb. butter or
2 C. Rice Chex	margarine
2 C. small wheat	2 T. Worcester-
biscuits	shire sauce
3 C. thin pretzels	½ t. celery salt
½ lb. large Span-	½ t. onion salt
ish peanuts	½ t. garlic salt

Combine all ingredients in a glass dish. Microwave 8 min. on HIGH. Stir well every 2 min.

Marilyn Ziegler
Monroe County

ZESTY SNACK MIX

¼ C. margarine	2 C. wheat cereal
½ t. paprika	squares
¼ t. seasoned salt	¼ C. coarsely
5 drops hot pep-	chopped wal-
per sauce	nuts (optional)
3 C. popped corn	2 T. Parmesan
2 C. mini-pretzels	cheese

Place margarine, paprika, salt, and hot pepper sauce in oblong baking dish. Microwave on HIGH 1 min. or until butter is melted; stir together with popped corn, pretzels, cereal, and nuts. Toss mixture until well coated; spread evenly in pan. Microwave 2–2½ min. on HIGH, stirring once. Remove from oven; toss with cheese, and cool. Store in airtight container. Makes 6 C.

Debbie Martin
Hancock County

CHOCOLATE FUDGE

½ lb. marshmal-	⅔ C. evaporated
lows (4 C. mini-	milk
atures or 32	¼ t. salt
large marsh-	1 12-oz. pkg.
mallows)	chocolate chips
¼ C. margarine	1 t. vanilla
or butter	½ C. nuts,
1½ C. sugar	chopped

Combine marshmallows, butter, milk, sugar, and salt in a 3 qt. bowl. Microwave on HIGH until mixture boils (8 min.). Stir. Cook 3 min. longer; remove from heat. Add chocolate chips; beat until chocolate chips melt. Add vanilla and nuts. Pour into buttered 9″ square pan. Cool until firm. Cut into squares. Makes 2½ lb.

Victory E. H. Club
Grant County

NO FAIL FUDGE

3 C. sugar	10 oz. marshmal-
¾ C. butter	low creme
5 oz. evaporated	1 C. chopped
milk	nuts
12 oz. chocolate	1 t. vanilla
pieces	

Combine sugar, butter, and milk in buttered large glass mixing bowl. Cover with plastic wrap. Microwave on ROAST for 10 min. Stir and continue cooking on ROAST 5–6 min., or until mixture forms a soft ball in cold water. Stir in chocolate pieces until melted. Fold in marshmallow creme, nuts, and vanilla. Pour into buttered 13x9″ pan. Chill until firm; cut into squares.

Linda Lizenby
Pulaski County

MICROWAVE QUICKIE FUDGE

1 lb. powdered sugar	¼ lb. butter or margarine
½ C. cocoa or peanut butter	½ C. chopped nuts (optional)
¼ C. milk	

Blend powdered sugar and cocoa (or peanut butter) in mixing bowl; add milk and butter. (Do not mix these ingredients; merely place in bowl.) Microwave on HIGH for 2 min. Remove bowl from oven and stir just to mix ingredients. Add vanilla and nuts and stir until blended. Pour into greased pan. Cool and cut into pieces.

Lois Shaw　　　　　　　　*Mrs. Herman Small*
Wells County　　　　　　　*Dubois County*

MICRO PEANUT BRITTLE

1 C. raw peanuts	1 t. butter or margarine
1 C. sugar	
½ C. light corn syrup	1 t. vanilla extract
⅛ t. salt	1 t. baking soda

Stir together peanuts, sugar, syrup, and salt in 1½ qt. casserole. Microwave on HIGH 7–8 min., stirring well after 4 min. Add butter and vanilla to syrup, blending well. Microwave 1–2 min. more. Peanuts will be lightly browned and syrup very hot. Add baking soda and gently stir until light and foamy. Pour mixture onto lightly greased cookie sheet; stretch by pulling with two metal spatulas. When cool, break into small pieces and store in airtight container. *Note:* If roasted salted peanuts are used, omit salt and add peanuts after first 4 min. of cooking.

Mary Smoker　　　　　　　*Opal Little*
Kosciusko County　　　　　*Parke County*

CHINESE CLUSTERS

12 oz. of morsels (chocolate, butterscotch, or ½ of each)	1 3-oz. can chow mein noodles
	6½ oz. peanuts

Microwave morsels in 1½–2 qt. dish on MEDIUM for 3–3½ min., or until melted. Stir until smooth. Stir in noodles and nuts; drop by teaspoon onto waxed paper. Let set until firm.

Loretta Byrne
Harrison County

DOUBLE PEANUT CLUSTERS

6 oz. chocolate chips	1 C. roasted peanuts
⅓ C. peanut butter	

Microwave chocolate and peanut butter on MEDIUM until melted. Stir until blended. Add peanuts, stirring to coat. Drop from teaspoon onto waxed paper. Chill until set.

Janean DePlanty
Starke County

Woks and Skillets

Stir-Frying

A fast, delicious, and vitamin-conscious way to prepare foods is to stir-fry. Stir-frying can be done successfully in either a skillet or a wok.

If you buy a conventional wok, don't buy one smaller than fourteen inches. To remove industrial oil from a new wok scrub it well with a soap-filled steel wool pad. Season by pouring about one inch of oil into the wok and heating it in a 275° oven for 1½ hours. Obviously, if your wok has wooden handles you will have to heat it on a stove top burner. Once it is seasoned, you no longer need to scrub the wok—merely wipe it out with a paper towel or cloth. When well seasoned, your wok will be black almost to its top. Once it is properly seasoned, you can use less cooking oil.

To stir-fry, heat your utensil before adding oil. Use the least expensive oil available—there is no one best kind. Add 1–2 tablespoons of oil, bringing oil up onto sides of utensil. Stir-frying requires that you keep the food moving all the time. Stir at a rate corresponding to the size of your food pieces. Sometimes you will have to stir furiously. Stir-fry vegetables only until crisp-tender.

Don't try to stir-fry more than one-half pound of food at a time, because larger amounts tend to reduce cooking temperatures too rapidly. Since quick changes of heat are difficult on an electric stove, regulate heat by simply moving the wok or skillet off the burner and placing it temporarily on a cold burner to cool.

The slicing, chopping, and dicing of foods for stir-frying can be time consuming. By preparing foods early in the day and keeping them covered and cold, the cook can eliminate a last-minute hassle.

Experiment with soy sauces—there are a variety. You might especially enjoy Tamari, a Japanese version of soy sauce. The difference between light and dark soy sauces is mainly aesthetic.

After a little practice you can forget stir-fry recipes and successfully use whatever ingredients you already have on hand.

STIR-FRIED BEEF WITH BROCCOLI

1 lb. round steak
2 T. soy sauce
1 T. sherry
1 t. sugar
1 clove garlic, minced
1 T. cornstarch
¼ C. water
1 beef bouillon cube
1 T. salt
1 bunch broccoli, chopped
1 C. sliced celery
1 T. oil

Slice steak in very thin slices. Combine soy sauce, sherry, sugar, and garlic. Coat meat well and marinate 30 min. Combine cornstarch, water, and bouillon cube; set aside. Cook broccoli 1 min. in boiling water. Add celery and cook 1 min. longer; drain. In hot oil, stir-fry beef until color is gone, about 3 min. Stir in cornstarch mixture. Add vegetables and cook until mixture is hot. Serve with rice. Serves 6.

Violet Crase
Clark County

STIR-FRIED BEEF AND CARROTS

2 T. vegetable oil
1 lb. lean beef chuck steak, cut into ½x2″ strips
1 C. carrots, sliced on diagonal
½ C. celery, sliced on diagonal
½ C. onion, chopped
1 C. seeded green pepper, sliced in ½″ strips
For sauce blend together:
2 T. soy sauce
2 T. water
½ t. minced garlic
½ t. cornstarch
⅛ t. ginger

Heat oil over high heat in wok or skillet. Add meat and stir-fry 2–3 min., or until meat has lost its pink color. Add carrots and celery and stir-fry 2–3 min. Add onions and stir-fry 2 min. Add sauce; add green pepper and stir-fry 1–2 min. until sauce is thick and vegetables are crisp-tender. Serves 4.

Pam Fausz
Huntington County

BEEF-VEGETABLE STIR-FRY

1 T. cornstarch	1 clove garlic,
1 t. sugar	minced
¼ t. ginger	1 large onion,
2 T. soy sauce	sliced in ¼"
½ C. beef broth	slices
1 lb. boneless	1¼ lb. mush-
beef (top	rooms, sliced
round, etc.)	in ¼" slices
5 T. vegetable oil	¾ lb. pea pods

Mix together cornstarch, sugar, and ginger. Blend in soy and beef broth; set aside. Cut beef, with grain, into 1½" wide strips. Cut each strip across grain in thin slanted ⅛" slices (easier if meat is partially frozen). Heat 2 T. of oil over high heat in wok or skillet; stir-fry ½ of meat and minced onion, until meat is lightly browned. Remove from pan and set aside. Repeat, using 1 T. oil and remaining meat. Heat remaining 2 T. oil and stir-fry onion and mushrooms, about 2 min. Add pea pods and stir-fry 1 min. Return meat to pan; add cornstarch mixture and stir until sauce boils and thickens. Serves 4.

Edna Marshall
Madison County

30-MINUTE CHOP SUEY

1 round steak,	1 T. brown sauce
cut in narrow	1 can chow mein
strips	noodles
½ C. margarine	soy sauce
1 C. chopped	**Paste:**
onion	⅓ C. water
1 C. sliced celery	2 t. soy sauce
1 can bean	2 T. corn starch
sprouts,	1 t. sugar
drained	

Brown steak in hot margarine; add onions and stir-fry 5 min. Add celery, salt and pepper to taste, 1 C. hot water, and brown

sauce; cover and cook 5 min. Add bean sprouts and bring to boil. Add paste; cook and stir until mixture thickens slightly. Serve over rice. Pass chow mein noodles and soy sauce. Serves 4.

Margaret Simmerman
Monroe County

SLICED STEAK ON A BUN

½ lb. round	1 T. water
steak	1 T. salad oil
2 T. soy sauce	2 green peppers,
½ t. sugar	seeded and
1 T. butter or	sliced into ¼"
margarine	strips
2 medium	6 hamburger
onions, thinly	buns
sliced	

Cut steak into thin slices, ⅛" thick, on the diagonal. Marinate steak in mixture of soy sauce, sugar, and water for 30 min. Sauté pepper and onion in hot butter until lightly browned; remove from pan and keep warm. Add oil to skillet; heat. Add steak slices and the marinade. Stir-fry on high heat until browned. Add onion and pepper. Cook until liquid in pan is almost gone, about 3 min. Serve in buns. Serves 6. *Note:* When returning the onion and pepper to the skillet, add a seeded and chopped tomato, if you like.

Wilma Linville
Decatur County

CHINESE PEPPER STEAK (1)

2 lb. flank steak,	1 clove garlic,
sliced in thin	finely chopped
strips	1 t. salt
1 T. vegetable oil	dash pepper

¼ t. ginger
¼ C. soy sauce
1 T. cornstarch
2 large green peppers, seeded, cut in 1" strips
2 medium tomatoes, quartered
1 1-lb. can bean sprouts, drained
¼ C. water

Sauté beef, garlic, salt, pepper, and ginger until browned. Add soy sauce; cook covered 5 min. Add green peppers, tomatoes, and bean sprouts. Bring to boil; cook, covered, over high heat 5 min. Meanwhile, make a smooth paste of cornstarch and water; stir into beef mixture and cook until mixture thickens. Serve over rice. Serves 8.

Variation: Omit bean sprouts and replace with ¼ lb. sliced mushrooms and 6 green onions, cut in ½" pieces.

Mrs. John Matzinger
St. Joseph County

CHINESE PEPPER STEAK (2)

1 lb. round steak, partially frozen for easier slicing
4 T. cornstarch, divided
water
2 T. dry sherry
2 T. soy sauce, divided
4 t. sugar, divided
1 t. ginger, fresh grated
¼ C. catsup
¼ t. pepper
2 T. vegetable oil
1 clove garlic, minced
1 bunch green onions, cut in ½" pieces
2 large green peppers, seeded, cut in chunks
3 medium tomatoes, cut in chunks

Cut steak in thirds lengthwise, then cut crosswise diagonally into thin slices. Mix 2 T. cornstarch, ¼ C. water, the sherry, 1 T. soy sauce, and 1 t. sugar; toss with beef to coat well; set aside. May be prepared up to 1 day in advance; covered and refrigerated. Mix remaining 2 T. cornstarch, ½ C. water, remaining T. soy sauce, remaining 3 t. sugar, the catsup and pepper; set aside. Stir-fry beef in 2 T. hot oil until it loses its pink color. Remove with slotted spoon; set aside. Stir-fry garlic and onions 30 seconds. Add green peppers and ¼ C. water; bring to boil and cook about 3 min., or until peppers are tender. Add tomatoes, beef, and ginger. Stir to reheat. Add cornstarch-catsup mixture; stir until sauce thickens. Serve over rice.

Nancy Wagner
Fountain County

SUKIYAKI

3 T. vegetable oil
1 medium onion, thinly sliced
1 4-oz. can mushrooms, drained, or 4 large fresh mushrooms
½ lb. round or sirloin steak, sliced into thin strips
½ C. celery, thinly sliced
¼ lb. fresh spinach, remove hard stems, tear into pieces
4 green onions, cut lengthwise into thin pieces (optional)
4 T. soy sauce
2 T. sugar
½ 10½-oz. can consommé

Heat oil over high heat in wok or skillet. Add onion and mushrooms; stir. Add beef and celery; stir-fry until beef loses red color. Add spinach, green onions, and celery; stir-fry. Next add soy sauce, sugar, and consommé. From start to finish cooking time is 10 min. Do not overcook. Serve with rice.

Marcia Ford
Jay County

CHICKEN CAULIFLOWER

1 chicken, skinned, boned, and chopped into 1½" pieces	½ head of cauliflower
	1 handful of fresh snow peas
	1 C. mushrooms

Oil wok and season with ginger root and garlic. Discard the ginger root and garlic. In hot oil, stir-fry chicken until nearly done. Place cauliflower and peas on top of chicken; cover and steam until tender. Add mushrooms and stir-fry until heated. Thicken juices with cornstarch (you may need to add some chicken stock for more liquid). Season with soy sauce and stir until every ingredient is coated. Serve immediately.

Janean DePlanty
Starke County

STIR-FRIED CHICKEN

2 chicken breasts, skinned, boned, and cut into cubes (partially freeze for easy cutting)	½ C. each of chopped onion and green peppers
	¾ C. chicken broth
1 C. each of cut up celery, carrots, broccoli and mushrooms	1–2 C. fresh or frozen snow peas
	1 T. cornstarch
	2 T. water
2 T. sherry	¼ t. ginger

In hot vegetable oil, stir-fry chicken until it loses its color and turns white. Make well in center and add separately the celery, carrots, broccoli, and mushrooms. Next add the onions and green peppers. Stir-fry until tender-crisp. Make well in center and add chicken broth, sherry, and snow peas; bring to boil and cook 1 min. In the center of the wok, combine cornstarch, water, and ginger and boil 1 min. Stir all ingredients together and simmer to desired doneness. Salt and pepper to taste. Serve over rice.

Ferne Savoie
Noble County

CHINESE ALMOND CHICKEN

1 whole chicken breast, boned, skinned, and cut into ¾" cubes	1 6-oz. pkg. frozen or ¼ lb. fresh Chinese peapods, blanched 1 min.
3 T. vegetable oil	½ C. sliced celery
½ C. blanched whole almonds	Sauce:
1 clove garlic, minced	3 T. soy sauce
	3 T. dry sherry
¼ lb. mushrooms, sliced	¼ C. water
	1 t. sugar
3 green onions, cut in 1" lengths	½ t. ginger
	1 T. cornstarch

Heat oil in wok over medium-high heat. Add almonds and toss until roasted, about 1 min. Add chicken and garlic and stir-fry until chicken turns opaque. Add vegetables and stir-fry until tender-crisp, about 3 min. Blend sauce ingredients together. Add sauce mixture, stirring constantly, until sauce thickens and clears.

Dianna Crouse
Union County

CHICKEN CHINESE STYLE

3 half breasts of chicken, skinned, boned, and cut in strips	1 C. sliced mushrooms
	2½ T. soy sauce
	2 t. cornstarch
	1½ C. snow peas
¾ C. chicken broth	1 C. celery, sliced
3 T. vegetable oil	rice or Chinese noodles

Marinate chicken in soy sauce. Heat oil and stir-fry chicken until browned and cooked through. Add vegetables and cook over medium heat 5 min. Mix cornstarch and broth; add to meat and vegetables. Cook until slightly thickened. Serve with rice or Chinese noodles. Serves 4.

Elaine Wells
Randolph County

CHICKEN TERIYAKI

2 whole chicken	½ C. soy sauce
breasts	½ t. powdered
2 T. sherry	sugar substitute
1 clove garlic,	1½ T. vegetable
minced	oil

Skin and debone chicken; cut into 1" cubes. Make a marinade by combining all remaining ingredients. Pour marinade over chicken pieces and refrigerate for 1 hr. Add additional oil to wok or skillet; when hot, stir-fry chicken for about 10 min. Serve with rice. Serves 5.

Sue Childes
Monroe County

CHICKEN YAKITORI

1½ lb. chicken	5 T. sugar
meat, skinned,	2 T. saki or rice
boned, cut into	wine
¾" squares	20 green onions,
3 T. vegetable oil	cut in 1" pieces
⅓ C. soy sauce	

Combine soy sauce, sugar, and saki; set aside. In hot oil stir-fry chicken for 6–7 min. Pour off excess oil. Pour soy sauce mixture in pan and cook 3–4 min. Add onions and cook until heated through. Do not overcook. Serve with rice. Serves 6.

Mary Frasier
Cass County

STIR-FRIED LIVER (1)

2 lb. beef or	3 large yellow on-
calves liver, cut	ions, sliced thin
in thin strips	3 medium green
2 T. vegetable oil	peppers,
2 t. flour	seeded, and cut
¼ t. pepper	into ⅛" strips
1½ t. salt	4 t. cider vinegar

Heat 1 T. oil and add liver; sprinkle with flour and pepper and cook 2–3 min., turning once. When liver is just pink in the middle, remove from skillet and keep warm. Add remaining 1 T. oil to skillet; fry vegetables over high heat 1 min., stirring constantly with 2 large spoons. Cover skillet, reduce heat, and cook about 2 min. until vegetables are crisp-tender. Return liver to skillet. Add vinegar and stir-fry over high heat for 1 min. to heat through and blend flavors.

Gretta Gehring
Steuben County

STIR-FRIED LIVER (2)

1 lb. liver, cut in	1 T. cooking oil
thin strips	1 5 or 6-oz. can
2 t. cornstarch	bamboo shoots,
¼ t. ginger	drained
2 T. dry sherry	1 3-oz. can mush-
⅓ C. green	rooms, drained
onions, sliced	1 T. soy sauce

Coat liver with mixture of cornstarch, ginger, sherry, and onions; stir-fry in hot oil. Add bamboo shoots and mushrooms; cook, stirring constantly, until heated through. Stir in soy sauce. Serve over rice. Serves 4.

Nancy Wagner
Fountain County

STIR-FRIED SWEET-AND-SOUR PORK

1½ lb. pork, sliced in thin strips	2 T. water
	¼ C. sugar
1 t. salt	1 T. cornstarch
2 t. soy sauce	1 T. soy sauce
2 t. cornstarch	8 oz. can pineapple chunks, drained
⅛ t. pepper	
2 T. oil	1 small green pepper, sliced
½ C. carrots, sliced	
	3 green onions, cut in 2″ pieces
1 C. pineapple juice	

Combine salt, 2 t. soy sauce, 2 t. cornstarch, and pepper. Marinate pork in mixture for 20 min. Heat oil and stir-fry pork until white; add carrots and water. Cover and cook for 2 min. Push mixture to side of wok or skillet and, in center of wok, make sweet and sour sauce with pineapple juice, sugar, 1 T. cornstarch, and 1 T. soy sauce. When sauce is thick and clear, return meat and carrots to sauce; add pineapple and bring to a boil. Add green peppers and onions. Cook ½ min. until bubbly. Serve with hot rice or fried noodles.

Dorothy Beck
Greene County

CHOP SUEY

1 lb. lean pork, beef, or chicken, sliced in thin strips	1 4-oz. can mushroom pieces, drained
½ t. salt	1 16-oz. can chop suey vegetables, drained
¼ C. cooking oil	
2 green onions, sliced diagonally	1½ C. chicken broth
	2 T. cornstarch
1 green pepper, cut in ¼″ slices	2 T. soy sauce
	2 T. water

Sprinkle meat with salt. Brown in hot oil;

remove from skillet. Add onions, green pepper, and mushrooms to skillet. Stir-fry 2 min., stirring constantly. Add chop suey vegetables, chicken broth, and meat. Combine cornstarch, soy sauce, and water; blend until smooth. Add to meat mixture; simmer until slightly thickened. Serve over chow mein noodles and/or hot rice. Serves 6.

Diana Yeager
Porter County

HAM-FRIED RICE

4 C. cooked rice	3 chopped mushrooms
½ lb. cooked sliced ham	
	½ lb. chopped bacon
1 medium onion, chopped	
	1 C. scrambled eggs
½ C. frozen or fresh peas	
	2 T. soy sauce

Heat wok or skillet to medium high (375°). Fry bacon and onion until onion is tender. Add mushrooms; stir. Add ham; stir. Add green peas; stir. Add eggs; stir. Add salt, pepper and 2 T. soy sauce. Add rice; stir a few min. Serves 6.

Variations: Use other cooked meats to make different kinds of fried rice. Suggestions: chicken, beef, luncheon meats, pork, etc.

Hiromi Burker
Brown County

STIR-FRIED PEA PODS

¼ C. salad oil	2 8-oz. pkg. frozen or 1 lb. fresh Chinese pea pods
3 T. finely chopped onion	
1 small can mushroom pieces, drained	
	1 t. salt
	⅛ t. pepper

Sauté onion in hot oil until golden; add pea pods and stir-fry until tender-crisp, about 5 min. for frozen or 8 min. for fresh; add mushrooms. Stir in salt and pepper and serve immediately. Serves 6–8.

Norma Sullivan
Carroll County

CHINESE FRIED RICE

3 T. bacon drippings	1 C. mushrooms, sliced
½ C. green onions, cut in ½" pieces	2 T. soy sauce
1 C. celery, diced	1 egg, slightly beaten
3 C. cooked rice	½ lb. crisp bacon, crumbled

Heat bacon dripings in skillet; add onions and celery and sauté until tender. Add mushrooms, rice, and soy sauce. Cook 10 min. on low heat, stirring occasionally. Stir in beaten egg and cook only until egg is done. Add bacon and mix well. Serves 6–7.

Variation: Substitute shrimp for the mushrooms, and omit the bacon.

Ellen Bess
Owen County

ART'S VEGETABLE SLUMGULLION

1 clove garlic, minced (optional)	1 "mess" okra, thinly sliced
1 medium zucchini, thinly sliced	3 medium, partially ripened, tomatoes
2 green peppers, thinly sliced	½ C. vinegar
	½ t. dry mustard
	½ t. thyme

In hot peanut oil, stir-fry vegetables, adding in order given. When crisp-tender, add seasonings; cover and simmer 5 min. Good served with rice. Serves 4–6.

Audrey Gehlbach
Harrison County

STIR-FRIED ZUCCHINI AND MUSHROOMS

1 C. sliced zucchini	garlic and soy sauce to taste
1 C. sliced mushrooms	Parmesan cheese

Stir-fry vegetables in skillet until tender-crisp. Add garlic and soy sauce; sprinkle with cheese. Serve immediately.

Juanita Russell
Lawrence County

Skillets

The skillet can make quick work of both cooking and serving main dishes, or one-dish meals. Skillet meals are great for those days when little food pre-preparation is possible. While many skillet meals require 1–1¼ hr. cooking time, others can easily be done in 45 min. The thermostatically controlled electric fry pan eliminates much of the need for constant "skillet watching." Meat can be skillet-cooked, starting from the frozen state with almost no loss of flavor. Frozen roasts will require ⅓–½ more cooking time; steaks and chops ¼–½ more time.

STEAK IN A SKILLET

1 lb. round or sirloin steak, cut into serving pieces	1 large onion, sliced
1 can beef broth	6 medium potatoes, peeled and sliced

Brown steak in cooking oil; drain. Add beef broth, and alternate layers of onion and potatoes. Cover and cook until tender, 45–60 min. Serves 6.

Jean Hudson
Orange County

BEEF STROGANOFF

1½ lb. steak, partially frozen	2 medium onions, diced
½ lb. mushrooms, fresh or canned	salt and pepper to taste
margarine to brown meat and vegetables	flour
	2 t. liquid garlic
	1 C. sour cream

Early in day cut meat into thin strips; coat with flour. Refrigerate. At dinner time melt margarine in skillet; sauté mushrooms and onion together until tender and remove from pan. Brown all meat quickly in hot pan until brown on all sides. Add mushrooms and onions to pan; stir well. Remove from burner; add salt, pepper, garlic, and sour cream. Stir well. Serve over hot buttered noodles or rice. Serves 5.

Bev McClure
Union County

VEAL MADAGASCAR FROM TRADER VIC'S (VEAL WITH MUSHROOMS IN A CREAM SAUCE)

8–12 slices veal scaloppine, about 1 lb.	salt and freshly ground pepper to taste
2 T. flour	¼ lb. thinly sliced mushrooms
3 T. butter	¼ C. dry white wine
1 t. crushed green peppercorns (found in gourmet section of grocery store)	½ C. heavy cream
	½ t. Worcestershire sauce
¼ C. finely chopped onion	juice of half a lemon

Pound pieces of meat lightly with a heavy mallet; sprinkle with salt and pepper and dust with flour. Sauté meat in butter 1½ min. to each side; remove from skillet. To the skillet, add the onion, mushrooms, and peppercorns; cook briefly and add the wine. Cook quickly to reduce liquid; add the cream. Bring to a boil; stir in the Worcestershire sauce and lemon juice. Add salt to taste; return the meat to the skillet and heat through. Serve with buttered fine noodles seasoned with salt, pepper, and freshly grated nutmeg. Serves 8.

Patsy Kirkendall
Howard County

MOCK CHICKEN PATTIES

½ lb. ground veal or pork	⅓ C. evaporated milk
½ t. salt	1 can cream of chicken soup
¼ t. pepper	½ C. water
¼ C. oats	
1 T. shortening	

Mix the meat, salt, pepper, oats, and milk together; shape into 4–6 patties. Brown slowly on both sides in hot shortening. Mix soup and water together; pour over patties. Cook slowly for 5 min., turning patties often.

Wanda Vincent
Warrick County

SPEEDY BEEF N' BEANS

1 T. instant	Kitchen Bouquet
minced onion	1 8-oz can spa-
½ C. milk	ghetti sauce
1½ lb. ground	with
beef	mushrooms
1 slightly beaten	1 8-oz. can kid-
egg	ney beans
½ C. quick oats	buttered, toasted
1–2 t. salt	French bread
¼ t. pepper	slices

Soak onion in milk 5 min. Mix in beef, egg, oats, salt, and pepper. Mound mixture in 10″ skillet. With wooden spoon handle score in 5 or 6 wedges. Brush top of wedges with Kitchen Bouquet. Combine spaghetti sauce and kidney beans; pour over beef mixture. Simmer uncovered 20–25 min., or until done. Serve wedges on French bread slices; spoon extra sauce over wedges. Serves 6.

Carol Vandeventer
Greene County

SKILLET CASSEROLE

1 lb. hamburger	2–4 carrots, sliced
1 large potato,	or chopped
sliced or	1 can cream of
chopped	mushroom
1 large onion,	soup
sliced or	1 can cream of
chopped	celery soup
¼-½ me-	(optional)
dium head	6 slices process
cabbage,	cheese food
shredded	(optional)

Pat hamburger into cold electric skillet. Layer potato, carrot, onion, and cabbage over hamburger. Pour soups over vegetables, spreading to edge of skillet. Top with cheese and cook at 300° for 30-40 min. Be sure to open vent slightly, or cheese, if used, will run out.

Evelyn Shumaker   *Thelma Bond*
Noble County   *Parke County*

SKILLET LASAGNE

1 lb. ground beef	1 t. basil
1 envelope spa-	1 t. salt
ghetti sauce	1 T. parsley flakes
mix	1 No. 2½ can
1 lb. cream style	tomatoes
cottage cheese	1 C. water
3 C. medium	1 8-oz. pkg.
noodles,	shredded moz-
uncooked	zarella cheese

Brown meat; drain. Sprinkle ½ spaghetti sauce mix over meat. Spread cottage cheese in layer over meat; arrange uncooked noodles in layer. Sprinkle with remaining spaghetti sauce mix and salt. Add tomatoes and water. Simmer covered 30–35 min. Sprinkle cheese over top; cover and let stand 10–15 min. before serving. Serves 8.

Edna Stetzel
Huntington County

MINUTE RICE MEATBALLS

1 can mushroom	1 egg, slightly
soup	beaten
1 C. water	2 t. grated onion
1 C. Minute Rice	⅛ t. marjoram
1 lb. ground beef	⅛ t. pepper
2 t. salt	

Mix soup with water. Combine remaining ingredients with ½ C. of the soup mixture; mix just to blend. Shape into 18 meatballs; cover with remaining soup and simmer in skillet 15 min.

Betty Christopher
White County

SKILLET MINI-MEAT LOAVES

2 slices bread, crumbled	Topping:
½ C. milk	1 1-lb. can tomatoes
½ t. basil leaves	2 t. prepared mustard
2 T. onion flakes	2 T. onion flakes
1 t. salt	½ C. pickle relish
¼ t. pepper	½ C. water
1 lb. ground chuck	

Combine meat loaf ingredients and shape into 4 portions; brown in hot fat. Mix topping ingredients together; pour over meat loaves and simmer covered 20 min. Serves 4.

Shelley Martinek
Fountain County

PIZZA MEATBALLS

1 lb. ground beef	½ t. oregano
1 C. dried bread crumbs	½ lb. mozarella cheese, cut into 12 cubes
½ C. milk	
2 T. instant minced onion	3 T. flour
1 t. garlic salt	2 T. salad oil
⅛ t. pepper	1 15½-oz. jar pizza sauce

Mix together beef, bread crumbs, milk, and seasonings. Shape into 12 meatballs with one cube of cheese in center of each. Dredge lightly with flour. Sauté in hot oil until browned. Add pizza sauce and simmer 10 min. Serve with rice. Serves 6.

Janice Dunn
Clark County

RICE OLÉ

½ C. raw rice	1 T. butter or meat drippings
1 lb. hamburger	
¾ C. onion, chopped	1 beef bouillon cube

¼ C. tomato paste	1 t. chili powder
1½ t. salt	½ lb. Velveeta, cubed
⅛ t. pepper	2¼ C. water

Brown meat and onion; drain. Stir in rice, water, bouillon cube, and tomato paste; add seasonings. Simmer for 25 min. Add cheese cubes and toss lightly. Serve at once. Serves 6.

Karen Brown
Parke County

GARDEN SPANISH RICE

2 C. cooked rice	1 large onion, chopped
1 8-oz. can tomato sauce	1 medium green pepper, chopped
¾ lb. ground chuck, browned and drained	4 whole tomatoes, cut in eighths
3 T. soy sauce	

Mix cooked chuck, onion, green pepper, and rice together; add soy sauce and simmer for 10 min. Add tomatoes and tomato sauce; warm together a few min. *Optional:* Top with Parmesan cheese. Serves 4.

Holly Custer
DeKalb County

SKILLET SPAGHETTI

1 lb. ground beef	4 oz. (1½ C.) dry spaghetti, broken in 2–3" lengths
1 clove garlic, minced, or garlic salt	
1 C. chopped onion	1½ t. salt (less if you use garlic salt)
¼ t. mace	
¼ t. allspice	3 C. tomato juice
½ t. dry mustard	Parmesan cheese, grated
¼ t. pepper	

Brown beef, garlic, and onion. Sprinkle mace, allspice, mustard, and pepper over meat. Place spaghetti over meat. Stir salt into tomato juice and pour over spaghetti. Simmer covered 35 min. Serve with Parmesan cheese. Serves 4–6.

Florence Ringel
Wabash County

SKILLET STEW (1)

1 lb. ground beef	8 oz. can tomato
6 oz. can mixed	sauce
vegetables,	½ envelope
drained	Sloppy Joe sea-
⅓ C. water	soning mix

Brown beef in skillet; drain. Add other ingredients. Cook over low heat until bubbly and hot.

Doris Nifong
Marshall County

SKILLET STEW (2)

1 lb. hamburger	1 C. diced carrots
½ C. chopped	1 C. red kidney
onion	beans
1 qt. tomato juice	1 t. salt
1 C. sliced	½ t. pepper
potatoes	

Brown hamburger and onion in skillet; drain. Add juice, salt, pepper, potatoes, and carrots; simmer until done. Add kidney beans and heat thoroughly. Serves 4.

June Corell
Wells County

CHICKEN CACCIATORE

1 fryer	oregano to taste
1 8-oz. can to-	1 T. Parmesan
mato sauce	cheese
½ C. white wine	½ green pepper,
1 T. sugar	chopped
½ lb. fresh	½ medium onion
mushrooms	chopped

Sauté chicken in vegetable oil; remove from pan. Add onion to pan and sauté. Arrange chicken over top of onion, sprinkle with oregano; add sauce and wine; cover and cook for about 45 min. Add rest of ingredients and cook until chicken is tender. Add water as needed to keep from scorching.

Minnie Colonese
LaPorte County

CHICKEN IMPERIAL

2 1-lb., 1-oz.	¼ t. salt
cans black	1 T. flour
cherries	1 t. sugar
1 fryer, cut up	⅛ t. allspice
salt	⅛ t. cinnamon
pepper	1 chicken bouil-
paprika	lon cube
3 T. butter	

Drain cherries, reserving liquid. Sprinkle chicken pieces with salt, pepper, and paprika; brown in butter. Remove chicken from skillet; add ¼ t. salt, flour, sugar, and spices to skillet and blend with drippings. Gradually stir in cherry liquid. Add chicken and remaining ingredients, except cherries. Simmer covered until chicken is tender, about 35 min. Add drained cherries and continue cooking for another 5 min. Serves 4–6.

Sharon Johnson
Porter County

CHICKEN MARENGO

1 fryer; skinned,	1 large onion,
boned, and cut	chopped
into cubes	1 T. fresh parsley,
flour, salt and	minced
pepper	¼–½ t. thyme

1 bay leaf, crushed	1 C. dry white wine
3–4 tomatoes, cut in wedges, or equal amount canned tomato wedges	½ lb. fresh mushrooms, sauteed ½–1 C. sliced ripe olives

Dredge chicken in seasoned flour. In skillet brown chicken and onion in hot oil; add seasonings, tomatoes, and wine and simmer for 30 min. Add olives and mushrooms; simmer additional 10 min. Add more wine if necessary. Serves 4.

Ingelore Welsh
Monroe County

PEPSI CHICKEN

1 stick margarine	1 20-oz. bottle ketchup
1 12-oz. can Pepsi	salt and pepper to taste
1 cut-up chicken	

Melt margarine in electric skillet. Place chicken in skillet and pour Pepsi and ketchup over chicken. Cook at 205° for 2 hr. (*Note:* May bake in oven at 350° for 1 hr.) Serves 4.

Cindy Franz
Warrick County

ROBIN HOOD'S CHICKEN

3 T. fat	½ t. pepper
chicken parts to serve 6	1 lb. can peas and carrots, drained
1 clove garlic, minced	3 C. cooked rice
2 t. salt	1 C. water
1 lb. can small onions, drained	2 T. catsup, optional

In large skillet, brown chicken in hot fat; add garlic, 1 t. of the salt and ¼ t. of the pepper. Cook slowly, until the chicken is tender, about 30 min.; add onions, peas, and carrots, the other 1 t. of salt and ¼ t. pepper. Top chicken with cooked rice; pour on water and catsup which have been mixed together. Cover and heat until most of liquid has been absorbed and vegetables are hot. Serves 6.

Carla Hoffman
Martin County

SKILLET CHICKEN AND RICE

¼ C. flour	2 C. water
1 t. salt	1 medium onion, sliced
1 t. paprika	½ t. salt
¼ t. pepper	¾ C. rice, uncooked
1 fryer, cut up	
¼ C. margarine	

Mix flour, 1 t. salt, pepper, and paprika. Dredge chicken pieces in flour mixture. Brown chicken in hot fat; drain. Add water, ½ t. salt, onion, and rice; stir with fork. Simmer covered 30 min., or until rice and chicken are tender and liquid is absorbed. Serves 4.

Marilyn Kelsch
Hancock County

LEMON CHICKEN BREAST

Cut 1 whole skinned, boned chicken breast to make 2 chicken cutlets. Place cutlets between waxed paper and pound to flatten. Salt cutlet on each side; dust lightly with flour. Sauté in melted hot margarine until golden brown on each side. Turn heat down; pour small amount of lemon juice on cutlets. Cover and simmer about 10–15 min., or until lemon juice is cooked into the chicken. Serves 2.

Esther Kersjes
Allen County

WINGS AND RICE

½ C. flour	3 T. butter
½ t. salt	⅔ C. thinly sliced
⅛ t. pepper	celery
6 chicken wings	1¼ C. chicken
½ C. each:	broth or water
chopped green	⅛ t. thyme
onions and un-	½ C. toasted
cooked rice	almonds

Combine flour, salt, and pepper in a paper bag. Add wings; shake to coat well. Heat butter to sizzling; brown wings slowly. Remove wings from skillet; add celery, onion, and rice. Cook and stir mixture gently until rice is golden; blend in chicken broth and thyme. Return wings to skillet. Cover and simmer 15 min. Top with almonds and serve hot. Serves 2.

Doris Shuppert
St. Joseph County

TEMPURA

fish fillets, cut into 1½x2" pieces	asparagus, cut into bite sizes (or use any garden
green peppers, cut into 1½x2" pieces	vegetables, such as onion, snow peas,
sweet potatoes or carrots, peeled and sliced on diagonal	cauliflower, broccoli, or mushrooms)
zucchini, unpeeled and sliced in ½" rounds	**Tempura Batter:** 1 large egg 1½ C. ice cold water
green beans or	2 C. sifted cake flour

Drain fish and vegetables thoroughly on paper towels; arrange on large platter. Pour vegetable oil at least 2" deep into electric frying pan or deep, wide frying pan. Heat to 400°. Beat egg thoroughly with wire whisk; blend with water. Sprinkle all flour over liquid. Stir in flour quickly. Batter should be lumpy. Dip vegetables and fish into batter, drain excess batter, and slide into hot oil. Fry 1 min. on each side. To serve, dip in catsup, hot mustard, soy sauce, or tempura sauce.

Hiromi Burker
Brown County

SWEET & PUNGENT PORK

vegetable oil for frying	1½ C. pineapple chunks,
1 egg, beaten	drained
⅔ C. flour	½ C. brown
½ t. salt	sugar
4 T. water	¾ C. vinegar
1 lb. pork shoulder, cut in ½" cubes	1 C. water 2 T. molasses
2 small green peppers, seeded, cut in ½" strips	¼ C. water 3 T. cornstarch 2 small tomatoes, cut in pieces

Combine egg, flour, salt, and 4 T. water to make thin batter. Add pork cubes and mix well until coated. Fry cubes in hot cooking oil until nicely browned; drain well and keep hot. Combine green peppers, pineapple, brown sugar, vinegar, 1 C. water, and molasses; bring to boil, stirring constantly. Combine cornstarch and ¼ C. water; add to hot mixture. Cook, stirring constantly until thickened. Add pork and cook 5 min. Add tomatoes on top and cook until heated through.

Betty Witmer
Whitley County

DA'NIN DING

2 lb. lean pork, cut in 1" squares
1 No. 303 can French-cut green beans, drained
1 No. 303 can bean sprouts, drained (or 1 lb. fresh)

½ C. catsup
¼ C. soy sauce
1 C. water
thinly slice fresh vegetables (any or all of them): cauliflower, bok choy, celery

Brown pork in skillet in hot oil. Add catsup, soy sauce, and water. Simmer ½ hr. Add fresh vegetables and simmer until tender-crisp. Add green beans and sprouts and heat thoroughly. Serves 4–6.

Dorothy Anderson
Grant County

MUSHROOM-SAUCED PORK STEAK

4 pork blade steaks, ½–¾" thick
¼ t. pepper

1 can cream of mushroom soup

Use a piece of pork fat to grease a medium hot skillet; discard fat. Brown steaks; sprinkle with pepper and add undiluted soup. Simmer covered 45 min., or until meat is fork-tender. Serves 4.

Diana Sibery
Jay County

PORK CHOPS, APPLES, AND KRAUT

4–6 pork chops
1 No. 2 or 2½ can sauerkraut
2 unpeeled apples, cored and chopped

3 T. chopped onion
½ C. brown sugar
1½ t. caraway seeds

Brown pork chops in skillet; drain. Add remaining ingredients. Cover and cook on low heat about 1 hr. Serves 6.

Mrs. Ruth Dospoy
Steuben County

SKILLET PORK CHOPS

6 pork chops
⅔ C. uncooked rice
1 C. water
2 t. salt
½ C. chopped onion

1 1-lb. can tomatoes, chopped
1 cup whole kernel yellow corn, cooked
¼ t. black pepper

Trim some fat from pork chops; fry out in a large skillet. Add chops and brown very slowly on both sides; lift out. Pour off excess fat. Spread rice over bottom of skillet. Add water. Sprinkle with 1 t. of the salt; arrange chops over rice. Sprinkle with the other 1 t. salt. Add the onion and tomatoes; spoon on the corn. Sprinkle with the black pepper. Cover and simmer 25–35 min. or until the rice is tender. Serves 6.

Carla Hoffman
Martin County

SPANISH PORK CHOPS

4 pork chops
2 T. salad oil
4 green pepper rings
4 slices of onion

⅔ C. long-grain rice
1 8-oz. can tomato sauce
1 C. water

Brown chops in hot oil (450° in electric fry pan); drain. Add salt and pepper as desired. Fit onion slice into green pepper ring on each chop. Sprinkle rice between chops. Spoon about 1 T. tomato sauce over each pork chop; add rest of tomato sauce to rice. Pour water over rice, being sure all is moistened. Bring to boil. Simmer covered 50–60 min. Serves 4.

Mildred Jones
Owen County

SAUSAGE STROGANOFF

1 lb. bulk sausage	1 can mushroom soup
¼ C. chopped onion	1 C. sour cream

Brown sausage and onion in skillet; drain. Crumble sausage with sharp edge of spoon; add soup and heat. Before serving, add 1 C. sour cream. Serve over 3 C. cooked rice. Sprinkle with parsley. Serves 6.

Ruth Guard
Jay County

SUPER SAUERKRAUT AND SAUSAGE

1 lb. smoked sausage or franks, cut in 1″ lengths	1 tart apple, cored and diced
1 qt. sauerkraut, drained and rinsed	¼ C. onion, chopped
2 T. butter	¼–½ C. brown sugar
	½–¾ C. ketchup

Combine all ingredients in skillet and simmer over low heat until apple and onion are tender, and sausage is heated through. Serves 6.

Joy LeCount
Wabash County

DEVILED OYSTERS

½ C. vegetable oil	¼ C. lemon juice
½ t. salt	2 eggs, slightly beaten with 2 T. water
½ t. paprika	
1 t. grated horseradish	24 oysters, drained
1 T. Worcestershire sauce	sifted bread crumbs

Combine oil, salt, paprika, lemon juice, horseradish, and Worcestershire sauce; pour over oysters and let stand 1 hr. Drain and wipe oysters dry; roll in crumbs, dip in egg and again in crumbs. May refrigerate at this point. Fry in hot fat (305°) 1″ deep in heavy frying pan until brown. Serves 4–6.

Charlotte Tobias
Delaware County

JAPANESE FRIED EGGPLANT

1 large eggplant	1 t. water
2 eggs	vegetable oil for frying
bread or cracker crumbs	shoyu sauce

Peel eggplant and cut into size of French fries. Beat eggs with water and dip eggplant into egg mixture; roll in crumbs and set on waxed paper for 10 min. Fry in hot oil until brown, about 4–5 min., turning once without pricking eggplant. Drain on paper towels and serve hot with shoyu sauce.

Jay County Extension Homemakers

CALIFORNIA MEDLEY

¼ C. melted butter	½ C. onion, chopped
4 C. unpared zucchini, sliced	⅓ C. green pepper, chopped
1½ C. fresh or frozen corn	½ t. salt

Combine all ingredients in skillet and cook 10–12 min. Serves 4–6. Freezes well.

Diana Yeager
Porter County

VEGETABLE MEDLEY

⅓ C. margarine	½ C. cubed
3 C. raw pota-	onion
toes, cubed in	1 t. dill weed
1″ cubes	1½ t. chicken
1 C. raw carrots,	bouillon
sliced in ½″	granules
slices	2 C. green beans

Melt margarine in skillet; add remaining ingredients. Mix together and simmer gently, covered, until vegetables are tender. Stir once or twice.

LaVonne Peterson
Pulaski County

FRIED TURNIPS

Peel turnips. Slice into ¼″ thick "rounds." Salt and pepper to taste; roll in flour. Heat shortening in skillet. Brown turnips on both sides; drain on absorbent paper towels.

Lorene Sallee
Lawrence County

ZUCCHINI ROUNDS

⅓ C. biscuit mix	2 C. shredded,
¼ C. grated Par-	unpared zuc-
mesan cheese	chini (2 me-
⅛ t. pepper	dium zucchini)
2 slightly beaten	2 T. butter
eggs	

Stir together biscuit mix, cheese, and pepper; stir in beaten eggs and continue mixing until moistened—do not overmix. Fold in zucchini. Melt butter or margarine in skillet over medium heat. Use only two T. mixture for each round, cook about 2–3 min. on each side. Serves 6.

Nancy Sharp
Cass County

Slow Cookers

With your slow cooker you can forget about watching foods as they cook; no turning, stirring, or adjusting the heat. You won't have to worry about whether the food and the family will be ready at the same time, because food in the cooker can wait and still be delicious. Slow cookers are made in different sizes, so buy the size that fits your needs and follow directions that come with your cooker.

Less expensive cuts of meat that require long slow cooking are obvious choices for slow cookers. Browning meat first is not necessary, although browning will eliminate some of the fat.

Because of slow-cooker design, meats generally cook faster than most vegetables. Vegetables should be cut in small pieces, or at least quartered and placed near sides or bottom of your cooker.

In most recipes it is to your advantage to cook on the Low setting as much as possible. On Low less liquid is needed as there is very little evaporation, and natural juices are retained. Most meat and vegetable combinations require at least 8 hr. on Low.

High does have an advantage in speeding up the cooking time since 1 hr. on High is equal to approximately 2–2½ hr. on Low. On Low you are cooking at about 200° (just below boiling); and approximately 300° on High.

In a slow cooker it is practically impossible to overcook. Foods that might be done enough to eat in 4 hr. may actually improve in flavor if cooked for 8 hr.

POT ROAST OF BEEF (1)

3–4 lb. rump or boneless chuck roast	1 stalk celery, cut into 2″ piece (optional)
2–3 potatoes, sliced	½ C. water or beef consommé
2–3 carrots, sliced	salt and pepper to taste
1–2 onions, sliced	

Put vegetables in bottom of slow cooker. Salt and pepper meat, and place on top of vegetables. Add liquid. Cover and cook on Low for 10–12 hr. or High for 4–5 hr. Serves 4.

Variation: Add 1 2-oz. jar drained mushrooms or ¼ C. mushroom gravy. To thicken gravy, make a smooth paste of 3 T. flour and ¼ C. water and stir into slow cooker.

Betsy Quakenbush
Monroe County

POT ROAST OF BEEF (2)

1 10¾-oz can beef consommé	3 lb. boneless chuck roast
1 t. salt	1 pkg. dry onion soup mix
½ t. pepper	

Pour half of the beef consommé into the slow-cooker. Season meat and put in cooker. Sprinkle soup mix over meat and pour remaining consommé over meat. Cover and cook on Low for 7 hr., or on High 4–4½ hr. Serves 4–6.

Meta Katter
Dubois County

BEV'S SLOW-COOKER BEEF AND NOODLES

arm or chuck roast	1 large pkg. frozen noodles
2 cans beef broth	salt and pepper to taste

Put meat in slow cooker with 1 can broth and cook until tender (Low for 10–12 hr.). Cool; remove bone from meat and shred with 2 forks into bite-sized pieces. Add 1 can broth and the noodles; cook on High until noodles are tender (45 min.). Flour from noodles will thicken broth. Serves 8.

Bev McClure
Union County

BEEF STEW (1)

3 carrots, cut up	1 clove garlic
3 potatoes, cut up	1 bay leaf
2 lb. stew meat, cut in cubes	1 T. salt
1 C. water or beef broth	½ t. pepper
1 t. Worcestershire sauce	1 t. paprika
	3 onions, quartered
	1 stalk celery, cut up

Put all ingredients in slow cooker in order listed. Stir just enough to mix spices. Cover and cook on Low for 10–12 hr. (High 5–6 hr). Serves 6–8.

Teresa Daniel
Monroe County

BEEF STEW (2)

2 lb. stew beef	3 T. Minute
1 large pkg.	Tapioca
frozen stew	¼ C. water
vegetables	1 t.–1 T. salt
2 16-oz. cans to-	½–¾ t. pepper
matoes with	1 small can
juice	mushroom
1 T. sugar	pieces, optional

Mix all ingredients together; pour into slow cooker and cook on High 5 hr. Serves 6.

Ruth Colbert
Daviess County

SNOWBALL (BEEF) STEW (3)

1 can mushroom	2 lb. stew meat
soup	1 4-oz. can sliced
1 pkg. dry onion	mushrooms,
soup mix	drained
¼ C. red wine or	(optional)
beef broth	

Combine all ingredients; place in slow cooker and cook on Low 8 hr. Serve over noodles or rice.
Note: Soup-broth mixture may be doubled depending on amount of gravy wanted.
Variation: Use round steak, cut into serving pieces.

Mrs. Lowell Roberts
Vermillion County

WALDORF-ASTORIA (BEEF) STEW (4)

2 lb. stew meat	1 large can toma-
5 stalks celery,	toes and 1 small
sliced	can tomato
4 or 5 carrots, cut	sauce, or 1 can
in 2″ pieces	tomato soup
3 or 4 potatoes,	and 1 soup can
cut in chunks	water
1 t. salt	½ t. garlic pow-
¼ t. pepper	der (optional)
3–5 T. tapioca	

Do not brown meat. Mix all ingredients together. Cook on Low in slow cooker for 6–8 hr.

Wanda Volbrecht
Boone County

BOEUF BOURGUIGNONNE

6 strips bacon,	1 t. salt
cut in ½″ pieces	½ t. pepper
3 lb. beef rump	2 cloves garlic,
or chuck, cut in	minced
1½″ cubes	6 whole black
12 small carrots,	peppers
sliced	4 whole cloves
12 small white	1 bay leaf
onions	¼ C. minced
12 small mush-	parsley
rooms, sliced	¼ t. marjoram
1 10½-oz. can	½ t. thyme
beef broth	1 C. red or bur-
¼ C. flour	gundy wine

Shake flour, salt, pepper, and beef cubes in bag. Cook bacon until crisp; remove from skillet. Add beef cubes and brown in bacon fat; add garlic and cook a minute or two longer. Put onions, carrots, and beef in slow cooker. Stir together broth, wine, parsley, marjoram, thyme, and bacon bits and pour over meat and vegetables. Tie peppers, cloves, and bay leaf in small square of cheesecloth and add to pot. Cover and cook on Low 8–10 hr. Sauté mushrooms in 2 T. butter and add to slow cooker about 1 hr. before serving. To thicken gravy, turn slow cooker to High. Cream ¼ C. flour and 2 T. butter; roll in pea-sized balls and drop into pot. Bring to boil and let thicken. Serves 6–8.

Marilyn Oliver
Wells County

ITALIAN ROUND STEAK

2 lb. round steak, cut in serving pieces	1¼ C. liquid (tomato juice, plus hot water)
2 beef bouillon cubes	1 garlic clove, minced
1 28-oz. can whole tomatoes, drained and liquid reserved	1 t. salt
	½ t. pepper
	½ t. oregano
	1½ t. Worcestershire sauce
1 C. chopped onion	¼ C. cornstarch
	¼ C. cold water

Place steak pieces in slow cooker. Dissolve bouillon cubes in liquid. Combine tomatoes, onion, garlic, salt, pepper, oregano, and Worcestershire. Pour over steak. Add bouillon-liquid mixture. Cook on Low for 8–9 hr. Turn cooker to High. Combine cornstarch and water. Stir into hot liquid and thicken.

Mrs. Norman H. Jones
Orange County

SWISS STEAK

2 lb. round steak, 1″ thick	1 4-oz. can sliced mushrooms, drained
1 t. salt	
¼ t. pepper	1 8-oz. can tomato sauce
1 medium onion, sliced (½ C.)	

Trim fat from meat. Pound meat with mal-let; sprinkle with salt and pepper. Layer meat, onions, mushrooms, and sauce in slow cooker, ending with tomato sauce on top. Cover and cook on High for 6–7 hr., or cook on High for 1 hr. and Low for 8–10 hr. Serves 6–7.

Marcia Ford
Jay County

GROUND BEEF DINNER

2 large potatoes, sliced	2 stalks celery, sliced
3 medium carrots, sliced	1½ lb. ground beef, browned
1 No. 2 can peas, well drained	1 can tomato soup
3 medium onions, sliced	1 soup can water

Layer vegetables in order given into slow cooker. Season each layer with salt and pepper. Put beef on top of celery. Mix tomato soup and water and pour into slow cooker; cover. Cook on Low for 6–8 hr. Serves 6–8.

Rozella Thornton
St. Joseph County

CHUCKWAGON BEEF

1 lb. extra-lean ground beef	½ C. rice, raw
	1 t. salt
1 16-oz. can whole tomatoes	½ t. basil
	⅛ t. pepper
1 green pepper, seeded and chopped	4 slices process cheese food, cut into triangles
1 onion, chopped	

Place all ingredients, except cheese triangles, in slow cooker. Stir thoroughly. Place 4 cheese triangles on top. Cover and cook on Low 7–10 hr. Before serving, top with remaining cheese. Serves 4–6.

Ruth Sallee
Martin County

CHILI (1)

1 2-lb. can chili beans	1 green pepper, coarsely chopped
2 1-lb. cans tomatoes, undrained	2 cloves garlic, crushed or minced
2 lb. beef, cut in large cubes and browned	3 T. chili powder
	1½ t. salt
2 medium onions, coarsely chopped	1 t. pepper

Put in slow cooker in order listed. Stir once. Cover and cook on Low 10–12 hr. (5–6 hr. on High). Serves 4–6.

Victory E.H. Club
Grant County

SLOW-COOKED CHILI (2)

2 lb. ground beef	1 28-oz. can whole tomatoes, undrained
1½ C. chopped onion	
1 C. chopped green pepper	2 16-oz. cans kidney beans, undrained
2 garlic cloves, minced	
2 t. salt	1 t. pepper
2 T. chili powder	1 t. cumin

Brown beef and place in slow cooker. Add all other ingredients, and stir to mix. Cover and cook on Low 7–10 hr. Serves 8–10.

Mary Bryant
Harrison County

VEGETABLE BEEF CHILI SOUP

1 lb. ground beef	1 8-oz. can tomato sauce
1 C. chopped onion	½ C. water
2 10-oz. pkg. frozen mixed vegetables	1 T. chili powder
	1 t. salt
1 16-oz. can tomatoes, cut up	1 t. sugar (optional)

Brown beef with onions; drain off excess fat. Transfer mixture to slow cooker. Place frozen vegetables in strainer, rinse with hot water to separate. Stir vegetables and remaining ingredients into beef mixture. Cover and cook on Low 8–10 hr. Serves 4–6.

Joyce Louck
Jay County

BAR-B-QUE HAMBURGER AND BEANS

1 lb. ground beef	¾ lb. bacon
1 C. onions, chopped	1 C. catsup
	¼ C. brown sugar
2 1-lb., 15-oz. cans pork and beans	3 T. vinegar
	1 T. liquid smoke
1 15-oz. can red beans	1 t. salt

Brown beef and onions; drain. Fry bacon; drain. Add the rest of ingredients and cook in slow cooker on High for 4 hr. Serves 8–10.

Jean Weaver
Delaware County

MEATBALLS

3 lb. ground beef	2 t. oregano
3 t. salt	Sauce:
3 t. pepper	2 8-oz. cans tomato sauce with herbs and spices
1 medium onion, chopped	
2 t. Italian seasoning	
	2 T. sugar
4–6 slices of bread, soaked in milk and squeezed dry	1 t. salt (or to taste)
	1 T. dry onion flakes

Combine all meatball ingredients; form into small balls and bake on cookie sheet at 400° for 25–30 min. Combine sauce ingredients and heat. Add meatballs to sauce; place in

slow cooker. Cover and cook on Low 6 hr.
or more.

Janice Lyon
Monroe County

MEAT LOAF

1½ lb. ground
chuck
½ C. cracker
crumbs, me-
dium fine
2 eggs, beaten
1 8-oz. can to-
mato sauce
½ t. sage

¼ C. chopped
onion
1 t. seasoned salt
Sauce (optional):
3 T. brown sugar
3 T. catsup
½ t. prepared
mustard

Combine all meat loaf ingredients to blend
thoroughly. Shape meat to fit the bottom of
the slow cooker. Cover and cook on Low for
6 hr. Combine sauce ingredients and pour
sauce over meat the last 15 min. of cooking
time. Serves 4–6.

Meta Katter
Dubois County

SPAGHETTI SAUCE

1½ lb. ham-
burger,
browned and
drained
2 No. 2 cans of
tomatoes,
sieved or
mashed
1 8-oz. can to-
mato sauce
1 6-oz. can to-
mato paste
1 C. water

1 t. basil
1 t. parsley flakes
1 crumpled bay
leaf
¼ t. oregano
1 chopped onion
⅛ t. rosemary
leaves
2 t. salt
¼ t. pepper
1 clove garlic,
minced

Combine all ingredients and cook in slow
cooker 6–8 hr. on Low.

Janet Sweeney
Noble County

BUSY DAY CHICKEN AND RICE

2 C. rice
1 pkg. onion
soup mix
5 C. water

1 chicken, cut
into serving
pieces

Place all ingredients in slow cooker on Low
and cook 8 hr.

Kay Kinnamon
Madison County

ORIENTAL CHICKEN

Marinate overnight 3½ lb. chicken (skinned
and excess fat removed, if desired) in the
marinade mixture:

2 t. frozen orange
juice
concentrate
1 t. salt
½ t. pepper
½ C. catsup

2 T. brown sugar
2 T. soy sauce
1 t. dry mustard
½ t. garlic salt
1 C. water
½ t. ginger

Put chicken and marinade in slow cooker.
Cover and cook on Low 6–8 hr. One hr.
before serving set heat on High. Add the
following ingredients:

1 11-oz. can man-
darin oranges,
drained
½ C. ripe pitted
olives, quartered

3 T. chopped
green peppers
3 T. cornstarch
mixed with 1 C.
water

Cook until bubbly and thickened. Serve with
rice or noodles. Serves 8.

Louise Nahrwold
Allen County

SLOW-COOKER CHICKEN

1 3-lb. chicken
2 chopped carrots
2 sliced onions
2 chopped celery
ribs

2 t. salt
pepper to taste
1 t. basil
½ C. white wine,
water or broth

Sprinkle chicken inside and out with salt,

pepper, and basil. Place in slow cooker with remaining ingredients. Cover and cook on Low 5 hr. Serves 6.

Patricia Harmon
Harrison County

CHICKEN LIVERS

1 lb. chicken livers	3 green onions with tops, chopped
½ C. flour	10 oz. can golden mushroom soup
1 t. flour	
¼ t. pepper	
3 slices bacon	4 oz. can sliced mushrooms
1 C. chicken bouillon	¼ C. dry white wine

Cut chicken livers in bite-size pieces; toss in flour, salt, and pepper. Fry bacon pieces in large skillet; remove when brown. Add chicken livers and green onion to bacon grease in skillet; sauté until lightly browned. Pour chicken bouillon into skillet and stir into drippings; pour mixture into slow cooker. Add bacon and all remaining ingredients. Cover and cook on Low 4–6 hr. Serve over rice, toast, or buttered noodles. Recipe may be doubled for 3½ or 5 qt. cooker.

Martha Daggy
Monroe County

LIVER AND ONIONS

1 lb. liver (medium sliced), beef or pork	1 large onion, sliced in rings
1 small can mushrooms, drained (optional)	salt and pepper to taste
	about 2 C. water
	¼ C. flour

Wash liver and pat dry. Mix salt, pepper, and flour together. Coat liver with flour

mixture. Place liver in alternate layers in slow cooker with onions and mushrooms, and cover with water. Cover and cook on Low 4 hr. Serves 4.

Betty Ratliff
Hendricks County

PORK CHOPS

9 medium potatoes, peeled and quartered	6 pork chops
	salt and pepper to taste
1 20-oz. pkg. frozen peas	1 can mushroom soup, undiluted
2 medium onions, sliced	

In bottom of slow cooker, place potatoes, peas, and onions. Next place the pork chops and seasonings. Spread the soup on top. Cover and cook on Low for 8 hr.

Diane Guyer
Wabash County

PLANTATION PORK CHOPS

4 double-cut loin pork chops	1 T. finely chopped pecans
2 C. corn bread stuffing mix	salt and pepper
2 T. melted butter	¼ C. light corn syrup
¼ t. salt	½ t. grated orange peel
⅓ C. orange juice	

Cut a horizontal slit in side of each pork chop. Combine stuffing with butter, ¼ t. salt, orange juice, and pecans. Fill pockets with stuffing. Sprinkle chops with salt and pepper. Place on metal rack in slow cooker. Brush with mixture of corn syrup and orange peel. Cover and cook on Low for 6–8 hr. Turn to High; brush with sauce again, and cook for 15–20 min.

Rita Carpenter
Pulaski County

PORK ROAST

2½–3 lb. pork   garlic salt to taste
   roast   pepper to taste

Place pork roast on broiler pan, fat side up. Broil for 15 min. to remove excess fat and brown meat. Place roast in slow cooker; sprinkle with seasonings. Cover and cook on High for 3 hr., or Low for 8 hr. (or until meat thermometer inserted in center of meat registers 185°). Serves 4–6.

Meta Katter
Dubois County

HAM AND HASH BROWNS

1 large pkg. fro-   1 C. milk
   zen hash brown   2 C. sharp Ched-
   potatoes   dar cheese
1 10-oz. pkg.   1 can ham or
   frozen peas   SPAM, diced
1 can mushroom   1 can Cheddar
   soup   cheese soup

Mix all ingredients in a slow cooker and season to taste. Cover and cook on High 4 hr., or Low 8 hr.

Darla Kay Cook
Starke County

HAM AND SCALLOPED POTATOÉS

6–8 slices ham   1 C. Cheddar
8–10 med.   cheese, grated
   potatoes,   1 can cream of
   thinly sliced   celery or cream
2 onions, thinly   of mushroom
   sliced   soup
salt and pepper   paprika
   (small amount)

Put half of ham and potatoes and onion in slow cooker. Sprinkle with salt and pepper and add grated cheese; repeat. Spoon undi-luted soup over top. Sprinkle with paprika. Cover and cook on Low 8–10 hrs., or on High 4 hr. Serves 6.

Myra Maxwell   *Riva Callahan*
Hancock County   *Huntington County*

BARBECUED SPARERIBS (1)

4 lb. country-   ½ C. brown
   style spareribs   sugar
1 can tomato   1 t. celery seed
   soup   1 t. salt
½ C. cider   1 t. chili powder
   vinegar   ⅛ t. cayenne
1 T. soy sauce   pepper

Layer spareribs in slow cooker. Combine remaining ingredients. Pour over spareribs. Cook on Low 6–8 hr.

Karen Brown
Parke County

COUNTRY-STYLE SPARERIBS (2)

1 C. beef broth   1 t. salt
½ C. peach   2½ lb. country-
   preserves   style spareribs
3 T. vinegar   1 medium onion,
2 T. Worcester-   thinly sliced
   shire sauce   ⅓ C. cold water
1 T. brown sugar   3 T. flour

Combine first six ingredients. Place ribs in cooker and pour broth mixture over. Lay onion on top. Cover and cook on Low for 8 hr., or on High for 4 hr. Remove ribs and keep warm. Skim fat from broth. Mix flour and water in a saucepan; blend with 1½ C. of broth and cook until thickened. Serve sauce over ribs.

Helen Brust
LaPorte County

COUNTRY-STYLE RIBS AND SAUERKRAUT (1)

2½–3 lb. country-style ribs	⅓ C. brown sugar
1 medium onion, sliced	3 T. catsup
1 1-lb., 11-oz. can sauerkraut, drained and rinsed	1½ t. salt ¾ t. caraway seed

Place ribs and onion in slow cooker. Combine sauerkraut, sugar, catsup, salt, and caraway seed; pour over meat. Cover and cook on Low 10–12 hr., or High 5-6 hr.

Maurine Shelby
Hancock County

MARY'S RIBS AND SAUERKRAUT (2)

4 lb. country-style pork ribs	2 large whole onions, peeled
1 large plus 1 small can sauerkraut, undrained	1 whole, unpeeled apple, cored
2 T. caraway seeds	

Layer ribs in slow cooker. Pour sauerkraut over ribs. Mix caraway seeds into sauerkraut. Push onions and apple down into kraut. Cook on Low 10–12 hr. *Serve over mashed potatoes.*

Mary Baxter
Monroe County

WIENER STEW

2 lb. potatoes, peeled and cut into 1″ chunks	1 T. dry basil
1 lb. carrots, peeled and cut into ½″ slices	1 T. dry parsley 2 qt. water 2 cans tomato soup
1 t. salt	1 lb. wieners, cut into fourths
¼ t. pepper	

Cook first 7 ingredients in slow cooker 3 hr. on High until vegetables are tender. Add last 2 ingredients. Cook 1 hr. on High. Serves 8.

Irene Campbell
Madison County

CREOLE RED BEANS WITH SAUSAGE

1 lb. dried red kidney beans, soaked overnight	6 green onions, chopped salt and pepper to taste
6 cloves garlic, peeled and pressed	⅛ t. onion salt ⅛ t. garlic salt water to fill slow cooker at ¾ capacity
1–1½ lb. sausage (bulk made into patties, or link)	

Put all ingredients in slow cooker. Cook on High 2–3 hr.; turn to Low and cook 3–4 hr. Stir 2 or 3 times. Mash a few beans toward the end of the cooking time to make a thicker gravy. Serve over rice. *Note:* It is not necessary to brown the sausage first.

This is a New Orleans washday dish and has many variations.

Betsy See
Clark County

SHRIMP CREOLE

1 28-oz. can tomatoes, cut up and undrained	1 t. oregano, crushed
½ C. chopped onions	1 t. thyme, crushed
½ C. chopped green pepper	½ t. salt 2 dashes bottled hot pepper sauce
2 bay leaves	
1 clove garlic, minced	1 10-oz. pkg. frozen shelled shrimp

In slow cooker, stir together all ingredients, except shrimp. Cover and cook on High for 3 hr. Stir in shrimp. Cover and cook 20 min. longer. Thicken with 1 T. cold water and 1 T. cornstarch. Serve over cooked rice.

Lorraine A. Nichols
Spencer County

BARBECUED BEANS AND BACON

1 lb. dried navy beans	1 C. catsup
½ lb. bacon, diced	½ C. brown sugar
3 C. tomato juice	1 T. Worcester-
1 large onion, chopped	shire sauce
	2 t. salt

Soften beans by putting into large saucepan with enough water to cover (3 C. water for each 1 C. beans). Heat to boiling; then simmer 30 min. Cover and let stand 1½ hr. or until beans are soft. Drain and put into slow cooker. Fry bacon until crisp; add bacon and drippings to slow cooker along with remaining ingredients. Stir to blend. Cover with a piece of aluminum foil, then with lid. Cook on Low up to 24 hr. Skim off excess fat, then stir before serving.

Marilyn J. Baker
Lawrence County

MEXICAN BEANS

2 C. dry horticulture or pinto beans	2½ C. water
	½ t. chili powder
3 C. diced fresh tomatoes	½ t. salt
	½ t. pepper
½ C. chopped green pepper	
⅓ C. diced onion	

Place all ingredients in slow cooker and mix. Turn cooker to High and cook for 20 min.; reduce heat to Low and cook 6–8 hr. Check at 5 hr. to see if more liquid is needed.

Mary Whitaker
Monroe County

SLOW-COOKER BEANS

1 1-lb. can pork and beans	¼–½ C. chopped onion
1 1-lb. can red kidney beans	4–8 slices of bacon, fried crisp
1 1-lb. can lima beans (butter beans)	¼–¾ C. brown sugar
	1 t. salt
2 t. vinegar	½ C. catsup

Drain lima and kidney beans. Mix in slow cooker and add remaining ingredients. Cook on Low for 8 hr., or High for 3–4 hr. Serves 10.

Variation: Add ½ lb. browned hamburger and 1 t. dry mustard and use ¼ C. vinegar instead of 2 t.

Mary Lou Young
Noble County

LIMA BEAN CASSEROLE

2 small onions, thinly sliced	1 2-oz. jar chopped pimiento, drained
3 10-oz. pkg. frozen baby lima beans, thawed	2 t. salt
2 cans cream of celery soup	⅛ t. pepper
	½ t. dill seed
2 4-oz. cans sliced mushrooms, undrained	½ C. heavy cream
	1 C. grated Parmesan cheese

Combine all ingredients, except cream and cheese in slow cooker; stir well. Cover and cook on Low 10–12 hr. Just before serving, add cream and stir well; sprinkle cheese on top. Serves 8–10.

Margaret Pinkerton
Grant County

STUFFED CABBAGE LEAVES

12 large cabbage leaves	¼ t. thyme
1 lb. lean ground beef	¼ t. nutmeg
½ t. salt	¼ t. cinnamon
⅛ t. pepper	1 6-oz. can tomato paste
	¼ C. water

Wash cabbage leaves. Boil 4 C. of water; turn heat off and soak leaves in the water 5 min. Drain and cool; set aside. Combine remaining ingredients, except tomato paste and water. Place 2 T. of the mixture on each leaf and roll firmly. Stack in slow cooker. Combine tomato paste and water; pour over the stuffed cabbage. Cover and cook on Low for 8–10 hr.

Hilda Dunfee
Huntington County

GERMAN RED CABBAGE

1 head red cabbage	salt and pepper to taste
⅓ C. shortening	3 tart apples
⅓ C. vinegar	sliced German sausage, optional
⅓ C. brown sugar	
1 C. red wine	

Choose a firm, glossy head of cabbage (quality of cabbage does make a difference). Shred cabbage evenly and thinly, discarding core. In a large kettle melt shortening; add cabbage turning over and over, until all shreds are coated with oil (this helps retain color of cabbage). Add vinegar, sugar, and wine; place mixture in slow cooker. Lay apples on top. Cook on High for 15 min. Turn mix-

ture over one time, turn cooker to Low and cook for 2 hr. Add sausage and cook on Low additional 30 min.

Cabbage can be served immediately, but will be even better if refrigerated overnight and reheated the next day.

Mary Whitaker
Monroe County

APPLE BUTTER (1)

12–14 cooking apples (about 16 C.), peeled and chopped	2 C. cider
	2 C. sugar
	1 t. cinnamon
	¼ t. cloves

Combine apples and cider in slow cooker. Cover and cook on Low for 10–12 hr. Puree in food mill or sieve. Return pureed mixture to pot; add sugar, cinnamon, and cloves. Cover and cook on Low 1 hr. Yield: 8 C.

Mildred Smith
Allen County

APPLE BUTTER (2)

apples, peeled, cored, and diced	2 t. cinnamon
	½ t. cloves
3 C. sugar	½ C. water

Fill cooker ¾ full with apples. Add remaining ingredients. Cover and cook on Low for almost 24 hr. Stir once during cooking process.

Barbara Fannin
St. Joseph County

CRANBERRY NUT BREAD

2 C. fresh cranberries	½ C. walnuts
1 medium cooking apple, peeled, cored, cut into chunks	2 C. flour
	1 C. sugar
	1½ t. baking powder
	½ t. soda

½ t. salt

6 T. soft butter

1 egg

1 T. grated orange peel

½ C. orange juice

Put cranberries, apple, and walnuts through coarsest blade of food grinder; set aside. Combine dry ingredients in a deep bowl. Cut in butter until size of peas. Stir in egg, orange peel, juice, and cranberry-apple mixture. Stir until blended. Spoon into greased 2 qt. mold or 2 1-lb. coffee cans. Cover with foil and tie; place on rack in slow-cooking pot. Pour 2 C. hot water around mold. Cover pot and cook on High for 2½–3 hr. Let stand several min., before turning out on cooling rack. Serve warm.

Betty J. Short
Hancock County

BOSTON BROWN BREAD

2 eggs

½ C. sugar

½ C. molasses

2 T. vegetable oil

2 t. soda

2 C. sour milk

2½ C. whole wheat flour

1½ C. white flour

½ C. raisins

1 t. salt

Beat eggs; add sugar, molasses, oil, and sour milk. Combine dry ingredients and raisins; add to first mixture. Pour batter into 2 lb. greased coffee can. Place can on trivet in slow cooker. Cook on High for 20 min., Low for 3 hr. Test for doneness after the 3 hr. cooking period. Continue cooking, if necessary, until cake tester comes out dry.

Becki Whitaker
Marion County

Whole Grains and Other

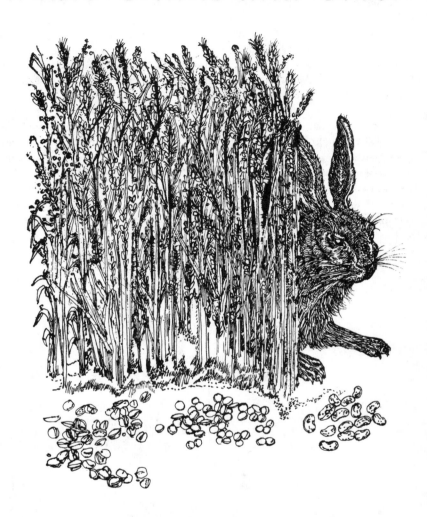

Many Americans are concerned about the continuing use of refined flours and overconsumption of sugars and animal fats in our diets. This concern has created a renewed interest in whole grains as a source of non-animal protein and more complex carbohydrates. The average American diet is low in fiber. Whole grains are an excellent source of bulk or dietary fiber.

Of the common grains, oats are the highest in protein. Since oats are a whole grain, they

Healthful Foods

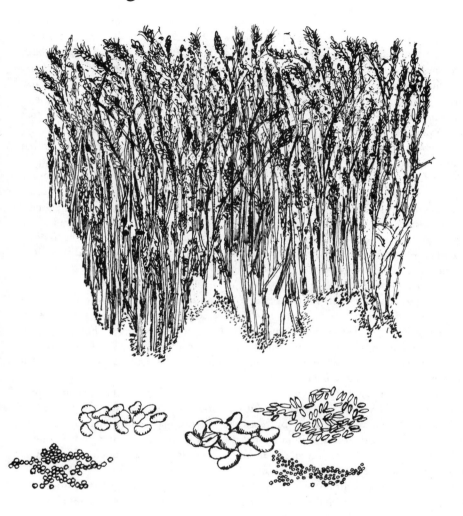

are complete. Nothing has been added to the grain, and nothing of consequence has been taken out. Oats still contain their original bran, germ, and endosperm. The bran is the outer covering of the grain and is an excellent source of fiber. Quick and old-fashioned oats have the same nutritional value.

Barley is a whole grain food that is coming into its own again. It is a source of protein, thiamine, niacin, phosphorus, and iron. Although traditionally used in soup, barley can be used in stews, casseroles, salads, and even desserts.

Home-baked breads with whole grain flours and bran help add the fiber lacking in many diets. Soy flour may be used as a replacement for up to 2–4 tablespoons in each cup of flour in a standard bread recipe. Since soy flour contains no gluten, it cannot be used alone to bake bread. Rye and whole wheat flours have less gluten so are usually combined with white flours if conventional bread texture is desired. Store whole wheat flour in your refrigerator or freezer.

Commercial granolas often contain saturated fat, generally coconut or palm oils, and two teaspoons sugar per ounce in the form of honey or brown sugar. Their salt content is often very high. You can make your own granola with less saturated fat, sugar, and salt.

Tofu, a soybean curd, is a food almost too good to be true. It is fast becoming a familiar food in supermarkets across the country. An increasing number of people are adding tofu to their diets because of its nutritional value. It can serve as the backbone of a meal in much the same way as meat and dairy foods. Tofu is a source of inexpensive protein that is low in saturated fats, sodium, and calories, and it contains no cholesterol. It is also easily digested.

Tofu's bland taste enables it to be used in a multitude of ways. Thin strips of tofu make a good topping for pizza. It is good in Mexican tacos, enchiladas, tostadas, and so forth. Tofu can be used in place of the ricotta cheese in lasagne, ravioli, and other Italian dishes. It is delicious in a quiche or a vegetable pie: cubed, laid in slices on top, or blended with other ingredients. Try tofu once, twice, and then again. You could become addicted.

The food value of yogurt will be the same as the milk from which it is made. Yogurt contains bacteria friendly to our digestive system. The cost of yogurt will equal the cost of milk, if the yogurt is made at home; purchased at a retail outlet the price is high. Yogurt is not a low-calorie food when made with half and half, or when sweetened and flavored with high-calorie additions. Read calorie information when buying your yogurt and monitor what you combine it with. One tablespoon of honey has 65 calories.

To salvage a batch of yogurt that won't thicken properly, try softening 1 package unflavored gelatin in ¼ cup cold water; heat gelatin mixture until dissolved and stir into 1 quart of yogurt. You may also start over again by reheating the original yogurt mixture to 180°, cooling to 106–109°, and adding a fresh starter. Failures in yogurt making may be due to killing the culture with too high a temperature in the mixing, using a poor culture, or using milk or utensils that were not absolutely clean.

Sprouts are a delicious addition to salads, soups, casseroles, and sandwiches. Sprout your own; it's fun, easy, inexpensive and there is no satisfactory substitute for fresh sprouts. Mung beans are a good choice for the first attempt at sprouting; they almost never fail to sprout.

MUNG BEAN SPROUTS

Purchase beans for sprouting at a health food store or Chinese grocery. Soak ⅓ C. beans overnight in water. Put 2 T. soaked beans in each of several quart-size canning jars. Cover top of jar with cheesecloth; screw on jar rings, or use a rubber band. Place jar on its side in a warm, dark place. Several times daily run warm water into jar, shake beans gently, and pour off water. When sprouts have grown to 1¼″ (3–5 days), remove beans from jar and refrigerate. If you prefer to remove green hulls, rinse sprouts repeatedly in cold water, lifting them out of water and discarding hulls as they sink. One-third C. beans yields 1 qt. sprouts.

REAL FRUIT POP

½ C. fruit juice   1 C. club soda

Pour juice and soda into a tall glass filled with ice; stir gently and serve. Proportions may need to be varied depending on the strength of the juice you use. With orange juice use a bit less soda, with apple a bit more, etc.

TOASTED PUMPKIN OR
SQUASH SEEDS

Separate the fiber from unwashed pumpkin or squash seeds. For each 2 C. of seeds, add 1½ T. melted butter or oil and 1¼ t. salt; spread seeds in a shallow pan. Bake at 250° until crisp and brown; stir occasionally.

TOASTED SUNFLOWER SEEDS

Wash seeds thoroughly; drain. Cover with brine (½ C. salt to 1 C. water). Bring to a boil; drain and spread seeds on a cookie sheet. Bake at 300° until desired degree of roasting is obtained.

Unfortunately, there is no easy way (yet) to remove the outer shell from sunflower seeds. No more efficient, effective way than the "crack and spit" technique which is recommended only if the "cracker and spitter" is going to eat the seeds himself.

Carol Turner
Vigo County

TOFU DIP

8 oz. tofu	1 T. onion salt
1 C. dairy sour cream	1 T. onion flakes
	1½ t. garlic salt

Blend all ingredients in blender until smooth; refrigerate for several hours.

Denise Kirby
Monroe County

DEL'S CORN BREAD

5½–6 C. unbleached white flour	2 pkg. dry yeast
	½ C. sugar
	1 T. salt
1 C. whole wheat flour	2 C. milk
	¾ C. butter or margarine
1½ C. whole cornmeal, not degerminated	4 eggs

Combine 3 C. flour, yeast, sugar, and salt; mix well. In saucepan, heat milk, and butter until warm (120°); add to flour mixture. Add eggs; blend at low speed in electric mixer until moistened. Beat 3 min. at medium speed. Stir in cornmeal and whole wheat flour by hand. Gradually stir in enough remaining flour to make a firm dough. Knead on floured surface until smooth and elastic, about 5 min. Place in greased bowl, turning to grease top. Cover; allow to rise in warm place until doubled, 1–1½ hr. Punch down dough; divide into 6 equal parts. Roll dough out on lightly floured surface. Fold to the center from 3 sides, tuck the ends under, put smooth side up. Place each into a greased 1 lb. coffee can. Let rise until dough reaches the top or slightly over the top of can. Bake at 375° for 25–30 min. until golden brown. Remove from oven and shake bread out of cans onto cake racks to cool.

Delbertine Coughlin
Vanderburgh County

EARLY COLONIAL BREAD

½ C. yellow cornmeal	2 pkg. active dry yeast
⅓ C. brown sugar	½ C. lukewarm water (105–115°)
1 T. salt	
¼ C. cooking oil	¾ C. whole wheat flour
½ C. rye flour	
2 C. boiling water	3¼–4¼ C. sifted white flour

Thoroughly combine cornmeal, brown sugar, salt, boiling water, and oil; cool to lukewarm, about 30 min. Soften yeast in the ½ C. lukewarm water; stir into the cornmeal mixture. Add whole wheat and rye flours; mix well. Stir in enough flour to make a moderately stiff dough. Turn out on lightly floured surface and knead until smooth and elastic, 6–8 min. Place dough in greased bowl, turning once to grease surface. Cover and let rise in warm place until double, 50–60 min. Punch down; turn out onto lightly floured surface and divide in half. Cover and let rest 10 min.; shape into 2 loaves and place in greased 9x5x3" loaf pans. Let rise again until almost double, about 30 min. Bake at 375° for 45 min. (Cap loosely with foil after first 25 min., if bread browns rapidly.)

Martha Stoner
Hancock County

EARTHBREAD

1 C. milk	½ C. wheat germ
1 C. water	2 C. rye flour
1 T. salad oil	2 C. 100% bran
2 pkg. active dry yeast	Glace and topping:
⅛ C. dark molasses	1 egg, well-beaten
2 t. salt	1 t. water
2 C. whole wheat flour	sesame seeds

(All flour used should be stone-ground with no additives or preservatives. The bran in the recipe is not cereal, and can be purchased in any grocery.) Scald milk and water and cool to 105°. (You should be able to touch it and keep your finger in it without burning, although it must be very warm.) Add yeast to milk and water; stir to dissolve. Add remaining ingredients in order listed and work into a dough. Knead dough for 10 min. on a floured surface. Let rise in warm place for 1 hr. Form into loaf and place in loaf pan. Allow to rise another hr. Before baking, glaze the dough with egg-water mixture. Sprinkle with sesame seeds and bake at 350° for 50 min.

This recipe will make 1 standard-sized loaf of bread. It will be a coarse bread and heavier than that purchased in a grocery or bakery.

Shari K. Price
Carroll County

HEALTH BREAD

2 pkg. dry yeast	3½ C. whole wheat flour
¾ C. honey	
3 C. warm water (105–115°)	3 C. white flour
	1 t. salt
½ C. wheat germ	

Mix yeast, honey, and water and let stand 5 min. Mix flours, wheat germ, and salt together. Add the dry ingredients to the warm water mixture and mix together thoroughly; add enough additional white flour to the dough to keep it from being sticky. Turn dough onto a floured board and knead for about 10 min. Place dough in a greased bowl and let rise until doubled in bulk; punch down, shape into loaves and place in pan(s). Let rise until doubled in bulk and bake at 350°. Bake small loaves 45 min.

and large loaves 60 min. Makes 2 large loaves and 1 small loaf.

Margaret Pund
Perry County

OLD-FASHIONED HONEY WHEAT BREAD

1½ C. water	3 C. whole wheat
1 C. cottage	flour
cheese	2 T. sugar
½ C. honey	1 T. salt
¼ C. margarine	2 pkg. dry yeast
4–5 C. white	1 egg
flour	

Heat first four ingredients in saucepan until very warm, 120–130°. Combine warm liquid, 2 C. white flour, and remaining ingredients in large electric mixer bowl. Beat 2 min. at medium speed. Stir in remaining flour by hand to form stiff batter. Knead on well-floured surface, about 2 min. Place in greased bowl. Cover; let rise until light and doubled in bulk, 45–60 min. Grease (not oil) 2 9x5″ or 8x4″ loaf pans. Punch down dough, divide, and shape into 2 loaves. Place into pans; cover and let rise until doubled, 45–60 min. Bake at 350° approximately 40 min.

Mary Ann Lienhart-Cross
Elkhart County

Variation: Use 5–5½ C. white bread flour in place of 4–5 C. white flour, 1 C. instead of 3 C. whole wheat flour. Add ½ C. wheat germ, substitute 2 T. light brown sugar for the 2 T. sugar, and use 2 t. salt instead of 1 T.

Ruth Burrus
Boone County

"HERMAN" SOURDOUGH STARTER

1 pkg. dry yeast	2 C. flour
2 C. warm water	¼ C. sugar

To make starter use a large glass or plastic container (do not use metal). The mixture will bubble up, so the container must be large enough to allow for that. Dissolve yeast in warm water. Stir in flour and sugar and beat until the mixture is smooth. Cover lightly and place in a warm place overnight.

The mixture will separate into a liquid on the bottom and a thicker substance on the top. There should be bubbles on the surface. It will have a yeasty aroma. Stir and refrigerate.

Stir each day for 5 days. On the fifth day, divide the mixture. Give one cup of starter to a friend and keep remainder as your starter. This starter must be fed and stirred for 10 days before it is ready to use.

FEEDING MIXTURE FOR SOURDOUGH

½ C. sugar	1 C. milk
1 C. flour	

Stir together sugar, flour, and milk. Always use this feeding mixture to feed sour dough on the day you get the starter and every 5 days after that. To feed: stir feeding mixture into starter (preceeding recipe) until smooth. Cover and refrigerate. Stir the mixture each day for 4 days. On the fifth day, feed starter again with feeding mixture. Cover and return to the refrigerator. Stir starter each day for 4 more days. On the tenth day (total of days since you began feeding the starter), sour dough is ready to be used for baking.

Use 2 cups in one of your favorite sourdough recipes. Give 1 cup to a friend and reserve remainder for yourself. The dough you keep for yourself must be fed again at this point. Follow the previous schedule, stirring for 4 days, feeding on the fifth day, stirring again for 4 days and using, dividing, and again feeding on the tenth day.

This procedure may go on indefinitely. The sourdough will stay active as long as it is fed every fifth day and stirred daily. The sourdough is kept alive by the starter yeast and scheduled feedings. It differs from regular sourdough in that it is sweeter and must be stirred and fed regularly, rather than put into the refrigerator and forgotten.

Donna Frye
Putnam County

WHOLE WHEAT SOURDOUGH BREAD

1½ C. boiling water	¾ t. salt
½ C. shortening	1 C. sourdough starter, at room temperature
1 pkg. dry yeast	
1 t. sugar	
1 egg, well beaten	2½ C. white flour
	2 C. whole wheat flour
½ C. sugar	½ C. white flour

Combine water and shortening in large bowl; allow to cool to 105–115°. Add yeast and sugar; let stand 15 min. Add remaining ingredients, except flours; beat at medium speed of electric mixer for 3 min. Stir in whole wheat and white flour by hand. Turn dough out on a floured surface and knead about 5 min., or until smooth and elastic. Put in a greased bowl, turning to grease top. Cover and let rise in a warm place (85°), 1½–2 hr., or until doubled in bulk. Divide the dough in half and shape each half for loaf pans. Put in 2 well-greased 9x5x3" loaf pans. Cover and let rise until doubled in bulk. Place in a cold oven. Bake at 400° for 15 min.; reduce heat to 350°, and continue baking for 15–20 min., or until loaves sound hollow when tapped. Remove from pans; cool on wire racks.

Donna Frye
Putnam County

SOURDOUGH OATMEAL WHOLE WHEAT BREAD

1 C. sourdough starter	⅓ C. safflower oil
2 pkg. dry yeast	1 T. salt
½ C. warm water (110°)	5–6 C. whole wheat flour
1¼ C. boiling water	2 eggs, beaten
1 C. quick oats	6 T. quick oats
⅔ C. light molasses	1 beaten egg white
	1 T. water

Soften yeast in warm water; set aside. Combine boiling water, the 1 C. oats, molasses, oil, and salt. Cool mixture to lukewarm; stir in 2 C. flour and beat well. Add oat mixture to sourdough starter; add softened yeast and eggs. Stir in enough flour to make a soft dough; turn onto a lightly floured surface and knead 5–8 min. or until smooth and elastic. Shape dough into a ball; place in greased bowl, cover and let rise 1–2 hr., or until doubled in size. Punch dough down; turn onto lightly floured surface. Divide dough in half; cover and let rest 10 min. Coat each of 2 well-greased loaf pans with about 3 T. oats. Shape dough into loaves; place in pans. Cover and let rise 1½ hr., or until doubled in bulk. Brush loaves with mixture of egg white and water. Sprinkle tops lightly with 3T. oats. Bake at 375° for 40–50 min. If tops are browning too rapidly, cover with a tent of aluminum foil for the last 15 min.

Donna Frye
Putnam County

WHOLE WHEAT BREAD (Molasses)

2 pkg. dry yeast	⅓ C. sugar
1 C. lukewarm water (105–115°)	⅓ C. shortening
	2 C. lukewarm milk

4 t. salt   2 C. whole wheat
⅓ C. molasses   flour
1 C. wheat germ   6 C. white flour

Dissolve yeast in lukewarm water. Stir in sugar, shortening, salt, milk, and molasses. Beat in wheat germ, whole wheat flour, and enough white flour to make a stiff dough. Turn out on floured board and knead 10–15 min., or until smooth and elastic. Cover dough and let rise in a warm place until double in bulk. Grease two 9x5x3" pans. Cut dough in half and shape into loaves; place in pans and let rise until double in size. Bake at 375° for 40 min.

Vernelda Ellermann
Knox County

WHOLE GRAIN BATTER BREAD

1½ C. boiling   2 C. oats
    water   2 C. whole wheat
½ C. margarine   flour
⅓ C. sugar   2 eggs
2 t. salt   3–4 C. white
2 pkg. dry yeast   flour
1 C. warm water

Combine boiling water, margarine, sugar, and salt in a large bowl, stirring until margarine melts; cool to lukewarm. Dissolve yeast in warm water. Stir dissolved yeast, oats, 2 C. whole wheat flour, and eggs into lukewarm mixture; mix well. Stir in enough remaining flour to make a stiff batter. Place in a large greased bowl. Cover; let rise in warm place about 1½ hr., or until double in size. Punch down. Spoon batter into 2 well-greased 9x5" loaf pans. Let rise uncovered in warm place 30–45 min., or until nearly double in size. Bake at 375° for 30–35 min., or until golden brown. Remove from pans. Cool at least 1 hr. before slicing.

Betty Hill
Hancock County

WHEAT GERM POCKET BREAD

2 pkg. dry yeast   1½ t. salt
1¼ C. warm   1½ t. oil
    water (105–   2½–3 C. flour
    115°)   sesame seeds
1 T. sugar   (optional)
½ C. wheat germ   cooking oil

Combine yeast and water; stir to dissolve. Stir in sugar and let stand 5 min. Add wheat germ, salt, and oil to yeast mixture; stir well. Beat in just enough flour to make a soft dough; turn onto floured board and knead until smooth and elastic, about 5 min. Divide dough into 10 equal pieces. Shape each piece into a ball, then roll into 5½–6" round. (Sprinkle with sesame seeds, if desired, before rolling.) Place rounds on greased and floured baking sheets. Brush lightly with oil. Do not cover. Let rise 1–1½ hr. until puffy. Bake 475° 5–7 min. Cool.

Dianna Crouse
Union County

WHOLE WHEAT REFRIGERATOR ROLLS

1 C. boiling   1 C. lukewarm
    water   water
½ C. butter   5 C. whole wheat
½ C. shortening   flour
½ C. honey   1 C. white flour
2 eggs, beaten   3 pkg. dry yeast

Combine boiling water, butter, shortening, honey, and salt; blend and cool. Add eggs. Sprinkle yeast into lukewarm water; stir until dissolved. Combine yeast with egg mixture. Blend in flour; cover and refrigerate for 4 hr. Dough should be in a large mixing bowl as it rises slightly in the refrigerator. This will keep a week to 10 days and may be used as needed. When needed, shape rolls, using only enough extra flour to make them easy to handle. Place on greased pan;

allow to rise for 3 hr. at room temperature, or until double in bulk. Bake at 425° for 12–15 min.

Jackie Sturgeon
Monroe County

BRAN BREAD

3 C. whole wheat flour	½ C. sugar
2 C. bran	1 t. salt
½ C. molasses	2 t. soda
	3 C. buttermilk

Mix all ingredients together and pour into 2 greased 7½x3½x3" pans. Bake 1 hr. at 300° (slow oven).

Ardelle Johnson
LaGrange County

DOUBLE CORN BREAD

1 C. flour	¼ C. shortening, melted
1 C. cornmeal	
¼ C. sugar	1 can whole-kernel corn, drained
4 t. baking powder	
¾ t. salt	½ C. shredded Cheddar cheese
2 eggs, beaten	
1 C. milk	

Stir dry ingredients together. Mix together eggs, milk, and shortening; stir in corn and cheese. Stir egg-corn mixture into dry ingredients. Pour into greased cake pan. Bake at 425° for 25 min.

Karen Saboski
LaPorte County

MIXED GRAIN CORN BREAD

1⅓ C. yellow cornmeal	2 T. sesame seed
⅔ C. whole wheat flour	2 T. soy grits (optional)
¼ C. wheat germ	2½ t. baking powder

½ t. soda	¼ C. cooking oil
½ t. salt	2 C. buttermilk
1 egg	

Stir together cornmeal, flour, wheat germ, sesame seed, soy grits, baking powder, soda, and salt. Beat together egg and cooking oil; add buttermilk. Stir buttermilk mixture into dry ingredients; blend until moistened. Bake in greased 9x9x2" pan at 400° for 25 min. Serve warm. Serves 8.

Mabel Mood
Monroe County

SPICY RAISIN BREAD

2 C. flour	½ C. oil or melted margarine
2 t. baking powder	
1 t. salt	1 C. milk
1 t. cinnamon	2 eggs, beaten
¼ t. nutmeg	¾ C. quick oats
½ C. brown sugar	½ C. nuts
	1 C. raisins

Sift dry ingredients together. Mix oil, eggs, and milk together and add to dry ingredients; mix well. Add oatmeal, nuts, and raisins. Makes 1 standard size loaf or two small loaves. Bake at 350° for 60 min. (large loaf) or 45 min. (small loaf). Remove from pan immediately.

Mary Catherine Farley   *Norma Hilgeman*
White County   *Dubois County*

WHOLE WHEAT QUICK BREAD

2 C. whole wheat flour	1½ C. milk, with 2 t. vinegar added
1 t. baking soda	
2 t. baking powder	½ C. honey
½ C. soy flour	¼ C. powdered milk
¼ C. wheat germ	

Combine all ingredients and stir well; pour into buttered loaf pan. Let stand 20 min. Bake at 350° for 35 min.

Victory Extension Homemakers
Grant County

WHOLE WHEAT NUT BREAD

²⁄₃ C. chopped pitted dates	1½ C. stirred whole wheat flour
½ C. chopped figs	¼ C. brown sugar
½ C. chopped nuts	1 egg, beaten
1½ C. sifted white flour	½ C. honey
3 t. baking powder	1⅓ C. milk
½ t. salt	3 T. melted shortening
¼ t. soda	1½ t. grated orange peel

Mix fruits and nuts with 2 T. of the white flour. Sift remaining white flour with baking powder, salt, and soda; mix in whole wheat flour. Add brown sugar gradually to egg, beat thoroughly. Add honey, milk, shortening, and orange peel to dry ingredients, mixing only enough to dampen all the flour. Add fruits and nuts. Pour into greased 9½x5¼x2¾" loaf pan. Bake at 350° for 1¼–1½ hr. Cool before slicing.

Ruby Hatton
Posey County

WHOLE WHEAT PANCAKES

2 C. whole wheat flour	1 t. salt
2 T. sugar	½ t. soda
1 T. baking powder	2 C. milk
	¼ C. oil
	2 eggs, beaten

Stir dry ingredients together. Combine milk, oil, and eggs; add to dry ingredients. Beat only until lumps disappear. Bake on a hot griddle. If batter seems too thick, add a little more milk.

Ardelle Johnson
LaGrange County

FIBER BRAN MUFFINS

1 C. whole wheat flour	2 C. 100% bran cereal
½ C. honey	1 C. milk
2½ t. baking powder	1 egg
½ t. soda	¼ C. oil
½ t. salt	¼ C. wheat germ

Stir together dry ingredients. Mix together liquid ingredients; add all at once to dry ingredients and mix only until moistened. Bake in muffin pans, filled ²⁄₃ full. Bake at 350° about 20 min.

Mrs. Kenneth Meyers
Marshall County

MORMON MUFFINS

1 C. boiling water	½ C. shortening
3 t. soda	2 eggs
1 C. chopped dates	1 C. sugar
½ C. chopped nuts	2½ C. flour
	1½ C. 40% bran flakes
	2 C. buttermilk

Mix together water, soda, dates, and nuts; set aside. Cream together shortening, sugar, eggs, and flour. Combine bran flakes and buttermilk; add to creamed ingredients and date mixture. Fill large muffin cups ²⁄₃ full. Sprinkle top with mixture of ½ C. sugar and 1 T. cinnamon. Bake 20 min. at 400°. Batter may be refrigerated up to 4 weeks.

Rosalie McGuire
Monroe County

GOLDEN OATMEAL MUFFINS

1 C. sifted flour	1 C. oats
1 T. baking	3 T. oil
powder	1 egg, beaten
½ t. salt	1 C. milk
¼ C. sugar	

Sift dry ingredients together; stir in oats. Combine liquid ingredients. Make a well in dry ingredients; add liquid ingredients and mix only until dry ingredients are moistened. Fill muffin pans ⅔ full. Bake at 400° for 15 min. *Optional Ingredients:* ½ C. raisins, dates, or nuts.

Sherry Hendricks
Marshall County

WHOLE WHEAT MUFFINS

1 C. whole wheat	1 egg
flour	3 T. melted fat
¾ C. white flour	1 T. baking
½ C. sugar	powder
1 t. salt	1 C. milk

Sift dry ingredients together. Combine liquid ingredients; add to dry ingredients. Mix just to moisten. Stir until blended. Put in greased muffin pans and bake at 350° about 25 min.

Ruth Ann Chitty
White County

YOGURT CHIVE MUFFINS

1 C. yogurt, plain	2 T. sugar
1 pkg. dry yeast	1 egg, beaten
1 t. salt	1–2 T. snipped
2 T. shortening	chives
½ C. warm water	2½ C. flour
(105–115°)	

Heat yogurt until warm. In large bowl dissolve yeast in water. Add yogurt, sugar, salt, shortening, egg, chives, and 1½ C. flour. Beat until smooth. Stir in rest of flour and stir until smooth. Cover and let rise until double, about 45 min. Stir down batter. Grease 16 medium muffin cups and fill ½ full with batter. Pat tops with floured fingers to level. Let rise until batter reaches top of cups, 20–30 min. Bake at 400° for 15–20 min. until golden.

Note: If you have a problem finding a good spot to let bread rise, set heating pad on low setting and place covered bowl of dough on it.

Julia Berry
Whitley County

WHEAT GERM PANCAKES

1 C. whole wheat	½ t. salt
flour	2½ C. milk
1 C. white flour	½ C. vegetable
⅔ C. wheat germ	oil
4 t. baking	2 eggs
powder	

In large mixing bowl, combine flour, wheat germ, baking powder, and salt; stir to blend. In separate bowl, beat together milk, oil, and eggs. Pour the liquid ingredients into the dry ingredients and stir only until moistened. Serves 4.

Mrs. Elton Williams
Boone County

TABBOULEH

1 C. cracked	1½ C. finely
wheat (ask for	chopped
bulgur for	parsley
salads)	1 C. finely
boiling water	chopped onion
(start with 2 C.)	or scallion
2 T.–½ C. finely	¾ C. peeled,
chopped fresh	chopped
mint	tomatoes

¾ C. olive oil
1 C. lemon juice
2 cloves garlic, pressed in garlic press (optional)

salt and freshly ground black pepper to taste
¾ chopped cucumbers (optional)

Place cracked wheat in a mixing bowl; add boiling water to cover. Let stand 30 min., or until all liquid is absorbed. The wheat should become tender, but still be somewhat firm *al dente.* If the wheat is too dry, add a little more boiling water. If excessive water is added, it may be necessary to drain the wheat and press it. Cool wheat thoroughly and mix well with remaining ingredients. Garnish with additional chopped tomatoes. Serves 6–8.

Doti Pozzatti
Monroe County

TOFU LASAGNE

1 T. olive oil
1 clove garlic, minced
1 onion, chopped
10 oz. pkg. frozen or fresh chopped spinach
1 lb. tofu
½ C. Parmesan cheese, grated

½-1 C. fresh parsley, chopped
2 eggs
nutmeg and white pepper to taste
1 lb. mozzarella cheese, grated
tomato sauce
8 lasagne noodles, cooked

Sauté garlic and onion in oil; add frozen spinach and cover skillet. When spinach is thawed sufficiently to break into pieces, remove cover and cook until water from spinach evaporates. Mix tofu, Parmesan, parsley, eggs, and spices in a bowl. Add spinach mixture to tofu mixture (tofu will mix easier if mashed with a potato masher first). Into a greased 10x14x2″ pan, spoon a small amount of tomato sauce. Make 2 layers of

noodles, tofu mixture, and tomato sauce. Sprinkle top layer of tomato sauce with extra grated cheese if desired. Bake uncovered at 350° for 45–50 min.

Janet Richards
Monroe County

TOMATO SAUCE

2 T. vegetable oil
½ C. onion
1–2 cloves garlic , minced
1 No. 2½ can tomatoes
2–4 8-oz. cans tomato sauce
2 t. salt
1 T. sugar (optional)

½ t. pepper
1 t. dried basil (optional)
3 t. dried oregano (optional)
1 chopped carrot (optional)
chopped celery (optional)
chopped parsley (optional)

Sauté onion and garlic in hot oil in large kettle. Add remaining ingredients; mix well, mashing tomatoes with fork. Bring to a boil; reduce heat and simmer, stirring occasionally, for 1 hr.

Jane Burgart
Monroe County

TOFU AND LENTIL PIE

pastry for one 9″ pie shell
2 C. cooked lentils, drained
1 t. Worcestershire sauce
⅓ C. chopped green pepper
¼ C. tomato paste
1 lb. tofu
2 eggs

½ C. cream-style cottage cheese
¼ C. sliced green onions
1 T. chopped parsley
1 clove garlic, minced
salt and pepper to taste
1 small green pepper, chopped

Line a 9″ quiche dish or pie pan with pastry.

Trim crust to ½" beyond edge and flute high. Bake at 450° for 8–10 min. Season lentils with salt and pepper; add Worcestershire sauce, the ⅓ C. green pepper, and tomato paste; spoon mixture into pie shell. Place tofu chunks, eggs, cheese, green onion, parsley, garlic, salt, and pepper into blender; cover and blend until smooth. Pour tofu mixture over lentil layer. Sprinkle with the chopped small green pepper and bake at 350° for 30 min.

Christine Wilkey
Vigo County

TOFU-CHEESE-EGG QUICHE

1 lb. tofu	1 tomato, thinly
½ onion, thinly	sliced
sliced	1 C. cottage
4–5 mushrooms,	cheese
thinly sliced	2 large eggs
1 T. oil	2 T. whole wheat
¼ C. wheat germ	flour
or 10" pie shell	¼–½ C. grated
2 T. sesame seeds	hard cheese

Sauté onion and mushrooms in oil; drain on paper towel. Lightly grease pie plate; sprinkle with wheat germ to cover, or use pie shell. Sprinkle with sesame seeds. Spread onion-mushroom mixture over seeds; top with half the tomato slices. Blend tofu, cottage cheese, eggs, and flour. Add hard cheese, reserving some for topping. Pour into pan and arrange remaining tomato slices on top. Sprinkle with reserved cheese. Bake at 350° for 30–40 min.

Alison Gibbs
Monroe County

WHOLE WHEAT PIZZA (1)

Crust:	1 pkg. dry yeast
1 C. warm water	1 t. sugar
(105–115°)	1 t. salt

2½ C. whole	Toppings:
wheat stone-	sausage and ham-
ground flour	burger mixed
	and browned
Pizza Sauce:	together
1 15-oz. can to-	onions, chopped
mato paste	mushrooms,
1½ C. water	sliced
1 t. salt	green pepper,
½ t. sugar	chopped
1 t. oregano	Parmesan cheese
1 t. sweet basil	mozzarella cheese
1 T. parsley flakes	other toppings to
dash of Worces-	suit yourself
tershire sauce	

Dissolve yeast in warm water; add remaining ingredients and form into dough. Knead 10 min. Place in greased bowl. Cover and let rise while you make the sauce and toppings. Mix all sauce ingredients together. Spread dough on 2 pizza pans and put half the sauce on each crust. Add toppings as desired. Bake at 450° for 20 min. *Note:* Size of pizza depends on whether you prefer thick or thin crusts.

Shari K. Price
Carroll County

WHOLE WHEAT PIZZA CRUST (2)

1 pkg. dry yeast	1 egg
¼ C. sugar	1 C. whole wheat
¼ C. warm water	flour
¾ C. hot milk	2½–3 C. un-
¼ C. oil	bleached white
½ t. salt	flour

Dissolve yeast and sugar in water; set aside. Mix together milk, oil, salt, egg, and whole wheat flour; add yeast mixture. Add unbleached flour, ½ C. at a time. Knead slightly. Divide in two. (One part may be frozen, thawed, and rolled out later.) Spread onto a 14" pizza pan. Brush with oil. Bake at 425° for 5 min. Press bubbles down. Cover with favorite toppings. Bake 15–20 min. Will be thick and chewy. Serves 4.

Becky Isfalt
Boone County

BARLEY CASSEROLE

¼ lb. butter
2 medium on-
  ions, chopped
¾ lb. mush-
  rooms, sliced
1½ C. quick
  barley

3 pimientos,
  chopped
2 C. chicken
  stock
salt and pepper

Sauté onion and mushrooms in melted butter until tender. Add barley and cook mixture until the barley is a delicate brown. Transfer mixture to a casserole; add pimientos, chicken stock, and salt and pepper to taste. Cover casserole and bake at 350° for 50–60 min. All liquid should be absorbed and the barley tender. Add more stock during baking period if needed. Oven time is based on "quick" barley; regular will take a little longer. This is a change of pace from potatoes. Good served with pork, chicken, turkey, or fish. Serves 8.

Mary Grott
LaPorte County

EARLY SPRING DANDELION GREENS

3–4 C. cooked
  dandelion
  greens
4 slices bacon
2 t. prepared
  mustard
Sweet-Sour
  Dressing:
1 egg

⅓ C. sugar
2½ T. flour
¼ C. vinegar
½ C. water
¼ t. dry mustard
½ t. salt
dash of pepper

Wash freshly gathered dandelions. Cook until tender; drain. To make the sweet-sour dressing: beat the egg with an electric beater; add remaining ingredients. Cook until thick. Fry the bacon; drain. Stir hot dandelions, bacon, and prepared mustard into the hot sweet-sour dressing. Serve hot. Serves 6.

Mrs. Clarence W. Gunter
Kosciusko County

TOFU MAYONNAISE

6 oz. tofu
1½–2 T. lemon
  juice or white
  wine vinegar

2 T. vegetable oil
½ t. salt
½ t. pepper

Blend in blender until smooth; chill.

Barbara Wells
Morgan County

COUNTRY APPLE PIE
(DRIED APPLES)

1¼ C. heavy
  cream
2 T. quick tapicoa
½ C. honey
½ t. freshly
  ground nutmeg

¼ t. cinnamon
2 t. lemon juice
1½ C. sliced
  dried apples
2 T. butter

Mix first six ingredients together in saucepan; heat to about 185° (just under boiling). Add apples and toss all ingredients, except butter, together. Pour into pie shell. Dot with butter. Top with top crust; cut vents and bake at 350° for 50–60 min.

Isabelle Oplinger
Noble County

SWIRLED STRAWBERRY PIE

1 pt. fresh
  strawberries
1 C. water
½ C. granulated
  sugar
3 T. cornstarch
1 C. yogo cheese

few drops red
  food coloring
  (optional)
1 T. powdered
  sugar
1 9" baked pie
  shell

Wash and hull strawberries. In a small saucepan, crush 1 C. of the smaller berries and cook in water about 3 min. Stir together granulated sugar and cornstarch; add to cooked berries. Cook mixture until clear and thickened; remove from heat. Stir in food coloring. Reserve 2 T. yogo cheese for glaze. Stir remaining yogo cheese with powdered sugar until creamy. Cover bottom of pie shell with yogo cheese mixture. Stand remaining berries, stem side down, over the cheese. Carefully swirl remaining 2 T. yogo cheese into cooled glaze. Pour glaze over berries. Refrigerate until firm, about 4 hr., before serving. Serves 6–8.

YOGO CHEESE
Line a colander with 4 layers of white paper towels. Place yogurt in colander; cover with more paper towels. Place colander in pan about 2″ deep. Refrigerate and allow to drain 8–10 hr. Check occasionally to remove excess liquid from pan. Carefully remove yogo cheese from paper towels. Place cheese in a container with a cover; sprinkle with salt and mix well. Yogo cheese will keep covered in refrigerator up to 4 weeks. Use as sour cream or cream cheese.
Note: 1 qt. yogurt makes about 1½ C. yogo cheese.

Mary Ann Lienhart-Cross
Elkhart County

TOFU ALMOND CREAM PIE
10″ baked pie shell or crumb crust in 10″ spring form pan	½ C. honey
	3 eggs, separated
	2 t. vanilla
	1½ t. almond extract
2 T. unflavored gelatin	1 C. whipping cream, whipped
¼ C. water	
1 lb. tofu	

Soften gelatin in water; heat to dissolve. In a blender, combine tofu, honey, egg yolks, vanilla, and almond extract; blend until smooth. Beat egg whites until stiff but not dry. Pour tofu mixture into a large bowl; fold in beaten whites and whipped cream. Turn mixture into prepared crust; chill.

Denise Kirby
Monroe County

Note: Raw eggs are safe to eat as long as the egg's shell is clean, uncracked, and unbroken. Use raw eggs in beverages or uncooked desserts that will be eaten promptly. There has been concern that eating raw eggs may prevent the absorption of biotin, one of the B vitamins. A human would probably have to eat 8–10 raw egg whites daily to develop any biotin absorption problems.

TOASTED OAT CRUST
1 C. quick oats	⅓ C. brown sugar
⅓ C. finely chopped nuts	3–4 T. butter, melted
½ t. cinnamon	

Combine all ingredients; mix well. Press onto bottom and sides of lightly oiled 9″ pie plate. Bake at 375° for 8–10 min., or until golden brown.
Note: If crust is flat on bottom of pie plate after baking, use back of spoon to push up onto sides of pan and to even out bottom of crust.

YOGURT HONEY CREAM PIE
1 envelope plus 1½ t. unflavored gelatin	dash of salt
	food coloring, if desired
½ C. water	1½ C. heavy cream, whipped
3 8-oz. cartons flavored yogurt	
½ C. honey	toasted oat crust

Soften gelatin in water. Stir over low heat

until dissolved. Combine yogurt, honey, salt, and food coloring, mixing until well-blended. Gradually add dissolved gelatin; mix well. Chill about 15 min., or until slightly thickened. Fold in whipped cream. Chill 45 min., or until mixture mounds when dropped from spoon. Mound into crust. Chill 4 hr. or until firm.

Note: To cut down on calories use 1 C. heavy cream. Also use unflavored yogurt and drained unsweetened crushed pineapple in place of flavored yogurt.

Dianna Crouse
Union County

"CHEESE" PASTRY

1 C. tofu,	2 c. sifted flour
crumbled	1 T. sugar
1 C. margarine	¼ t. salt

Drain tofu well to remove excess moisture. Cream margarine and tofu together until smooth and creamy. Sift together flour, sugar, and salt; work into creamed mixture with pastry cutter or wooden spoon. Mold into a ball; wrap in plastic wrap and chill several hr. Pastry may be used for cookies, pies, or tarts.

Cookies: Roll dough about ⅛" thick; cut into 2½" squares. Place a teaspoonful of tart jam or preserves in the center of each square. Fold corners to center to enclose filling. Bake 15 min. at 425°, or until lightly browned. Cool. Sprinkle with confectioners' sugar.

Mini-Meat Pies: Brown ½ lb. lean ground beef with 1 small chopped onion. Add ½ t. salt, ¼ t. marjoram, dash of pepper, and 1 t. dried parsley. If filling is very moist, add 1 T. bread crumbs or flour. Roll dough; cut into 4" squares; place about 1 T. filling on each. Fold in half diagonally and press edges with fork tines to seal. Bake at 425° 15 min., or until lightly browned.

Mrs. John Hensel
Hamilton County

CHEDDAR CHEESE PIE CRUST

¾ C. whole	1 C. grated Ched-
wheat flour	dar cheese
½ t. salt	¼–⅓ C. water
¼ t. dry mustard	

Stir together the dry ingredients; add the Cheddar cheese and enough water to allow the dough to "gather together." Roll dough out, and place in an oiled 9" pie plate. Fill and bake.

Victory Extension Homemakers
Grant County

TOFU CHEESECAKE

24 oz. tofu, or	1 T. vanilla
1 lb. tofu and	2 T. vegetable oil
8 oz. cream	1 T. lemon juice
cheese	⅛ t. nutmeg
2 eggs	¼ t. salt
⅔ C. honey or	1 9" graham
½ C. sugar	cracker crust

Combine all cheesecake ingredients in a blender and mix until smooth. Pour the filling into crust and bake at 350° for 40 min., or until golden brown.

Dianna Crouse
Union County

TOFU ICE CREAM

16 oz. fresh tofu	1½ bananas
½ C. peanut	2 T. lemon juice
butter	1–2 T. honey

Place all ingredients in blender and "blend-erize" until smooth; freeze. Top with shaved bitter chocolate and pecan pieces.

Mildred MacKenzie
Monroe County

CREAMY VANILLA YOGURT

3¾ C. milk   ½ envelope un-
¼ C. non-instant   flavored gelatin
   powdered milk   2 T. yogurt
2 t. vanilla

In blender combine 2 C. milk, non-instant
powdered milk, gelatin, and vanilla; blend
until well-mixed. Pour mixture into large
saucepan and add the remaining milk; stir
until mixed. Place over medium heat; stir
constantly and bring to almost a boil (mixture will almost double in bulk). Remove
from heat and cool to lukewarm (approximately ½ hr.). Add the yogurt and mix
well; pour into yogurt maker containers and
process according to yogurt maker instructions.

Ellen Hummel
Marshall County

FRUIT YOGURT SHERBET

1 C. yogurt   1 T. honey
juice of one   16 oz. can
   orange   crushed pine-
2 C. fresh, or   apple,
   frozen,   unsweetened
   strawberries   ½ C. non-instant
1 banana   dry milk
   (optional)   powder

Blend all ingredients together until smooth.
Freeze in ice cube tray.

Teresa Hildebrand
Vigo County

YOGURT ICING

½ C. yogurt   ⅓ C. non-instant
¼ C. honey   milk powder
1 T. lime juice   1 T. butter

Beat all ingredients together until smooth.
Thicken if necessary with up to ¼ C. more
milk powder.

Teresa Hildebrand
Vigo County

BUTTERSCOTCH BROWNIES

¼ C. vegetable   2 t. vanilla
   oil   1 C. raw wheat
1 T. dark   germ
   molasses   ¼ t. salt
⅞ C. sugar (1 C.   ½ C. dry milk
   minus 2 T.)   powder
½ C. chopped   ½ t. baking
   nuts   powder
2 eggs

Combine all ingredients, except milk powder and baking powder. Stir well; sift in
milk and baking powder. (*Note:* This recipe
contains no flour.) Spread in a greased and
floured 8″ square pan. Bake for 30 min. at
350°. Be careful not to overbake. Cut into
squares immediately while still hot.

Janet L. Bedel
Decatur County

CAROB NUT BROWNIES

½ C. butter or oil   2 T. whole milk
½ C. honey   powder or 3½
2 eggs   T. instant
½ t. salt   1½ t. baking
1 t. vanilla   powder
⅓ C. carob   ⅔ C. sunflower
   powder   seeds
⅔ C. whole   ½ C. roasted pea-
   wheat flour   nuts, chopped

Use a greased 8 or 9″ pan, or a 7x11″ pan.
Cream butter (or oil) and honey; beat in the
eggs, salt, and vanilla. Stir together the
carob powder, whole wheat flour, and baking powder; blend into the creamed mixture. Stir in sunflower seeds and peanuts.
Turn into prepared baking pan. Bake at 325°
for 20–25 min.; cool and cut into bars.

Victory Extension Homemakers
Grant County

GRANOLA

7 C. quick oats	½ t. salt
1 C. coconut	1 C. all-bran
½ C. wheat germ	½ C. sunflower
½ C. nut meats	seeds
1 C. cornmeal	1 C. poppy seeds
1 C. soy grits	½ to ¾ C. saf-
	flower oil
	½ C. water

Mix all ingredients together with hands. Set oven at 325°. Put on cookie sheet or pan and bake at 325° for 20 min. Stir every 5–10 min. Add 1 C. seedless raisins and ½ C. chopped dates, if desired, after removing mixture from the oven.

Agnes Mawhorter
Noble County

GRANOLA BARS

½ C. light corn	3 C. granola
syrup	1 carrot, grated
⅔ C. peanut but-	(optional)
ter (10 T.)	

Butter a 9″ square pan. In a 3 qt. saucepan, boil corn syrup for 1 min. only, stirring constantly; remove from heat. Stir in peanut butter; stir in granola and carrot. Work fast as mixture hardens quickly. Transfer to pan. Spread and pat in place with a spoon or dampened spatula. Cool for 1 hr. before cutting into bars.

Mary Ann Lienhart-Cross
Elkhart County

BREAKFAST COOKIES

¾ C. butter or	2 t. prepared
margarine	mustard
⅔ C. brown	1¼ C. flour
sugar	½ C. cornmeal
1 egg	1 t. soda

¼ t. salt	2 smoked pork
1 C. instant oats	sausage links,
1 C. raisins	finely chopped

Beat together butter and sugar until light and fluffy; blend in egg and mustard. Add combined flour, cornmeal, soda, and salt; mix well. Stir in remaining ingredients. Drop by heaping tablespoonfuls onto ungreased cookie sheet about 2″ apart. Bake at 375° about 12 min. or until edges are golden brown. Cool thoroughly on wire rack. Store in lightly covered container in refrigerator. Makes about 2 doz. cookies. To reheat cookies, bake in toaster oven or in oven at 300° about 5 min.

Janet Gordon
Boone County

MONSTER COOKIES

12 eggs	1 lb. butter
2 lb. brown sugar	18 C. oats (whole
4 C. white sugar	42-oz box of
1 T. vanilla	quick oats)
flavoring	1 lb. chocolate
1 T. corn syrup	chips
8 t. soda	1 lb. M & M
3 lb. peanut	candies
butter	

Beat the eggs in a large pan; add and mix remaining ingredients in order listed. (*Note:* the recipe contains no flour.) Use an ice cream scoop to drop mixture on cookie sheets. Place about 6 cookies to a sheet; flatten. Bake for 12 min. at 350°. Do not overbake.

Leah Lash　　　　*Lorraine A. Nichols*
Steuben County　　　*Spencer County*

NUTRITIOUS COOKIES

⅔ C. honey	2½ C. whole
½ C. oil	wheat flour
1 egg, beaten	1 t. baking soda

½ t. salt
1 C. cooked
  pumpkin, or
  1 C. mashed
  banana, or
  1 C. applesauce

1 t. baking
  powder
1 t. cinnamon
1 t. vanilla
1 C. nuts and/or
  raisins

Stir together dry ingredients. Combine honey, oil, and egg; add to dry ingredients. Mix well. Blend in pumpkin, nuts, and raisins. Drop by teaspoon on a greased cookie sheet. Bake at 350° for about 10 min. *Note:* May add about 5 T. wheat germ.

Nancy Buckland
Owen County

PEANUTTY GIANT COOKIE

2 C. brown sugar
¼ C. shortening
¾ C. peanut
  butter
½ C. finely
  chopped apples
1 t. vanilla

2 eggs
2 t. soda
¾ t. salt
1¾ C. flour
1 C. oats
¼ C. wheat germ

Cream shortening and sugar and add rest of ingredients. Measure in amounts of ¼ C., and place on cookie sheet. Press down. Bake at 350° for 10–12 min.

Mary Catherine Sheldon
Carroll County

TOFU SPICE COOKIES

1½ C. whole
  wheat flour
¾ C. raisins
¼ C. chopped
  dates or prunes

½ C. chopped
  nuts
½ t. baking soda
½ C. honey
½ lb. tofu

1 egg
½ C. soft butter
  or oil
1 t. ginger

1 t. cinnamon
1 t. nutmeg
½ t. salt
1 t. vanilla

In a 2 qt. bowl, mix flour, raisins, dates, nuts, and baking soda together. In a blender or food processor, blend the remaining ingredients. Mix wet and dry ingredients together. Drop by teaspoonfuls onto oiled cookie sheet. Bake at 350° for 10–15 min. These cookies can be made ahead of time and frozen, or kept in a tin box for a few days.

Alison Gibbs
Monroe County

WHOLE WHEAT SUGAR COOKIES

1 C. sugar
1 t. baking
  powder
½ t. salt
½ t. soda
½ t. nutmeg
½ C. butter,
  softened
2 T. milk

1 T. grated lemon
  or orange peel
1 t. vanilla
1 egg
2 C. whole wheat
  flour
2 T. sugar
½ t. cinnamon

Combine first 10 ingredients in large bowl; blend well. Lightly spoon flour into measuring cup; level off. Stir in flour. Shape into 1″ balls. Place 2″ apart on ungreased cookie sheets; flatten slightly. Combine 2 T. sugar and cinnamon, sprinkle over cookies. Bake at 375° 8–10 min.

Jeanette Becker
Marshall County

Foods for the Calorie Conscious

The American Medical Association says 40 percent of Americans are overweight. Almost one half of adult menu planners are concerned with weight. There are no magic foods or diets which will cause weight loss. When the total number of calories from any food source exceeds the number of calories expended, the excess will be stored as fat. To reach and maintain your ideal weight, cut back on fats, sugar, and alcohol in your diet. While you are cutting back on serving sizes, you should increase your physical activity.

Artificial sweeteners are used to reduce the proportion of calories consumed as sugar. Saccharin is relatively calorie-free, but its safety is still questionable. A new sugar substitute, aspartame, cannot be used in cooking or baking. It is no doubt wise to use all artificial sweeteners sparingly. We need to guard against a false sense of calorie reduction when using artificial sweeteners in baked goods because these foods may still be high in calories due to the eggs, flour, and fats used.

Cooking with sugar substitutes requires the willingness to experiment. You will have to vary the amounts you use when substituting them for sugar in your own recipes. Recipes for cakes, yeast breads, and cookies require the carbohydrate of sugar for balance, so you cannot easily substitute saccharin for sugar in these recipes. Quick breads often require no adjustments. Be prepared for some early failures as you try to adapt recipes.

ORANGE JEWEL DRINK

1 orange, peeled and seeded	1 can orange diet soda
artificial sweetener to taste (optional)	⅓ C. nonfat dry milk
	6 ice cubes

Place all ingredients except ice cubes in blender, blend 1 min. Add ice cubes, 1 at a time, until mixture is frothy.

Strawberries, blueberries, or pineapple with the appropriate flavored soda may be used in place of the orange.

Rita Carpenter
Pulaski County

MUSKMELON SOUP

When melons are plentiful, do some for the freezer. For each quart of pureed melon add ¼ C. lemon juice and freeze. To serve, thaw and stir in chopped apples, peaches, or cherries and top with yogurt. Can be used plain as breakfast juice.

Jennette Shull
Noble County

DIETER'S SOUP (1)

1 head cabbage	2 bouillon cubes
3 large onions	2 C. water (optional)
1 stalk celery	
1 green pepper	salt and pepper to taste
1–2 large cans tomatoes	garlic salt (optional)
2 pkg. dried onion soup mix	

Chop vegetables. Bring all ingredients to a boil; simmer 1 hr., or until vegetables are done. Serves 4–6.

Bertha Corcoran
Brown County

DIETER'S SOUP (2)

1 qt., 14-oz. can tomato juice	½ head cabbage, cut up
½ C. water	2 small carrots, sliced
4 beef bouillon cubes	1 can French-style green beans, drained
4 chicken bouillon cubes	
⅓ C. dehydrated or fresh chopped onion	½ head cauliflower, cut up

Mix the first 7 ingredients together in a large pot; simmer for ½ hr. Add green beans and cauliflower. Simmer for another 30 min., or until cauliflower is tender.

Juanita Colvin
Ripley County

MOLDED APPLE SALAD

1 envelope gelatin, unflavored	2 T. lemon juice
1¾ C. unsweetened apple juice	½ C. diced celery
	dash salt
1 C. unpared, diced apples	few drops red food coloring (optional)

Sprinkle gelatin over ¾ C. apple juice; let soften 5 min. Heat remaining apple juice until it boils; pour over gelatin and stir until dissolved. Add remaining ingredients; stir. When about the consistency of egg whites, pour into 5½ C. pan. Chill until firm. When ready to serve, top with pineapple "yogurt."

"YOGURT":

½ C. water	2 C. buttermilk
1 envelope gelatin, unflavored	1 C. unsweetened crushed pineapple, drained
6 T. powdered artificial sweetner	1 t. vanilla

Dissolve gelatin in water. Heat until gelatin is dissolved. Add remaining ingredients; chill.

Ann Weltzen
Pulaski County

GREEN BEAN SALAD

1 28-oz can French-style green beans	1 medium onion, minced
3 stalks celery, chopped	1 2-oz. can pimiento
1 medium cucumber, diced	¼ C. tarragon vinegar
1 small green pepper, chopped	¼ C. white vinegar artificial sweetener to taste

Mix ingredients. Chill before serving. Serves 6 at 37 calories per serving.

Mary Bryant
Harrison County

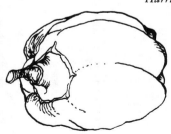

LOW-CAL BEAN SALAD

1 16-oz. can green beans, drained	Dressing: ¼ C. lemon juice ½ t. salt
1 16-oz. can wax beans, drained	½ t. pepper ½ t. garlic powder
1 C. chopped mushrooms	1½ T. liquid or 6 packets sugar
⅓ C. chopped pepper	substitute
⅓ C. chopped onion	

Combine all ingredients. Mix dressing and add. Serves 6 at 45 calories per serving.

Sally Slater
Grant County

MARINATED LOW-CAL VEGETABLE SALAD

2 large carrots	2 medium onions, sliced
6–8 pieces of celery	2 green peppers, cut into strips
small head cauliflower	1 small bottle low-cal Italian dressing
small bunch broccoli	

Cut vegetables into bite-sized pieces; cover with water and bring to boil. Remove from heat immediately; drain and run cold water over vegetables to cool. Put vegetables into bowl and add onions and peppers. Pour dressing over vegetables and refrigerate. Will keep in refrigerator 2–3 weeks.

Mary Condon
LaPorte County

EGGPLANT SALAD

1 medium eggplant	3 medium tomatoes, peeled and cubed
4 scallions, chopped	3 T. vegetable oil

¼ C. cider   ½ t. sugar
   vinegar   dill weed to taste
salt and pepper to   (fresh or dried)
   taste

Wash eggplant; dry, but do not pare. Bake at 375° for 45 min., or until tender. Cool, pare, cut into cubes, and chill. Make dressing of the oil, vinegar, salt, pepper, sugar and dill. Gently combine salad ingredients with dressing; chill several hours before serving. Serves 4–6.

Harriet Curry
Monroe County

LOW-CALORIE COOKED SALAD DRESSING

1 T. flour   1 T. salad oil
2 T. sugar   1 C. water
1¼ t. salt   2 eggs
1 t. prepared   4 T. vinegar
   mustard   dash red pepper

Blend together all ingredients except eggs and vinegar in top of double boiler. Cook over hot water, stirring constantly, until slightly thickened. Beat eggs lightly in small bowl; add vinegar gradually. Add ½ of hot sauce to egg mixture stirring constantly; return to double boiler. Stir and cook over hot (not boiling water) until mixture coats spoons. Note: overcooking after eggs are added will cause dressing to curdle. Remove from heat; pour into glass jar. When cool, cover and refrigerate.

Variations:

Russian—add 1 T. ketchup per ¼ C. dressing. Gourmet—add ¼ t. horseradish and ½ t. Worcestershire sauce per ¼ C. dressing. Thousand Island—add 2 T. chili sauce, 2 T. chopped green pepper, and ½ chopped hard-cooked egg per ¼ C. dressing.

Betty Sendmeyer
Putnam County

ZERO DRESSING

¼ C. lemon juice 1 C. tomato juice
   or vinegar   salt & pepper to
2 T. finely minced taste
   onion

Combine in jar with tight-fitting lid. Shake well before using.

Sheila Whitehead
Clay County

NEXT TO NOTHING DRESSING

1 12-oz. can or   2 T. chopped
  1 ½ C. tomato   green pepper
  juice   2 t. lemon juice
⅓ C. chopped   1 t. sugar
  celery   1 t. garlic salt
¼ C. chopped   ¼ t. Worcester-
  onion   shire sauce

Place all ingredients in blender container. Process until smooth; cover. Refrigerate at least 4 hours to blend flavors. Keeps well for 2 weeks. 3 ½ calories per tablespoon.

Jane Rodman
Monroe County

WAIST WATCHER DRESSING

1 C. low-fat cot- 1 T. any dehy-
  tage cheese   drated salad
3–5 T. skim milk   dressing

Place all ingredients in blender; blend at high speed until smooth.

Alice Sink
Parke County

LOW-CAL SKILLET STEAK

1 round steak,   1 onion, chopped
  cut into ½x2″ 1 C. beef
  strips   bouillon

2 16-oz. cans French-style green beans, drained

1 4-oz. can mushrooms, drained

1 T. cornstarch

Spray skillet with non-stick vegetable spray; brown steak and onion. Add bouillon and simmer until tender, approximately 30 min. Add beans and mushrooms; thicken with cornstarch. Serve over rice.

Betty Feldmeyer
Marion County

LOW-CAL BEEF STROGANOFF

1½ t. butter
1½ t. cooking oil
1 lb. lean round steak, trimmed of fat and cut into cubes
1 4-oz. can mushroom stems and pieces
2 T. cornstarch

½ C. chopped onion
1 t. fresh ground pepper
1 beef bouillon cube
1 C. boiling water
1 C. plain yogurt

Heat butter and oil in heavy skillet. Sauté meat and onion until meat loses its redness. Mix the bouillon cube and cornstarch in water; add cornstarch mixture and remaining ingredients (except yogurt) to meat and simmer about 1 hr. until meat is tender. Stir in yogurt and heat thoroughly. Serve over hot rice. Serves 4 at 285 calories per serving.

Dorothea Wenning
Decatur County

SLIM ENCHILADAS

6 soft tortillas
¼ lb. lean hamburger
4 T. minced onion

1 T. vinegar
1–2 t. chili powder
¼ t. oregano
2 C. tomato juice

1 t. cumin seed or ½ t. ground cumin
garlic salt
1 C. water

diced green pepper
2 T. shredded cheese

Brown hamburger; drain. Add onion and vinegar and stir until vinegar evaporates. Stir in spices and ¼ C. of tomato juice and water combined. Stir until juice evaporates. Divide meat filling on tortillas and roll like crepes. Arrange in skillet. Pour on remaining juice. Add green peppers. Cover and simmer 10–15 min. Uncover and simmer until sauce is thick. Sprinkle with cheese. Serve with a dollop of sour cream on top (lowfat yogurt for fewer calories). Serves 6.

Ruth M. Burrus
Boone County

BROILED SAUERBRATEN

1 C. water
1 C. cider vinegar
artificial sweetener to equal 3 T. sugar
1 T. dehydrated onion flakes
2 t. pickling spices

1 t. salt
1 bay leaf
½ t. ginger
½ t. peppercorns
2 lb. lean beef, cut into 1½″ cubes
parsley sprigs, radish slices

Make marinade by mixing together water, vinegar, sugar substitute, onion, and seasonings. Marinate beef for 1–2 days in refrigerator. Turn meat frequently to season evenly. Transfer meat to broiling pan; strain marinade. Broil meat about 4″ from source of heat for about 10 min. Serve garnished with radish slices and parsley sprigs. Serves 4.

Deloris Wallace
Posey County

CALORIE-CONTROLLED MEAT LOAF

½ C. minced celery
2 oz. finely minced onion
1 pkg. instant chicken broth mix
1 C. unsweetened applesauce
1 T. plus 1 t. catsup
½ t. thyme
¼ t. garlic powder
½ medium green pepper, minced
½ C. water
2 lb. ground beef
2 slices bread, crumbed
1 t. Worcester-shire sauce
½ t. salt
⅛ t. pepper

In a small saucepan combine celery, green pepper, onion, water, and broth mix; cook until celery is tender. Add remaining ingredients and mix well. Divide into two small loaves; place on a rack in a baking dish. Bake at 375° for 45–60 min.

Deloris Durham
Randolph County

Pat Niedermeyer
Whitley County

CHICKEN BREAST IN FOIL

1 T. whipped margarine
1 T. chopped green onions
4 chicken breast halves
4 pieces of foil, each 12x12"
8 canned or fresh mushrooms
½ C. white wine
pinch of tarragon
vegetable salt to taste
chopped parsley to taste

Sauté onions and chicken in melted margarine for 1 min. Grease each piece of foil lightly with vegetable oil and place a chicken breast in the center. Add 2 mushrooms for each breast. Fold edges of foil upward to form individual cooking pans. Add cooking wine to skillet and deglaze; add seasonings. Pour liquid into each foil "pan." Fold edges together tightly. Bake at 350° for 1 hr. Serves 4 at 205 calories per serving.

To deglaze, remove cooked food from pan and keep warm. Add your choice of liquid to hot pan; scrape up crusty bits with a spatula while liquid boils, stirring in additional liquid and seasonings as needed. Pass the rich-tasting sauce as a meat accompaniment.

Sue Childes
Monroe County

MUSHROOMS & CHICKEN

1 12-oz. can mushrooms, drained
2 C. cooked diced chicken
½ C. diced celery
½ C. plain yogurt
2 T. orange juice
1 t. tarragon leaves, crushed
1 t. salt
⅛ t. black pepper

Mix all ingredients together. Serve on lettuce leaf. Serves 4 at 161 calories per serving.

Mary Taylor
Warrick County

BEAN SPROUTS AND CHICKEN SALAD

2 C. cut-up chicken
2 C. fresh bean sprouts (¾ pound), or 1 16-oz can, drained
½ C. sliced water chestnuts (½ of 8 oz. can)
2 green onions with tops, minced
½ C. chopped green pepper
Dressing:
¼ C. vegetable oil
3 T. soy sauce
2 T. vinegar
2 t. ginger
1 t. sugar
salt and pepper to taste
5–6 lettuce cups

Combine chicken and vegetables (except lettuce). Mix dressing ingredients and pour over salad; toss lightly. Spoon into lettuce cups. Serves 5–6.

Faye Ice
LaGrange County

DIET FRIED SHRIMP

½ lb. cleaned and cooked shrimp, drained and dried	¼ C. low-calorie Italian salad dressing

Heat dressing in a skillet; add shrimp and stir-fry until lightly browned. Remove from skillet and drain. Serve with soy sauce or low-calorie seafood cocktail sauce. Serves 3. One serving contains about 80 calories.

Patricia Marshall
Morgan County

SPICY BAKED FISH

1 lb. frozen cod fillets, thawed	2 t. vegetable oil
¼ C. chopped onion	1 8-oz. can tomatoes
¼ C. chopped green pepper	¼ t. salt
	⅛ t. pepper

Grease a 9x9x2″ baking pan with ½ t. oil. Cut fish into 4 servings; place in pan. Bake at 350° 20 min., or until fish flakes easily. Drain cooking liquid from fish. While fish bakes, sauté onion and green pepper in remaining oil until onion is translucent; add tomatoes, salt, and pepper. Simmer sauce 20 min.; pour over fish and bake additional 10 min. Serves 4 at 110 calories per serving.

Shirley Ruark
Putnam County

DIETER'S BARBECUED TUNA OR CHICKEN

6 oz. water-packed tuna or chicken	¼ C. dehydrated onion flakes
½ C. chopped celery	2 t. prepared mustard
½ t. oregano	1 T. vinegar
artificial sweetener to equal 6 t. sugar	2 T. Worcestershire sauce
	½ C. tomato juice

Combine all ingredients and bake at 350° about 45 min., or until the celery is tender. Enough filling for 4 large sandwiches.

Leona Rhodes
Greene County

CURRIED TUNA

1 T. plain gelatin	½ t. paprika
¼ C. cold water	1 T. lemon juice
½ C. boiling water	1 T. curry powder
1½ C. water-packed tuna, flaked	1 C. cottage cheese
¼ C. minced onion	1 C. part-skim yogurt
1 T. margarine	¼ C. chopped parsley
½ t. Tabasco	

Soften gelatin in cold water; dissolve in boiling water. Sauté onion in margarine until barely tender. Put tuna, cottage cheese, and yogurt in blender; blend 30 seconds. Add gelatin, onion, and seasonings to tuna mixture; pour into greased 1 qt. mold and chill overnight. Serve with tomato, zucchini, and green pepper slices. Serves 4 at 200 calories per serving.

Irma Spear
Clark County

ORIENTAL TURKEY

8 oz. cooked tur-
  key, cut into 1"
  cubes
½ C. canned
  pineapple
  chunks,
  unsweetened
½ C. canned
  mushrooms,
  drained
½ C. canned car-
  rots, drained
2 oz. canned
  water chest-
  nuts, drained
  and sliced

2 oz. onion,
  thinly sliced
¼ C. cider
  vinegar
¼ C. water
  artificial sweet-
  ener to equal
  2 t. sugar
1 garlic clove,
  minced
1 T. cornstarch,
  dissolved in 1
  T. soy sauce
1 C. cooked rice,
  cooked without
  added salt

Combine all ingredients except cornstarch
mixture and rice in a medium saucepan.
Cover and cook, stirring occasionally, until
mixture is hot and onion is tender-crisp.
Stir in dissolved cornstarch; continue to stir
and cook until thickened. Divide in half
and serve each portion over ½ C. cooked
rice. 433 calories per serving.

Della Menchhofer
Ripley County

HARVARD BEETS

3 C. sliced
  cooked beets
2 t. powdered
  sugar substitute
1 T. cornstarch

½ t. salt
½ C. beet liquid
  or water
½ C. cider
  vinegar

Mix sweetener, cornstarch, salt, liquid, and
vinegar in a saucepan and let boil for 5
min., stirring constantly. Add beets and pour
into serving dish. Serves 4 at 50 calories per
serving.

Juanita M. Evans
Marion County

OVEN FRENCH FRIES

3 med. potatoes,
  unpeeled, cut
  in strips

1 T. vegetable oil
1 T. water

Mix oil and water together; add potato strips
and stir to coat. Place in a shallow pan;
bake at 475° for 30 min. If more browning
is necessary, place under broiler. Salt to taste.

Shirley Ruark
Putnam County

LAZY DAY TACOS

1 9½-oz. can
  water-packed
  tuna, drained
  and flaked
1 C. chopped
  celery
¾ C. plain yogurt
6 large olives,
  chopped
1 T. instant
  minced onions
1 t. chili powder

½ t. salt
6 taco shells; pre-
  pared according
  to pkg.
  directions
2 C. shredded
  lettuce
1½ oz. shredded
  Cheddar cheese
3 oz. pimiento
  strips, optional

Combine tuna, celery, yogurt, olives, onion, chili powder, and salt in a bowl; chill.
Spoon tuna mixture, lettuce, cheese, and
pimiento into taco shells. Serves 6.

Treva E. Beam
Grant County

CAULIFLOWER ITALIANO

1 T. chopped
  onion
1 small clove
  garlic, crushed
2 T. low-calorie
  Italian dressing
3 C. small fresh
  cauliflowerets

2 T. chopped
  green pepper
1 C. cherry toma-
  toes, halved
½ t. salt
⅛ t. dried basil
  leaves, crushed

In 8″ skillet cook onion and garlic in salad dressing until tender; add cauliflowerets and ¼ C. water. Cook, covered, over low heat for 10 min. Add green pepper; cook until cauliflower is tender, about 5 min. Stir in remaining ingredients; heat through. Serves 6 at 35 calories per serving.

Marcia Ford
Jay County

SPICY APPLE CAKE

2 T. butter	¼ t. baking
¼ C. light brown	powder
sugar	½ t. cinnamon
¼ C. dark brown	¼ t. ginger
sugar	2 small apples,
½ C. beaten eggs	peeled, cored,
½ C. flour	and sliced
⅛ t. soda	

Cream butter and sugars. Beat in eggs. To measure ½ C. beaten eggs, beat eggs lightly and measure. Sift dry ingredients together; stir into creamed mixture. Fold in apples. Spoon into greased pie tin. Bake at 350° for 30–35 min., or until cake starts to shrink from the side of pan. Serves 9 at 104 calories per serving.

Mary Bryant
Harrison County

DIABETIC BANANA BREAD

1¾ C. sifted cake	2 eggs, well
flour	beaten
2 t. baking	liquid sweetener
powder	to equal ½ C.
¼ t. soda	sugar
½ t. salt	1 t. vanilla
¼ C. shortening,	2 medium ba-
melted	nanas, mashed

Sift together flour, baking powder, soda, and salt. Combine shortening, eggs, sweet-

ener, and vanilla; add to flour mixture and stir only until flour is moistened. Fold into mashed bananas. Pour into a well-greased 8x4″ loaf pan. Bake at 350° for 60–70 min.

Pauline Summers
Owen County

BANANA TEA BREAD

1¾ C. sifted flour	2 eggs, well
2 t. baking	beaten
powder	2 T. liquid artifi-
¼ t. soda	cial sweetener
½ t. salt	1 t. vanilla
¼ C. melted	2 medium ba-
shortening	nanas, mashed

Sift flour, baking powder, soda, and salt together. Combine shortening, eggs, sweetener, and vanilla; add to flour mixture, stirring only until flour is moistened. Fold in bananas. Put into well-greased loaf pan (7½x3¾x2½″). Bake 60 min. at 350° or until done. Makes 12 servings, at 123 calories per serving.

Phyllis J. Stevens
Posey County

SLIM GOURMET CHEESECAKE

3 eggs, separated	⅛ t. salt
2 C. low-fat cot-	½ C. sugar
tage cheese	sweetener to
½ C. skim milk	equal ½ C.
1 T. lemon juice	sugar
¼ C. cornstarch	

Set aside egg whites. Put all other ingredients in blender or food processor and beat until smooth and creamy. Whip egg whites until stiff but not dry. Fold into cheese mixture. Spoon into springform pan or 2 qt. round casserole. Bake at 275° for 1 hr. Turn off heat and allow cake to cool gradually in oven for additional 1–1½ hrs. Serve chilled.

If a topping is desired, spoon on sugarless or low-sugar preserves. Serves 12 at 92 calories a slice, without preserves.

Eleanor Arnold
Rush County

CHOCOLATE SWISS ROLL

⅓ C. dry pow-	½ banana,
dered milk	mashed
2 t. cocoa	1 t. vanilla
3 small pkg. arti-	Filling:
ficial sweetener	⅓ C. ricotta
½ t. soda	cheese
1 slice bread,	½ t. vanilla
crumbled in	1 pkg. artificial
blender	sweetener
1 egg	

Blend dry ingredients, banana, egg, and vanilla. Stir until blended smooth. Spread on nonstick baking pan. Bake at 325° for 10 min. While still hot, turn out onto waxed paper. Mix filling and spread evenly over cake; roll up in waxed paper and chill. Serves 1.

Wanda Sherman
Harrison County

LOW-CALORIE BAKED CUSTARD

1 egg, lightly	¾ t. powdered
beaten	sugar substitute
1 C. skim milk	½ t. vanilla

Combine beaten egg with sugar substitute; slowly add skim milk and vanilla, blending well. Pour mixture into 2 custard cups; top with a sprinkling of nutmeg. Bake in pan of hot water at 325° about 1 hr., or until mixture does not adhere to knife. 82 calories per serving.

Lois Cole
Grant County

BREAKFAST CUSTARD

2 C. skim milk	½–1 t. vanilla
2 beaten eggs	2 packets artifi-
4 thin slices	cial sweetener
bread	(individual size)
½–1 t. butter	½ t. cinnamon
flavoring	½ t. nutmeg

Beat and mix all ingredients together (except cinnamon and nutmeg). Pour mixture into greased 1 qt. casserole and sprinkle with cinnamon and nutmeg. Bake at 350° for 20–25 min.

Marjorie Toole
Monroe County

DANDY DIET DESSERT

1 20-oz. can un-	½ of 6 oz. can
sweetened	orange
crushed	concentrate
pineapple	⅔ C. nonfat
1 banana	dried milk

Blend in blender and freeze. Serves 6.

Hallie Tyson
Greene County

PROCESSOR PUMPKIN PIE FOR CALORIE COUNTERS

3 eggs	¾ t. cinnamon
¼ C. brown	½ t. orange peel,
sugar twin	grated fresh or
(don't	dried
substitute)	¼ C. margarine
¼ t. nutmeg	½ C. biscuit mix
1 C. skim milk	1 No. 303 can
(1% or 2%)	pumpkin
¼ t. cloves	

Put eggs in food processor and process until blended. Add the next 6 ingredients and process until blended. Add margarine and process until small curds appear. Add biscuit mix and process until blended. Add pumpkin and process until blended. Pour into 8″ greased pie pan. Allow to set for 5 min. Bake at 350° for 40 min. When done, a silver knife inserted in center of pie should come out clean. Pie will have cracks on top in circular pattern.

Lois Thomas
LaPorte County

PINEAPPLE BOATS

fresh pineapple, cut into 1″ cubes	sliced strawberries
lemon juice	½ C. blueberries
	cantaloupe balls

Remove fruit from fresh pineapple, leaving ¼″ shell intact. Combine fruits; sprinkle with lemon juice and place fruit in pineapple shells. Chill.

Sherry Dowell
Clay County

PINEAPPLE-COCONUT DELIGHT

1 C. crushed unsweetened pineapple	⅓ C. cold water
	1 T. lemon juice
½ envelope (1½ t.) unflavored gelatin	¼ t. vanilla
	2 T. sugar
	2 T. shredded coconut, toasted
¼ C. instant nonfat dry milk	6 whole strawberries

Drain pineapple, reserving syrup. Add water to syrup to make 1 C. liquid. Soften gelatin in syrup-water mixture; stir over low heat until gelatin dissolves. Chill mixture until partially set. Dissolve dry milk in ⅓ C. water. Whip gelatin with rotary or electric beater to soft peaks; slowly add milk and continue beating to stiff peaks. Add lemon juice and vanilla. Gradually beat in sugar. Fold in pineapple. Pile into sherbets and sprinkle with coconut; chill. Garnish with strawberries. Serves 6 at 83 calories per serving.

Marilyn Meyer
Madison County

FRUIT PUDDING

2 C. fruit	¾ C. flour
2 packets powdered sweetener	2 t. baking powder
	¼ t. salt
¼ C. margarine	½ C. milk
1 T. liquid sweetener	1 C. water or fruit juice

Butter a deep 8″ square dish. Place fruit in dish and sprinkle with powdered sweetener. Cream margarine and liquid sweetener. Sift dry ingredients together and add alternately with milk to margarine mixture. Spread batter over top of fruit. Pour water or fruit juice over batter; don't stir. Bake at 275° for 40 min., or until done. Serves 6.

Avis Risk
Putnam County

PERSIMMON PUDDING

2 C. persimmon pulp	1 t. nutmeg
	1 t. soda
⅔ C. dry powdered milk	1 t. salt
	1 t. baking powder
3 T. powdered sugar substitute	
	4 slices bread, crumbled
¼ t. cinnamon	
¼ t. cloves	4 eggs

Blend all together. Pour into two 8 or 9″ baking dishes that have been sprayed with vegetable spray. Bake at 350° for 45 min. Serves 4–6.

Wanda Sherman
Harrison County

APPLE-ORANGE FROST

1 No. 2 can applesauce (about 2 C.)	1 small can orange juice concentrate
3 T. sugar, or equivalent of artificial sweetener (if desired)	2–3 T. lemon juice
	3 egg whites, beaten stiff

Combine applesauce, orange juice, lemon juice, and sugar. Fold in beaten egg whites; freeze until solid. This will keep 2–4 weeks in the freezer and may be used as a meat accompaniment, a salad, or a dessert. May be frozen in paper cupcake liners, dropped in a plastic bag, and stored—or frozen in a pan and cut into servings. Remove from freezer about ½ hr. before serving. Serves 6–8.

Janet Krumme
Hendricks County

OATMEAL DIABETIC COOKIES

¾ C. powdered sugar substitute	1 egg
1¾ C. sifted flour	½ c. raisins
1 t. cinnamon	1 t. baking soda
¼ t. ground cloves	1¼ sticks margarine
½ t. nutmeg	1 C. applesauce
½ t. salt	1 C. oats

Combine eggs, margarine, raisins, oats, and applesauce. Mix remaining ingredients together and sift into the egg mixture. Mix well. Drop by spoonfuls onto greased cookie sheet. Bake at 375° for 15–20 min.

Mary Jane Reuter
Lawrence County

FROZEN "MOUND" BARS

½ C. unsweetened crushed pineapple	⅛ t. vanilla
	⅛ t. coconut extract

1 .75-oz. pkg. Alba '66 or '77 chocolate flavor	artificial sweetener to taste (optional)

Mix all ingredients together. Drop from a teaspoon onto waxed paper and freeze solid. Makes 10 bite-sized pieces. May pour into plastic sandwich box; freeze and cut into bars.

Dorina Frye
Putnam County

PINEAPPLE SHERBET

10 slices unsweetened pineapple, drained	2 T. powdered artificial sweetener
10 T. pineapple juice	1½ t. vanilla
	1½ C. buttermilk

Blend all ingredients in blender. Freeze in tray. Stir when partially frozen and refreeze. (I often put it in five paper cups and freeze to eat as a popsicle.)

Margery Might
Noble County

LOW-CAL COOKIES OR CAKE

1 C. raisins	2 eggs, well beaten
½ C. dates, chopped	⅜ t. liquid or 3 t. powdered artificial sweetener
1 C. water	
½ C. vegetable shortening	1 t. soda
1 t. vanilla	1 C. flour

Combine first three ingredients; boil together for 3 min. Add vegetable shortening; stir and cool. Add remaining ingredients; chill in refrigerator before dropping by teaspoonfuls onto cookie sheet. Bake 10 min. at 350°.

To make a cake, place batter in a lightly

greased 9x13" cake pan and bake about 20 min. at 350°. Cut into squares when cool.

Phyllis J. Stevens
Posey County

COCONUT MACAROONS

2 egg whites	½ t. each vanilla
⅛ t. salt	and almond
½ C. sugar	extract
2 C. flaked	15 candied cher-
coconut	ries, halved

Grease large cookie sheet well. Dust with flour; shake off excess. Beat egg whites until foamy; add salt and beat until soft peaks form. Gradually add sugar, 1 T. at a time. Beat until very stiff; fold in extracts and coconut. Place rounded teaspoonfuls 1" apart on cookie sheets. Top each with halved cherries. Bake at 300° for 20 min., or until surface is firm. Makes 30 macaroons at 41 calories each.

Lee Evans
Benton County

ORANGE COOKIES

1¼ C. flour	⅓ C. flaked
1 t. baking	coconut
powder	1½ t. liquid
¼ t. soda	sweetener
¼ t. salt	(Sweet 10, etc.)
⅓ C. margarine	or ⅓ C. pow-
½ C. unsweet-	dered sweet-
ened orange	ener (Sprinkle
juice	Sweet, etc.)
2 t. grated fresh	1 t. orange
orange peel	extract
(optional)	1 egg

Combine first four ingredients; cut in margarine until crumbly. Stir in remaining ingredients all at once, stirring with fork until dough holds together. Drop by teaspoonfuls 2" apart onto ungreased cookie sheet. Bake

at 400° for 10–12 min., or until golden brown. Makes 36 cookies. Store in refrigerator. Each cookie is 36 calories if made with liquid sweetener or 37 calories if made with powdered sweetener.

Lois Redman
Marshall County

MERINGUE COOKIES

4 egg whites	2 T. sugar
¼ t. cream of	½ C. chopped
tartar	nuts or coconut

Add cream of tartar to egg whites and beat until foamy. Add sugar 1 T. at a time and continue beating until stiff. Fold in nuts or coconut. Line a cookie sheet with foil; sprinkle with cornstarch. Drop meringue by teaspoonfuls. Bake 1 hr. at 250°. Cool slightly and peel off foil. Makes 36 cookies at 15 calories each.

Patricia Harmon
Harrison County

PISTACHIO ANGELS

3 egg whites, at	green food color-
room	ing (make them
temperature	pale)
⅛ t. salt	¾ C. finely
1 C. sugar	chopped pista-
½ t. almond	chio nuts or
extract	blanched
	almonds

Line 2 cookie sheets with foil. In large mixer bowl on high speed beat egg whites and salt until frothy; gradually add sugar, 2 T. at a time. Add almond extract; beat 5 min. until stiff peaks form. Beat in food coloring; fold in nuts and drop in rounded teaspoonfuls 2" apart. Bake at 300° for 30 min. Cool and peel off foil. Makes 40 "angels" at 35 calories each.

Lee Evans
Benton County

From The Pantry Shelf

A well-stocked pantry makes it possible to feed family or friends nutritious and satisfying meals at times when shopping is impossible. Even the lowly pancake mix can help answer the question, "What's to eat?" when unexpected guests arrive late Sunday morning. Experiment with the recipes that follow; team them with an appropriate accompaniment from the Fast Foods section and you should be prepared for most meal emergencies.

HERB "BOUQUETS" FOR SOUP OR GRAVY

1 t. dried parsley	¼ t. dried sage
1 t. dried marjoram	½ t. dried savory
1 t. dried thyme	2 t. dried celery leaves

Divide mixture evenly into three 2″ squares of cheese cloth. Each "bouquet" is enough to season about 2 qt. liquid. Drop the bag into boiling soup toward the end of cooking, or place in gravy for total cooking time.

HOMEMADE PASTRY MIX

6 C. sifted flour	2⅓ C. vegetable
1 T. salt	shortening

Mix flour and salt in large bowl. Cut in shortening until mixture resembles coarse meal. Store covered in a cool place. Makes 8–9 C.

To make a 1-crust pie use 2–4 T. cold water and:

1¼ C. mix for 8″ pie
1½ C. mix for 9″ pie
1¾ mix for 10″ pie

To make a 2-crust pie use 4–6 T. cold water and:

2–2¼ C. mix for 8″ pie
2¼–2½ C. mix for 9″ pie
2½–2¾ C. mix for 10″ pie

Measure mix into bowl. Sprinkle on a small amount of water at a time, mixing evenly and quickly with fork until dough just holds together in a ball. Use no more water than necessary. Proceed as with traditional pastry.

WHITE SAUCE MIX

1 C. flour	4 t. salt
4 C. instant non-fat dry milk granules	1 C. margarine, cut up

Combine flour, milk, and salt; mix well. Add margarine and cut in with pastry blender until crumbly. Store in tightly covered container in refrigerator.

Basic Sauce Directions: Combine mix and milk in heavy saucepan. Cook over medium heat until thickened, stirring constantly with a wire wisk or wooden spoon. Stir while boiling gently for 2 min.

WHITE SAUCE CHART

Type of Sauce	Amount of Mix	Amount of Milk
Thin	⅓ C.	1 C.
Medium	½ C.	1 C.
Thick	1 C.	1 C.

Note: May use ⅔ C. water as a substitute for 1 C. milk. Use thin sauce for soups; medium for sauces, creamed vegetables, fish, poultry, meat, or pasta; thick for souffles and croquettes.

CHEESE DIP

1 8½-oz. can artichoke hearts, drained and chopped	1 8-oz. can mushroom pieces, drained (optonal)
1 8-oz. can Parmesan cheese	1 8-oz. jar mayonnaise

garlic salt to taste

Mix all ingredients together. Bake for 15–20 min. at 350°.

Peg Weller
Greene County

PANTRY SHELF DIP

1 t. garlic powder	1 t. vinegar
1 t. curry powder	1 C. mayonnaise
1 t. horseradish	

Mix all ingredients together and refrigerate. Good with raw vegetables, party crackers, or potato chips.

Jean LaRowe
DeKalb County

SWISS MOCHA

1 lb. instant caffeine-free coffee	1 lb. powdered sugar
1 lb. non-dairy creamer	1½ lb. instant dry milk
2 lb. Quik	

Mix all ingredients together. Use 2 heaping teaspoons per cup boiling water.

Marie Campbell
Warrick County

EGGNOG MIX

11 oz. powdered milk	2 small pkg. French vanilla instant pudding mix
6 oz. non-dairy creamer	

nutmeg if desired

Mix all ingredients together dry. Store covered until ready to use. To make 1 C. eggnog put a scant ½ C. mix and ½ C. water in blender; blend 5–6 sec. May also add 1–2 ice cubes.

Rebecca Standish Wilson
Orange County

SPICED TEA

Mix:	
4 sticks cinnamon, coarsely chopped	¼ C. shredded orange peel
2 t. whole cloves, coarsely crushed	1 t. candied ginger, finely chopped
	8 oz. (3 C.) orange pekoe tea

Combine all ingredients in 1 qt. casserole. Bake covered for 15–20 min. at 300°. Store in jar with tight-fitting lid for at least 1 week in a cool place. Use 1–2 teaspoons tea mixture for each 6 cups water.

Elaine Lumbra
Monroe County

BISCUIT MIX

8 C. flour	4 t. salt
⅓ C. baking powder	up to 8 t. sugar (optional)
2 C. shortening	

Stir dry ingredients together. Cut shortening into dry ingredients with a pastry blender until the consistency of corn meal. Store in airtight containers.

To make biscuits, add ⅓ C. milk for each 1 C. mix. Method: make a well in the center of dry ingredients; pour all the milk in at once. Stir vigorously a scant ½ min. Turn onto lightly floured board; knead gently another scant ½ min. Roll or pat out, to ¼" for plain biscuits, ½" for tea biscuits. Cut and bake at 450° for 12–15 min., depending on their thickness.

Goldie Jones
Pike County

PANCAKE MIX

6 C. flour	**Batter:**
1 T. salt	1 egg, beaten
6 T. baking	with fork
powder	1 C. water
6 T. sugar	2 T. melted fat or
2 C. powdered	oil
milk	1½ c. pancake
	mix

Combine the first 5 ingredients in large bowl. Mix well and store in an airtight container on cupboard shelf. (*Note:* This recipe doubles easily.)

To use: combine egg, water, fat or oil and pancake mix in bowl. Fry on hot ungreased griddle. Serves 3–4.

Option 1: Replace ⅓ white flour with buckwheat flour, whole wheat flour, oatmeal, or rye flour and cornmeal.

Option 2: Add 1 C. wheat germ.

Florence Coldren
Jay County

SALAD DRESSING MIXES

Prepare several pkg. of mix at one time, so they will be available when needed. For either mix cut a 6" square of heavy-duty foil. Place all ingredients in center of foil. Fold foil to make an airtight pkg. Label with date and contents. Store in a cool dry place; use within 6 mo.

1. GARDEN HERB DRESSING MIX

2 t. dried parsley	pinch oregano
leaves	⅛ t. garlic
2 t. dried basil	powder
leaves	pinch pepper
pinch cumin	¼ t. dried
1 t. spike	minced onion

Makes 1 pkg. of 2 T.

Note: Spike, an herbal seasoning salt, can be purchased in health food stores.

GARDEN HERB DRESSING

1 pkg. Garden	¼ C. cider
Herb Dressing	vinegar
Mix	2 T. water
¾ C. oil	

Combine ingredients in a 2 C. container with a tight-fitting lid. Shake until blended. Refrigerate 30 min. before serving. Makes ¼ C.

2. FRENCH-ITALIAN SALAD DRESSING MIX

3 T. sugar	½ t. paprika
¾ t. salt	½ t. dried ore-
⅛ t. pepper	gano leaves,
½ t. dry mustard	crushed
1½ t. dried	⅛ t. dried
minced onion	minced garlic

Makes 1 pkg. of 4 T.

FRENCH-ITALIAN SALAD DRESSING

1 pkg. French-Italian Salad Dressing Mix	¼ C. red wine vinegar
½ C. oil	½ C. ketchup

Process in a blender 5–7 sec. on high speed. Pour into a 2 C. container with a tight-fitting lid. Let stand at room temperature for 5 hr. Refrigerate 30 min. before serving. Makes 1¼ C.

Mary Ann Lienhart-Cross
Elkhart County

CANNED BEEF BAR-B-QUE

1 can roast beef	2 T. brown sugar
1 onion, chopped	2 T. vinegar
2 T. butter	2 T. Worcester-shire sauce
½ C. chopped celery	½ T. prepared mustard
¾ C. catsup	
¾ C. water	

Sauté onion in melted butter. Add remaining ingredients, except beef, and simmer 20–30 min. Add beef; simmer additional 10–20 min.

Josephine Gould
St. Joseph County

CORNED BEEF CASSEROLE

1 8-oz. pkg. noodles, cooked and drained	1 C. milk
	1 can cream of chicken soup
1 12-oz. can corned beef, diced	½ C. chopped onions
¼ lb. Cheddar cheese, diced	¾ C. buttered bread or cracker crumbs

Mix all ingredients together, except crumbs. Pour into a 2 qt. casserole. Top with crumbs. Bake 45 min. at 350°. Serves 6.

Jane Clayton
LaPorte County

CHICKEN CASSEROLE

5 oz. can boned chicken	1 small can evaporated milk
1 can chicken-rice soup	1 small can chow mein noodles
1 can cream of mushroom soup	2 T. Minute Rice, optional

Stir all ingredients together; place in a greased 1½ qt. casserole. Top with crushed potato chips. Bake 45 min.–1 hr. at 325°. Serves 6.

Mrs. Fred L. McCain   *Mrs. Otto H. Pierson*
Carroll County   *Greene County*

EASY CHICKEN CASSEROLE

1 stick margarine, melted	1 can mushroom or onion soup
1 C. long-grain rice	1 jar mushrooms
1 soup can water	2 5-oz. cans boned chicken

Mix all ingredients together. Bake in covered casserole dish for 1 hr. at 325°. Serves 4.

Roxanne Fike
DeKalb County

MONDAY NIGHT SCALLOPED CHICKEN

1 canned whole chicken, boned and cubed, broth reserved	milk to make 2 C. of broth
	2 T. margarine
2 T. cornstarch	salt and pepper to taste

Make a white sauce by adding cornstarch and margarine to milk-broth mixture. Add salt and pepper and bring to a boil over medium heat, stirring constantly; boil 1 min. Add chicken and pour into 2 qt. casserole. Top with buttered crumbs. Serve over cooked rice or noodles, if desired. Serves 8.

Kay Kinnamon
Madison County

MACARONI-HAM BAKE

1 C. elbow macaroni
1 can cream of celery soup
1 small onion, grated
¼ C. milk
1 C. diced canned ham
1 C. grated sharp cheese

Cook macaroni for 2 min. only. Remove from heat; let stand 10 min. Drain; stir in soup, milk, onion, ham, and half of cheese. Turn into buttered 1½ qt. casserole and top with remaining cheese. Bake at 350° for 25–30 min. Serves 6–8.

Luella Newman
Noble County

SOMETHING SPECIAL CASSEROLE

1 7½ oz. pkg macaroni and cheese dinner, cooked
1 C. cooked vegetables (peas, corn, or green beans)
1 T. minced onion (optional)
1 can cream of celery, chicken, or mushroom soup
¼ C. milk (optional)
1 C. chopped tomato, fresh or canned (optional)
1 T. chopped parsley (optional)
½ C. green pepper, chopped (optional)
1 12-oz. can Spam, cut into strips, or 2 C. cooked meat, or tuna fish

Combine macaroni, vegetables, and soup; mix well. Layer half of mixture and ½ of meat in 1½ qt. casserole; repeat layers. Bake at 350° for 25–30 min. May also combine all ingredients and mix well; heat on top of stove. Serves 6.

Florence Cassidy
Hendricks County

Opal Neff
Fulton County

RICE CASSEROLE

1 C. raw rice
1 can consommé
1 can onion soup
1 8-oz. can mushrooms, drained
1 stick margarine

Combine ingredients in 2 qt. covered casserole dish. Bake at 325° for 1 hr. Serves 4–6.

Audrey Gehlbach
Harrison County

UPSIDE DOWN SUPPER

1½ C. canned cooked ham
1 C. cooked lima beans
1 8-oz. can cream-style corn
1 t. Worcestershire sauce
2 T. minced onion
1 C. sharp Cheddar cheese, shredded (about 4 oz.)
⅔ C. biscuit mix
⅓ C. cornmeal
1 egg
¼ C. milk

Mix ham, beans, corn, cheese, onion, and Worcestershire sauce. Turn into greased 1½ qt. casserole, cover, and bake at 375° for 15 min. Mix remaining ingredients; spoon over hot meat mixture, spreading batter to edge of casserole. Bake uncovered 20 min. Cut into wedges; invert onto plate. Serves 4.

Lillian Randall
Posey County

SALMON LOAF

1 16-oz. can salmon, drained, liquid reserved
4 slices day-old bread, cubed
3 eggs, slightly beaten
1 can cream of celery soup
1 T. chopped onion
½ t. salt
⅛ t. pepper
⅛ t. Tabasco sauce

Add salmon liquid to bread cubes. Mix in eggs, soup, onion, and seasonings. Fold in salmon (broken into large chunks). Put mixture into greased loaf pan. Bake at 375° for 1 hr., or until firm.

Mrs. Billy Beach
Knox County

CREAMY SALMON CASSEROLE

1 8-oz. pkg. fine noodles, cooked and drained	3 C. milk
	1 3-oz. pkg. cream cheese, cubed
4 T. butter	¼ C. dry bread crumbs, mixed with 2 T. melted butter
2 large celery stalks, sliced	
2 green onions, chopped	1 7¾-oz. can salmon, drained and flaked
¼ C. flour	
1½ t. salt	
¼ t. pepper	

Melt 4 T. butter in large saucepan; sauté celery and onions. Stir in flour, salt, and pepper until blended. Gradually stir in milk; cook, stirring constantly until thick and smooth. Stir in cream cheese and cook until melted. Remove pan from heat; stir in salmon and noodles. Pour into 8x12″ baking dish. Sprinkle with bread crumbs and bake at 350° for 25–30 min. Serves 6.

Nancy Moore
Wabash County

SALMON FRITTERS

1 7¾-oz. can salmon	2 T. finely chopped green pepper
milk	
1 C. biscuit mix	2 T. finely chopped onion
1 egg, slightly beaten	
1 t. lemon juice	2 T. minced parsley
¼ C. finely chopped celery	½ t. seasoned salt

Drain and flake salmon, reserving liquid. Add milk to salmon liquid to make ½ C. Add egg, lemon juice, and salmon liquid to biscuit mix. Blend in salmon, vegetables, and salt. Drop batter by spoonfuls into deep fat heated to 375°. Fry 3 min., or until golden brown on both sides; drain on paper towels. Serve with lemon wedges and seafood or tartar sauce. Serves 4.

Mary Oler
Randolph County

TUNA CASSEROLE (1)

1 can mushroom soup	½ C. dry noodles
	½ soup can water
1 large can tuna, drained	16 crackers, crushed
1 15-oz. can peas	½ stick butter or margarine, melted
1 4-oz. can mushrooms	

Mix together soup, tuna, peas, mushrooms, and water. Place in greased 1½ qt. casserole. Mix crackers with butter and sprinkle over top of casserole. Bake at 350° for 45 min.

Muriel Brewer
Lawrence County

TUNA CASSEROLE (2)

1 12-oz. pkg. egg noodles, cooked and drained	1 C. cubed Velveeta
	½ C. milk
1 large can tuna	1 small jar mushrooms
1 can cream of chicken or celery soup	canned onion rings (optional)

Pour noodles into greased 9x13″ baking dish. Stir in soup, tuna, cheese, and milk. Cover with foil. Bake at 350° for 30 min. Add onion rings last 10 min. Serves 5.

Lottie Wise
Clark County

SALMON PATTIES

1 lb. can salmon, drained, flaked, and liquid reserved	¼–½ C. chopped onion
	¼–½ t. salt
	½ C. fine cracker crumbs
2 beaten eggs	

Combine all ingredients; mix well and shape into 8 patties. Place on waxed paper and let stand about ½ hr. at room temperature (longer if refrigerated). Fry in ⅛" of oil at medium heat; drain on paper toweling.

Wanetta Denbo
Posey County

CHERRY PUDDING

½ C. butter or margarine	2 t. baking powder
1 C. sugar	1 lb. can red sour pitted cherries
1 C. flour	
¾ C. milk	½ C. sugar

Melt butter in a 9" square pan. In a bowl combine the next 4 ingredients; mix until well blended. Pour mixture over melted butter; do not stir. Pour undrained cherries over batter; do not stir. Sprinkle ½ C. sugar over cherries; bake at 325° for 1 hr. Serves 9.

Georgia Davis
Monroe County

DUMPLINGS IN CHERRY SAUCE

1 can cherry pie filling	Dumplings:
	1 C. biscuit mix
1¼ C. orange juice	2 T. brown sugar
	¼ C. milk

Combine cherry pie filling with 1 C. orange juice in large, heavy skillet (or in electric skillet). Simmer while making dumplings. Combine biscuit mix and sugar. Make a well in center of mixture; add milk and ¼ C. orange juice all at once. Stir with fork until mixed. Divide mixture into 6 portions; drop into simmering sauce. Cover and cook 10 min. Remove cover and cook 10 more min.

Marilyn Fulk
Noble County

CURRIED FRUIT

1 large can cling peach halves	⅓ C. butter
	¾ C. light brown sugar
1 20-oz. can pineapple slices	2–4 t. curry powder
1 large can pear halves	

Drain fruit and dry on paper towels; arrange in 1½ qt. casserole. Melt butter, add sugar and curry; spoon over fruit. Bake uncovered for 1 hr. at 325–350°. Serves 4–6.

Sheila Whitehead
Clay County

NUTTY PEACH CRISP

1 29-oz. can sliced peaches, undrained	½ C. melted butter
	½–1 C. coconut
1 box butter pecan cake mix	½–1 C. nuts

Place ingredients in a 13x9" pan in order listed. Bake at 350° 35–40 min.

Rachel Roudebush   *Liz Shell*
Tippecanoe County   *Howard County*

MAKE YOUR OWN COOKIE MIX

2 C. flour	1 C. dark brown sugar
1 t. soda	
1 t. baking powder	3½ C. quick oats
	1 C. raisins
1¼ t. salt	1 C. chocolate chips
1½ C. shortening	
1 C. sugar	

Sift together flour, soda, baking powder, and salt. Stir in sugars; cut in shortening until blended. Stir in oats. Makes about 10 C. Divide the mixture in half and put in plastic storage bags, or other storage containers. Add ½ C. raisins and ½ C. chocolate chips to each batch. Close containers tightly. Will keep at room temperature for several weeks.

To bake: Empty one batch of cookie mix into a bowl. Make a "hole in the center of the mixture" and add 1 egg, ⅓ C. milk, and ½ t. vanilla. Mix the liquids well; gradually stir in the dry ingredients. Drop from a teaspoon onto ungreased cookie sheets. Bake at 350° 12–15 min. Makes 4½ doz.

Vivian Tesdahl
Grant County

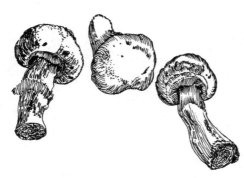

BASIC PUDDING MIX

Vanilla:	1 t. salt
1½ C. sugar	2½ C. nonfat dry
1¼ C. flour	milk

Mix all ingredients together and store in tightly covered container.

Variations:

Caramel: Substitute 1½ C. brown sugar for white sugar in the vanilla mix.

Chocolate: Add ¾ C. cocoa to the vanilla mix.

Pudding:

1½ C. pudding mix	1 T. butter
2½ C. warm water	1 t. vanilla
1 egg, beaten in bowl	

Mix the pudding mix with water in saucepan; cook over low heat until thickened. Beat half of hot mixture into the beaten egg; pour slowly into the remaining hot pudding mixture, and cook for 1 min. Stir in butter and vanilla. Serves 6.

Frances Kissel
Hancock County

Fast Foods

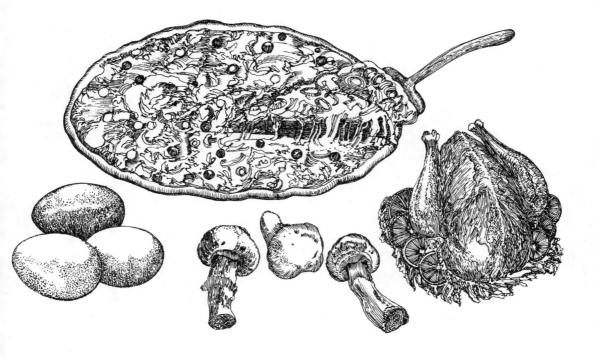

There will undoubtedly be as many definitions for the term "fast food" as there are individuals willing to attempt a definition. Fast may mean that preparation time is minimal, as in the recipe for Chicken and Rice, or that from start to finish you spend no more than 20–25 min., as in Quickie Cheese Potatoes. Whatever the definition today's busy and over-extended homemaker has created a demand for easy and uncomplicated foods. Even though the foods are "fast," the challenge still remains to serve nutritionally well-balanced meals. When prepared by you in your own kitchen, your "fast foods" can be better calorie and nutrition controlled.

RAW VEGETABLE DIP
Mix together:

2 C. sour cream   1 8-oz. bottle
2 dashes Worces-   Thousand Is-
   tershire sauce   land dressing

Mrs. Tom Hampton
Starke County

SAUSAGE TACO-MIX DIP

1 lb. sausage   1 8-oz. jar mild
                 taco sauce

Fry sausage in skillet; drain. Add taco mix and heat. Dip with chips.

Barbara Wells
Morgan County

TAILGATE SOUP

1 can tomato   1 pt. half and
   soup   half
1 can pea soup 1 7-oz. can crab
                   meat

Mix soups in double boiler and heat. Scald cream and add to soup mixture. Add shredded crab meat and garnish to taste.

Donna McDowell
Johnson County

QUICK MONKEY BREAD

4 cans refriger-   1 stick butter or
   ated biscuits   margarine,
¼ C. sugar   melted
2 t. cinnamon

Mix sugar and cinnamon in a 1 qt. bowl. Spray bundt pan with vegetable cooking spray; add 3 T. butter to bottom of pan. Take 2 cans biscuits; cut each biscuit into 4 pieces. Roll each piece in cinnamon-sugar and place in bundt pan and pour half of butter over biscuits. Repeat procedure with next 2 cans biscuits. Bake at 400° for 10 min.; reduce heat to 350° and bake for 15–

20 min. Watch carefully after 15 min. as top burns easily. Cool 1 min. and invert onto serving platter.

Georgia Davis
Monroe County

MAYONNAISE BISCUITS

2 C. self-rising   2 T. mayonnaise
   flour   1 C. milk

Mix all ingredients together well. Fill greased muffin tins about ½ full. Bake at 450° for 15–20 min., or until brown.

Grace Deal
Carroll County

FAST "BEEF STEW"

1 lb. ground beef   16 oz. can mixed
1 T. instant onion   vegetables,
¼ t. salt   drained
⅛ t. pepper   4 oz. can mush-
1 can tomato   rooms
   soup   (optional)

Brown beef and onions; drain and add seasonings. Stir in vegetables, soup, and mushrooms. Put in 1½ qt. casserole. Bake at 400° for 15 min.

Janet Bedel
Decatur County

BEEF AND CHEESE CRESCENT PIE

1–1¼ lb. ground   1–1½ C. cooked
   beef   green beans
⅓ C. chopped   ¼ t. cumin seed
   onion or 4 t. in-   (optional)
   stant minced   ¼–½ t. salt
   onion   8 oz. can quick
¼ C. chopped   crescent rolls
   green pepper   1 egg, beaten
8 oz. can tomato   8 oz. shredded
   sauce   Cheddar cheese
¼ t. garlic salt   paprika

Brown beef, onion, and green pepper; drain. Stir in tomato sauce, beans, cumin seed, garlic salt, and salt; simmer while preparing crust. Separate crescent dough into 8 triangles. Place triangles in ungreased 9" pie pan; press over bottom and up sides to form crust. Combine egg and 1 C. cheese; spread over crust. Spoon hot meat mixture into crust. Sprinkle with remaining cheese; sprinkle with paprika. Bake at 375° for 20–25 min. Let stand 5 min. Cut into wedges. Serves 5–6.

Afra Mauder
Martin County

BUTTER DIPS

⅓ C. butter
1 T. sugar
1½ t. salt
1¼ C. sifted flour
3½ t. baking powder
1 C. milk

Mix all ingredients together. Roll out to ½" thick; cut into strips, place on greased jelly roll pan. Baste with butter and bake at 375° about 10 min. Turn strips over (a pancake turner does this nicely) and bake another 10 min. Serve with jam, jelly, or honey.

Carolyn Harcourt
Hendricks County

REUBEN ROLL-UPS

1 pkg. refrigerated crescent rolls
1 8-oz. can sauerkraut, well-drained
1 T. Thousand Island dressing
8 thin slices cooked corned beef
2 slices Swiss cheese, cut into ½" strips

Separate rolls into 8 triangles. Snip sauerkraut, in can, to cut long strands; combine with salad dressing. Place one slice beef across wide end of triangle. Spread 2 T. sauerkraut on beef; top with 2 strips of cheese. Roll up beginning at wide end of triangle. Bake on ungreased baking sheet at 375° for 10–15 min., or until golden brown. Serve hot.

Donna Brown
White County

CHEESEBURGER CASSEROLE

1 can biscuits
1 lb. ground beef
¼ C. chopped onion
salt and pepper to taste
¼ C. catsup
1 8-oz. can tomato sauce
5–6 slices process cheese food

Brown beef and onion in skillet. Add salt and pepper; drain. Stir in catsup and tomato sauce. Heat through. Turn into 1½ qt. casserole, or leave in oven-proof skillet. Place cheese slices over meat. Top with biscuits. Bake at 425° for 20 min., or until biscuits are golden brown. Serves 4–6.

Nancy Carlisle
LaGrange County

HAMBURGER CASSEROLE

2 lb. ground beef
1 can mushroom soup
1 can cheese soup
1 large pkg. Tater Tots

Put meat in 9x13" baking dish. Mix soups together and pour over meat. Lay Tater Tots close together on top. Bake 1–1½ hr. at 350°.

Marjorie Umbaugh
Marshall County

MACARONI STROGANOFF

1 7-oz. pkg. macaroni (2 C. dry), cooked and drained
1 lb. ground beef
1 can cream of mushroom soup

1 C. chopped onion
1/2 t. pepper
1 t. salt
1 C. sour cream
1 17-oz. can sweet peas, drained

Combine ground beef, onion, and seasonings; if desired, shape into 16 meatballs. Brown beef mixture in small amount of hot vegetable oil. Stir in soup; cover and simmer 10 min. Remove from heat; stir in sour cream, macaroni, and peas. Pour into a 2 1/2 qt. casserole. Bake at 350° for 35 min. Serves 8.

Patricia Marshall
Morgan County

QUICK AND EASY SLOPPY JOE MIX

1–1 1/2 lb. ground beef
1 can tomato soup
1/2 soup can water
1/2 pkg. dry onion soup mix
1/2 t. chili powder
1/8 t. pepper
1/4 t. salt

Brown beef in skillet; drain. Add the remaining ingredients. Stir well; simmer ingredients, until mix reaches desired consistency (5–10 min.). Serve on buns. Serves 4–6.

Sarah Kesterson
Hancock County

TACOS—TEXAS STYLE

1 lb. ground beef
1 small onion, diced
1 13-oz. can of refried beans or bean and bacon soup
1 pkg. tortilla shells
sour cream (optional)
1/2 C. oil
2 C. grated or sliced cheese (your favorite kind)
2 C. shredded lettuce and chopped tomatoes
taco sauce (any kind)

Brown beef and onions; add beans (without draining grease) and mix together. Keep warm until needed. Heat oil hot enough to bubble when shell touches it. Fry shells for 20 sec. on each side. Drain on paper towels. Place shells on individual plates; fill with desired amount of cheese, beef filling, lettuce, tomatoes, sour cream, and taco sauce. Fold. Serves 6.

Sandra A. Gunter
Kosciusko County

PIZZA BY THE YARD

1 unsliced loaf French bread
1 6-oz. can tomato paste
1/3 C. grated Parmesan cheese
1/4 C. finely chopped green onion
1/4 C. chopped pitted ripe olives
1/2 t. dried oregano, crushed
3/4 t. salt
1 lb. ground beef, browned and drained
2 tomatoes, sliced
1 green pepper, cut in rings
1 C. shredded mozzarella cheese (4 oz.)

Cut bread loaf in half lengthwise. Combine tomato paste, Parmesan cheese, onion, olives, oregano, salt, and beef. Mix well. Spread on top of loaf halves. Place on baking sheet and bake at 400° for 20 min. Remove from oven and top with tomato slices and green pepper rings. Sprinkle with shredded cheese and bake 5 min. Serves 4–5.

B. J. McElroy
Monroe County

VERY EASY FRIED CHICKEN

1 cut-up fryer
1 C. flour
1 t. salt
1/2 t. pepper
vegetable oil

Rinse chicken under running water and pat dry. Combine flour, salt, and pepper in paper bag; shake chicken pieces in closed bag. Heat oil (¾–1″ deep) in electric skillet to 350°. Place flour-coated chicken pieces skin side down in hot oil; cover (vent in cover should be partially open). Cook for 20 min.; turn chicken and cook for 20 more min. Extra thick chicken pieces may require longer cooking.

Penny Few
Monroe County

CHICKEN AND RICE

1½ C. Minute Rice	3 lb. cut-up chicken
1 can cream of celery soup	salt and pepper to taste
1 can cream of chicken soup	1 pkg. dry onion soup mix
1 soup can milk	

Sprinkle rice over bottom of greased 9x13″ baking pan. Mix cream soups and milk together and pour over rice. Salt and pepper chicken pieces; layer chicken skin side up on rice and soup mixture. Sprinkle dry soup over chicken; cover with foil (do not open until done). Bake at 325° for 2 hr. When frozen, bake for 2½ hr. Serves 4.

Verona Lemmon
Daviess County

CHICKEN NOODLE CASSEROLE

¼ C. diced green pepper	1 can cream of mushroom soup
2 t. chopped onion	½ C. sour cream
2 T. butter	2 C. cooked noodles
1 C. cooked diced chicken	

Sauté pepper and onion in butter. Combine soup and sour cream; mix in pepper, onion, chicken, and noodles. Pour into buttered 9x12″ casserole. Bake at 350° for 30 min., or until hot and bubbling. Serves 4.

Irene Roser
St. Joseph County

CALICO CASSEROLE

2 C. macaroni, cooked and drained	1 C. sliced celery
	⅛ t. basil leaves, crushed
¼–1 C. diced green pepper	1 can Cheddar cheese soup
2 T. butter	2 5-oz. cans chicken
1 16-oz. can tomatoes, cut up	⅛ t. pepper
¼ t. salt	

Sauté celery, green pepper, and basil in butter until tender. Add remaining ingredients; heat. Serves 6–8.

Kathryn Jessup
Randolph County

BUTTER HERB BAKED FISH

½ C. butter or margarine	½ t. each: basil, oregano, and salt
⅔ C. crushed saltine crackers	1 lb. frozen sole or perch fillets, thawed and drained
¼ C. grated Parmesan cheese	
¼ t. garlic powder	

In a 9x13″ baking pan, melt butter in preheated oven 5–7 min. Combine cracker crumbs, cheese, basil, oregano, salt, and garlic powder. Dip fish in butter and then in crumb mixture; place in baking pan. Bake at 350° for 25–30 min., or until fish is tender and flakes with a fork. Serves 3.

Carolyn Wuethrich
Pulaski County

SOLE ALBERT

½ C. dry vermouth	½ t. dried tarragon, crushed
4 T. butter, melted	1½ C. soft bread crumbs (2 slices)
3 chopped shallots (4 t.)	2 T. butter, melted
1 T. snipped parsley	6 sole filets (1½–2 lb.)
½ t. lemon juice	

In 9x13x2″ baking dish, combine vermouth, the 4 T. melted butter, shallots, parsley, and tarragon; spread evenly in dish. Combine bread crumbs and the 2 T. melted butter. Sprinkle over fish. Place fish, crumb side up, atop the butter mixture. Bake at 425° for 15 min., or until the fish flakes easily with a fork. Remove to a serving plate. Strain juices; stir in lemon juice, and pour over each serving. Serves 6.

Rita Huntzinger
Madison County

SALMONBURGERS

1 lb. can salmon, drained	2 eggs, beaten
½ C. chopped onion	1 t. mustard
¼ C. melted fat or oil	½ t. salt
⅓ C. salmon liquid	½ C. dry bread crumbs (for rolling)
⅓ C. dry bread crumbs	⅓ C. mayonnaise
¼ C. chopped parsley	1 T. chopped sweet pickle
	6 buttered hamburger rolls

Flake salmon. Cook onion in hot fat until tender. Add salmon, crumbs, eggs, parsley, mustard, salt, and salmon liquid; mix well. Shape into 6 burgers. Roll in crumbs. Pan-fry in hot fat until brown on both sides. Drain on absorbent paper. Combine may-

onnaise and pickle. Place burger on bottom half of each roll. Top with 1 T. mayonnaise mixture and top half of roll. Serves 6.

Vivian Shortridge
Henry County

TUNA CASSEROLE

1 13-oz. can tuna, drained	¾ C. frozen peas

Mix tuna and peas with enough mayonnaise to moisten. Put in casserole dish. Crumble potato chips over top. Bake at 350° for 25–30 min. Serves 2–3.

Joy Harris
Brown County

TUNA SANDWICHES, OPEN FACE (1)

1 6½-oz. can tuna	½ t. grated onion
	8 oz. Velveeta

Melt cheese with a little milk or ⅓ C. mushroom soup. Add onion and tuna; spread on split buns and brown in oven or under broiler about 5 min., or until a little brown. Garnish with chopped parsley. Serve warm.

Dorothy Coe
Noble County

TUNA SANDWICH (2)

6 oz. can tuna, drained	3 T. skim milk
3 oz. Swiss cheese	½ t. prepared mustard
3 T. mayonnaise	3 slices toast

Combine cheese, mayonnaise, and milk. Cook at medium heat, stirring constantly until smooth. Place 2 oz. tuna on each slice of toast; cover with cheese sauce. Broil 1–2 min. Serves 3.

Glenda Reynolds
Washington County

BANANAS AND BACON

Lay thin slices of bacon in a baking pan and on each place a half banana. Bake at 350° until the bacon is crisp and bananas are browned well.

Wilma Runyan
Dubois County

BOLOGNA RAREBIT

6 slices bread	1 can Cheddar
6 bologna slices,	cheese soup
outer rind	½ C. dry white
removed	wine
dash cayenne	

Arrange bread slices on a cookie sheet. Broil 3″ from heat for 4 min., or until toasted. Turn bread slices; top with bologna slices. Broil 3 min., or until bologna is hot. In small saucepan, combine soup, wine, and cayenne; heat, stirring just to boiling. Pour sauce over bologna. Serve at once. Serves 6.

Sheila Whitehead
Clay County

PIZZA DOGGIES

1 large clove	¼ t. leaf oregano,
garlic, minced	crushed
2 T. olive oil	8 frankfurters,
1 can tomato	slit lengthwise
soup	8 frankfurter
¼ C. water	buns, slit
2 T. chopped	6 oz. sliced moz-
parsley	zarella cheese

Cook garlic in olive oil until lightly browned; add soup, water, parsley, and oregano. Cook over low heat 15 min.; stir often. Place frankfurters on buns in large shallow baking pan. Fill franks with sauce; top with cheese. Place under broiler about 1 min., or until cheese melts. Serves 8.

Patricia Marshall
Morgan County

LAZY DAY LASAGNE

6 oz. lasagne noo-	1 15½-oz. can
dles, cooked	spaghetti sauce
and drained	with meat
¼ t. oregano	1 6-oz. pkg.
1 C. cream-style	sliced mozza-
cottage cheese	rella cheese

Combine oregano with spaghetti sauce. In greased 10x6x2″ baking dish, alternate layers of noodles, cottage cheese, mozzarella, and sauce, using sauce for top layer. Bake at 375° about 30 min. Serves 4.

Margaret E. Heim
St. Joseph County

FAST LAST MINUTE SUPPER

1 can Spam, cut	2 C. cubed
in strips	cooked potatoes
1 medium onion,	(4 medium-
thinly sliced	sized)
2 T. butter	2 T. chopped
1 can cream	parsley
soup, any flavor	dash of pepper
½ C. milk	

Lightly brown meat and onion in butter until onion is tender. Blend in soup, milk, and remaining ingredients. Cook over low heat for 10 min. Stir often. Serves 4–6.

Juanita Rees
Rush County

BROCCOLI CASSEROLE

¼–½ lb. Vel-	¼ lb. party
veeta, cubed	crackers (Ritz,
2 10-oz pkg.	etc.), crushed
broccoli,	1 stick marga-
cooked and	rine, melted
drained	

Make 2 layers of broccoli, cheese, and crackers alternately in shallow baking dish, ending with crumbs on top. Pour melted margarine over top. Bake at 350° until bubbling hot.

Geraldine Banta
Switzerland County

EVERYBODY'S FAVORITE CABBAGE

1 large head cabbage (about 3½ lb.)	1 lb. Velveeta
	½ lb. saltine crackers
1 C. milk (approximately)	plenty of pepper

Cut cabbage into bite-sized pieces and cook until tender; drain. Cut cheese into small chunks; add to cabbage. Add milk. Add crackers, crumbling as you go. Season with pepper and salt. Stir and cook until thick. These amounts are not exact. You may have to add more or less crackers, or milk, depending on size of cabbage.

Mary Stenger
Franklin County

GREEN BEANS IN ITALIAN TOMATO SAUCE

1 10-oz. pkg. frozen green beans, partially thawed	1 onion, finely chopped
	garlic salt
	pepper
1 8-oz. can tomatoes	¼ C. water
	½ t. oregano

Combine all ingredients, except beans. Cover and simmer 10 min.; add beans. Simmer uncovered, stirring often, until beans are tender. Serves 6.

Frances Pickens
Fulton County

MUSHROOMS BAKED IN FOIL

Line a baking pan with aluminum foil. Place mushrooms, caps down, in one layer. Sprinkle lightly with salt. Cover with a second sheet of foil; crimp edges of both sheets together. Bake at 350° for 20 min.

Sue Childes
Monroe County

CHEESY PEAS

2 10-oz. pkg. frozen peas, cooked and drained	1 T. flour
	½ t. salt
	1 large can evaporated milk
1 C. sliced mushrooms	½ t. lemon peel
½ C. sliced green onions	1 C. shredded Swiss cheese
2 T. butter or margarine	

In small saucepan, cook mushrooms and onions in butter until tender, but not brown. Add flour, salt, milk, and lemon peel. Cook and stir until thickened; add cheese. Cook and stir until cheese is melted. Heat to steaming but do not boil. Stir into peas. Serve immediately.

Thelma Hardwick
Rush County

CRUNCH TOP POTATOES

⅓ C. margarine	1½ t. paprika
6 medium baking potatoes, pared and sliced into ½" rounds	1½ C. shredded sharp Cheddar cheese

Topping:
¾ C. crushed corn flakes

Melt margarine in jelly roll pan. Place potatoes in margarine and turn to coat both sides. Mix the topping and sprinkle over potatoes. Bake at 375° for 30 min. Serves 4–6.

Ardelle Johnson
LaGrange County

LIGHTNING POTATOES

2 pkg. frozen French fries (8 or 9 oz.)	1 can Cheddar cheese soup, undiluted
2 cans cream of celery soup, undiluted	1 T. minced onion
2 T. parsley flakes	2 T. Parmesan cheese

Mix potatoes, soups, and onion; put in baking dish. Combine parsley and cheese. Sprinkle over potato mixture. Bake at 350° for 1 hr. Serves 8.

Jeanette Shaw
Randolph County

QUICKIE CHEESE POTATOES

1 lb. frozen French-fried potatoes	½ t. instant minced onion
½ C. Italian salad dressing	1 C. shredded sharp process cheese
1 t. parsley flakes	

Put potatoes in skillet with Italian dressing, onion flakes, and parsley. Stir until well-covered with dressing. Let cook 10–15 min. Add cheese last. Let melt slightly. Serve at once.

Betty Sendmeyer
Putnam County

LAYERED SPINACH SUPREME

1 pkg. crescent rolls	½ C. grated Parmesan cheese
1 10-oz. pkg. frozen chopped spinach, thawed and drained	1 12-oz. carton creamed cottage cheese
4 oz. Monterey Jack cheese, cut into ½" cubes	½ t. salt
	2 cloves garlic, crushed
	2 eggs

Grease 12x7½x2" dish. Cover bottom of dish with rolled-out crescent rolls. Mix remaining ingredients; spoon evenly over rolls. Bake at 375° until set, about 30 min. Let stand 5 min. before cutting. Serves 6–8.

Becky Bryan
Monroe County

PLAIN CAKE

3 C. flour	¾ oil
2 C. sugar	4 T. vinegar
4 T. cocoa	1 t. vanilla
2 t. soda	2 C. water
1 t. salt	

Use a 9x13" ungreased pan. Sift dry ingredients together into pan. Add remaining ingredients and beat together with wire whisk, making sure you get into corners of pan. Bake 30 min. at 350°.

Alice Feller
Hendricks County

QUICK APPLE COBBLER

3 C. apples, pared, cored, and sliced	1 t. baking powder
1 stick margarine, softened	⅛ t. salt
½ C. sugar	1 t. vanilla
1 C. flour	½ C. milk
	1 C. sugar
	½ C. water

Place apples in an 8x8" pan. Cream margarine and the ½ C. sugar. Mix together flour, salt, and baking powder; add to creamed sugar mixture alternately with milk and vanilla (this makes a thick batter). Spread batter over apples. Mix the 1 C. sugar and water; pour over top of batter. Bake at 350° for 1 hr.

Belle Freddle
Delaware County

HOT FRUIT COMPOTE

1 No. 2 can pears, drained	3½ oz. pkg. blanched almonds, chopped lengthwise
1 No. 2 can chunk pineapple, drained	
2½–3 doz. macaroon cookies	1 T. butter brown sugar
1 No. 2 can apricots, drained	⅓ C. sherry

In a baking dish alternate layers of well-drained fruit, almonds, and crumbled macaroons. Dot each layer with butter and sprinkle with brown sugar. Pour sherry over the entire dish. Bake covered at 350° for 45 min., or until bubbly. Serve hot. Serves 12.

Virginia Luck
White County

24 GRAHAM CRACKER DELIGHT

2 sticks margarine	1 C. chopped nuts
½ C. sugar	24 graham crackers
1 t. vanilla	

Mix margarine and sugar together; boil for 2 min. Add vanilla. Arrange graham crackers on a cookie sheet. Pour mixture over crackers. Sprinkle with nuts and bake at 350° for 10 min. Remove at once with spatula to cool.

Jeannie Jacob
Clay County

TUTTI-FRUITTI DELIGHT

1 8¾-oz. can pineapple tidbits	½ C. flaked coconut
1 11-oz. can mandarin oranges	2 bananas, sliced
1 17-oz. can fruit cocktail	1 3-oz. pkg. French vanilla instant pudding

Combine undrained fruit, coconut, and bananas. Sprinkle pudding mix over fruit and toss. Chill. Serves 6–8.

Sheila Whitehead
Clay County

CHERRY DESSERT

1 can cherry pie filling	1 t. baking powder
1 C. flour	2 T. margarine, softened
½ C. sugar	milk to moisten
1 egg	

Spread cherry pie filling in greased 9x13″ pan. Mix remaining ingredients together and spoon over filling. Bake at 400° for 30 min. Serves 8.

Angie Smith
Brown County

JIFFY PUMPKIN PIE

1 3¾-oz. pkg. instant vanilla pudding	1 C. cooked pumpkin
1 C. frozen dessert topping, thawed	⅔ t. pumpkin pie spice
⅔ C. milk	1 baked pie shell, plain or graham cracker

Blend pudding with dessert topping. Add milk, pumpkin, and spice. Pour into pie shell. Refrigerate until ready to serve.

Gloria Huey
Greene County

COOKIES MADE FROM CAKE MIX

1 pkg. cake mix, any flavor	2 T. water for crisp cookies, or 4 T. water for soft cookies
1 or 2 eggs	
2 T. shortening	

To cake mix, add 1 or 2 eggs, shortening, and 2 T. or 4 T. water. The batter can be formed into a roll and chilled; dropped by spoonfuls for drop cookies; or rolled into balls and flattened for decorative cookies. Bake at 375° for 8–10 min.

By adding nuts, fruit, chips, etc., this recipe will make an endless variety of cookies.

Opal Neff
Fulton County

QUICK COOKIES

1 3-oz. pkg. in-	¼ C. vegetable
stant pudding	oil
mix (any flavor)	¾ C. biscuit mix
1 egg	

Combine all ingredients and shape into small balls. Place on greased cookie sheet. Press down; bake at 375° for 10 min.

Catherine Deems
Switzerland County

NO-BAKE OATMEAL COOKIES

2 C. sugar	½ C. milk
1 stick margarine	2 C. quick oats
2 T. peanut	3 T. cocoa
butter	1 t. vanilla

Mix together sugar, margarine, milk, and peanut butter; boil 1 min. Remove from heat and add oats, cocoa, and vanilla. Blend thoroughly. Drop by teaspoonfuls onto waxed paper. Cool thoroughly. Makes 4 dozen.

Carrie Dawson   *Bertha Corcoran*
Franklin County   *Brown County*

Variation: Add 1 C. coconut and 1 C. chopped pecans to mixture.

Lenora Graw and Ilone Kiff
LaPorte County

NO-BAKE PEANUT BUTTER COOKIES

1 C. peanut	½ C. sugar
butter	2 C. corn flakes
½ C. corn syrup	

Combine first 3 ingredients over low heat until blended (not cooked). Stir in corn flakes. Drop by teaspoonfuls onto waxed paper or cookie sheet. Makes about 3 doz.

Kitty Pettit
Clay County

Variation: 1 C. sugar, 1 C. syrup, 1 C. peanut butter, 6 C. corn flakes.

Geneva Michael
Monroe County

SNEAKY DEVILS

1 pkg. devil's	8 oz. marshmal-
food cake mix	low cream
½ lb. melted but-	½ C. peanut
ter or	butter
margarine	

Combine cake mix with butter and spread ½ of combination over bottom of 9x13″ pan. Combine marshmallow cream and peanut butter; spread over pan mixture. Top with remaining cake mixture. *Note:* Mix small amount of marshmallow cream with peanut butter at a time. This mixture does not spread smoothly over cake mixture. Bake at 350° for 20–30 min. Cool and cut into bars.

Carol Ford
Monroe County

WHIPPERSNAPPER COOKIES

1 lemon with	2 C. frozen
pudding cake	whipped top-
mix	ping, thawed
powdered sugar	1 egg, beaten

Grease cookie sheet. Mix together cake mix, topping, and egg. Drop a teaspoon of dough into powdered sugar and roll into a ball. Bake at 350° for 12 min. Makes 3–4 doz.

Marcia Ford
Jay County

"DOUGHNUTS"

1 can refrigerated biscuits	2 t. milk (optional)
½ C. confectioners' sugar (optional)	½ C. sugar (optional)
fat for frying	½ t. cinnamon (optional)

Cut each biscuit into 4 pieces with scissors. Deep-fat fry at 375° for 2–4 min., or until golden brown. Drain. While still warm (if desired), roll in a sugar glaze made by mixing the confectioners' sugar and milk together, or mix sugar and cinnamon together and roll doughnuts in mixture.

Note: Use your mini-fryer when making "doughnuts" for 1 or 2.

Carolyn Harcourt
Hendricks County

PORTUGUESE DOUGHNUTS

1 egg, slightly beaten	2 C. biscuit mix
1 C. milk	4 slices white bread
½ t. lemon extract	½ C. sugar

Combine egg, milk, and flavoring. Add all at once to biscuit mix. Trim crusts off bread. Cut each slice into 9 squares and dip each square into biscuit mix batter. Drop into hot oil (370°) and cook until golden brown. Drain. Put sugar in paper bag; shake doughnuts and serve immediately.

Joyce Frederick
St. Joseph County

QUICK-GLAZED YEAST DOUGHNUTS

1½ C. milk	2 eggs, beaten
¾ C. sugar	5½ C. flour
2 t. salt	
¼ lb. butter or margarine	Glaze:
4 pkg. dry yeast	1 lb. powdered sugar
½ C. lukewarm water (105–115°)	1 T. flour water sufficient to make creamy

Scald milk; add sugar, salt, and butter. Cool mixture until lukewarm. Soften yeast in water. Combine milk mixture, yeast, eggs, and flour. Mix very well. Turn dough onto floured board and pat out to desired thickness. Cut with doughnut cutter and lay on cookie sheet. Cover and set in warm place. By the time grease is hot, doughnuts can be fried. Glaze while hot.

Ethelmarie Kirby
Wabash County

Recipe Potpourri:
Parties and Everyday

Appetizers, Beverages, and Soups

Appetizers should be used to create a mood. Attractively and imaginatively served they will whet the appetite for the meal that follows. Be cautious in the number and amount of appetizers served less you overindulge your guests and lessen their enjoyment of the meal itself. Avoid repetition of appetizer foods in the dinner menus.

Soups can begin a meal, be the meal itself, or even be served as dessert. Serve icy cold Gazpacho, Spain's liquid salad, in place of an appetizer; or make a meal of Meatball Minestrone. Hot or cold, creamed, a bouillon or a broth, or whatever, soups can add an interesting dimension to your recipe repertory.

Appetizers

ASPARAGUS ROLLS

sandwich bread (white)	4 T. melted butter
6 oz. cream cheese	1 can asparagus spears, drained
3 oz. bleu cheese	

Trim crusts from bread; roll out flat using a rolling pin. Mix cream cheese and bleu cheese with enough milk to spread. Spread on bread slices; place asparagus spear on top and roll up. Dip in melted butter. Cut into 4 pieces. Bake at 350° for 15 min., or until brown. To freeze, place on cookie sheet until frozen; transfer to moisture/vapor proof container. Makes 4 dozen.

Mildred Hoeing
Rush County

DRIED BEEF HORS D'OEUVRES

6 oz. dried beef, spread out flat	¼ t. salt
1 8-oz. pkg. cream cheese	⅛ t. pepper
½ t. Worcestershire sauce	1 small onion, minced very fine

Mix together cream cheese, Worcestershire, salt, pepper, and onion. Thin with milk, if necessary. Spread on dried beef and roll up jelly-roll fashion. Place in freezer for 30 min. Cut into ¼" slices. Serve with cocktail picks.

Dorothy V. Knapp
Hendricks County

DILLED BRUSSELS SPROUTS

2 pkg. frozen Brussels sprouts, cooked, drained	2 T. vinegar
	½ small onion, minced
	1 t. dill weed
¼ C. salad oil	salt and pepper to taste

Combine oil, vinegar, onion, dill, salt, and pepper; pour over cooked Brussels sprouts. Cover and chill overnight.

Elizabeth Pitser
Vigo County

CHEESE BALL

1 8-oz. pkg. cream cheese	1 T. Worcestershire sauce
1 6-oz. jar Old English spread	½–1½ C. pecans, chopped
1 6-oz. jar blue cheese spread	chopped parsley, optional
1 t. garlic powder	

Mix cheeses with fork and refrigerate 3–4 hr. Add garlic powder and Worcestershire sauce; refrigerate 12 hr. Form ball; cover with pecans and parsley.

Liz Fountain
White County

CRAB SNACK SQUARES

1 7½-oz. can crab, drained	1 egg, slightly beaten
1½ C. grated Cheddar cheese	2 c. biscuit mix
3 T. minced green onions	½ C., minus 2 t., cornmeal
3 T. finely sliced green olives	⅔ C. water
¼ C. mayonnaise	3 T. margarine, melted

Combine biscuit mix with cornmeal, water, and margarine; spread mixture in bottom of greased 9x13" pan. Mix crab, cheese, onions, and olives together; stir in egg and mayonnaise. Spread crab mixture over top of biscuit layer and bake at 375° for 20–30 min. May be frozen before baking.

Charlotte Klootwyk
Monroe County

CHICKEN CURRY
CREAM CHEESE BALL

1 pkg. 8-oz. cream cheese	⅓ C. mayonnaise
1 C. cooked, finely chopped chicken	2 t. chutney, chopped
	1 t. curry powder
	½ t. salt
¾ C. almonds, toasted and finely chopped	chopped parsley or flaked coconut

Mix cream cheese, chicken, almonds, chutney, curry, and salt. Chill several hours. Shape into ball; roll in parsley or coconut.

Florence Talbot
Wayne County

CRUNCHY CHEESE BALL

1 8-oz. pkg. cream cheese, softened	1 t. minced onion
	½ t. dry mustard
¼ C. mayonnaise	¼ t. hot pepper sauce
2 C. ground cooked ham	½ C. chopped peanuts or pistachio nuts
2 T. chopped parsley	

Beat cream cheese and mayonnaise until smooth. Stir in next 5 ingredients. Cover; chill several hours. Form into ball; roll in nuts to coat. Serve with assorted crackers.

Rose Lee Barker
Hendricks County

CANTONESE CHICKEN WINGS

4 lbs. chicken wings	2 jars Jr. Apricots
	1 T. ginger
1 C. soy sauce	1 clove garlic

Line 17x11″ cookie sheet with foil. Mix sauce ingredients and spread over chicken. Marinate overnight. Bake uncovered at 325° for 1 hr.

Mary Stull
Clark County

CHEDDAR CHEESE TIDBITS

¾ C. margarine, softened	½ t. salt
	½ t. Tabasco sauce
9 oz. sharp Cheddar cheese, grated	3 C. Rice Krispies
1½ C. flour	

Cream margarine and cheese until well blended. Add flour and blend. Knead in the Rice Krispies. Form into tiny balls and place on cookie sheet. Press down with fork. Bake 10 min. at 400°.

Lebanonette E. H. Club
Boone County

HOT HORS D'OEUVRES

1½ C. grated sharp cheese	1½ t. capers
1 C. mayonnaise	6 scallions, chopped fine

Mix all together and spread on English Muffins. Bake at 350° until bubbly. When ready to serve, cut muffins into quarters.

Ruth Plumbeck
St. Joseph County

COCKTAIL MEATBALLS (1)

1 lb. ground beef	1 t. salt
½ C. dry bread crumbs	¼ t. pepper
⅓ C. minced onion	½ t. Worcestershire sauce
¼ C. milk	¼ C. shortening
1 egg	1 12-oz. bottle chili sauce
1 T. snipped parsley	1 10-oz. jar grape jelly

Mix ground beef, bread crumbs, onion, milk, egg, and next 4 ingredients; shape gently into 1″ balls. Melt shortening; brown meatballs. Remove meatballs from skillet; pour off fat. Heat chili sauce and jelly in skillet; stirring constantly until jelly is melted. Add meatballs and stir until thoroughly coated; simmer uncovered 30 min.

Patti Williams
Henry County

MEATBALL APPETIZERS (2)

1 lb. ground beef	1 C. bread
1 lb. ground pork	crumbs
½ C. milk	½ C. sherry
2 T. finely	½ C. ketchup
chopped onion	Sauce:
several dashes salt	1 C. sherry
and pepper	1 C. ketchup
¼ t. oregano	½ t. oregano

Mix all meatball ingredients together; shape into 1″ meatballs. Brown meatballs; drain. Mix together the sauce ingredients and pour over meatballs in skillet. Cover and simmer 20 min. May be frozen; if dry when reheating, add more wine or ketchup.

Christina Ott
Noble County

HOT MUSHROOM CANAPES

9 slices sandwich	15 medium large
bread, crusts	mushrooms,
removed	minced
8 oz. cream	1 T. butter
cheese,	1 egg yolk,
softened	beaten
3 T. onion,	salt and pepper to
minced	taste

Cut each slice of bread into quarters; place on cookie sheets and bake at 250° until browned lightly. Set "toasted" bread aside. Sauté the mushrooms and onion in melted butter; drain. Combine mushroom mixture with cream cheese, egg, salt and pepper. Spread mixture on bread quarters and broil until puffed and browned. May be frozen. To freeze, do not broil; place on cookie sheets

until frozen. Store in freezer in moisture/vapor proof bags or containers. Do not defrost before broiling.

Joan Abbott
Monroe County

PICKLED FISH

fresh fish fillets:	White Vinegar
bluegill, trout,	Mixture:
whiting, carp,	2 C. white
or buffalo fish	vinegar
saltwater solution	1 C. sugar
(strong enough	1 C. white port
to float an egg)	wine
white vinegar	2 t. pickling spice
onions	

Cut fish into 1″ squares, ¼″ thick. Prepare 1 gal. fish at a time. Soak in heavy saltwater solution 24 hr. Drain; pour enough white vinegar into container to cover fish and refrigerate 24 hr. Mix white vinegar mixture ingredients and bring to a boil; chill. Drain fish; put in jars. Layer onions on top of fish; pour enough cold vinegar mixture into jars to cover fish. Seal jars; refrigerate 2 weeks before eating. Keep stored in refrigerator.

Alma Small
Dubois County

PARTY PIZZAS (1)

1 lb. mild	1 t. Italian
sausage roll	seasoning
1 lb. hot sausage	½ C. chopped
roll	onion
1½–2 lb. shred-	2–3 loaves party
ded mozarella	rye bread
and Cheddar	
cheese	

Brown sausage; drain. Add onion and cook with sausage. Melt cheese in double boiler. Mix cheese, sausage, and Italian seasoning.

Spread on party rye and freeze. Remove from freezer and bake at 400° for 10 min.

Susie Jameson
Hancock County

PARTY PIZZAS (2)

1 lb. hamburger	1 t. oregano
1 lb. sausage	1 t. Worcester-
(mild or hot)	shire sauce
1 lb. cubed	1 t. garlic powder
Velveeta	2 loaves party rye

Brown the meats in separate skillets; drain. Combine meats in one skillet and add all other ingredients, except bread. Cook over low heat until cheese melts. Place slices of party rye on cookie sheets; spread each slice with meat mixture. Bake at 350° for 10–15 min. Freeze pizzas on the cookie sheets; bag or put into other freezer containers. Remove from freezer and bake at 400° for 10 min.

Variation:

2 lb. ground beef	1 lb. Velveeta
1 15-oz. can pizza	½ t. garlic salt
sauce	½ t. oregano

Use same method as above.

Barbara Skinner
Hendricks County

SUMMER SAUSAGE

5 lb. hamburger	2½ t. mustard
5 rounded t.	seed
Morton's Tender	1 t. hickory
Quick Salt	smoke salt
2½ t. garlic salt	

Mix all ingredients well; cover and refrigerate. Take out once a day for 3 days and mix well. On the fourth day, form into 4–5 long rolls and place on rack in broiler pan. Bake for 8 hr. at 140–150°. Turn once during baking. Freezes well.

Mary Ann Wright   *Marie Mann*
Delaware County   *Posey County*

Variation: Use 1 t. liquid smoke in place of 1 t. Hickory smoke salt.

Gerri Ruby
St. Joseph County

SAUSAGE BALLS (1)

1 lb. hot bulk	2 C. shredded,
sausage	sharp Cheddar
2 C. biscuit mix	cheese
2 T. grated onion	

Combine all ingredients; mix well. Roll into walnut-sized balls. Place on an ungreased baking sheet and bake at 400° for 15 min. Drain on paper towels; serve hot. Makes 48 balls.

Fern Johnson   *Maudie Scott*
Crawford County   *Benton County*

SAUSAGE BALLS (2)

1 lb. bulk	½ t. sage
sausage	½ C. catsup
1 egg, beaten	1 T. brown sugar
⅓ C. bread	1 T. cider vinegar
crumbs	1 T. soy sauce

Combine sausage, egg, bread, and sage. Shape into 1″ balls. Brown on all sides; drain. Mix catsup, brown sugar, vinegar, and soy sauce together; pour over meat balls and simmer 30 min. Makes 20–25 balls. If more liquid is needed, mix together and add additional sauce.

Linda L. Shirk
Decatur County

ZUCCHINI APPETIZERS

3 C. thinly sliced, unpared zucchini (about 4 small ones)
1 C. biscuit mix
½ C. finely chopped onion
½ C. grated Parmesan cheese
2 T. snipped parsley
½ t. seasoned salt
½ t. dried marjoram or oregano
½ t. salt
dash of pepper
1 clove garlic, finely chopped
4 eggs, slightly beaten
½ C. vegetable oil

Grease 13x9x2″ pan. Mix all ingredients together; spread in pan. Bake at 350° about 25 min. Cut into 1x2″ pieces.

Mrs. John Hensel
Hamilton County

HOT BROCCOLI DIP

1 12-oz. pkg. frozen chopped broccoli, cooked and drained
1 small onion, chopped
2 T. margarine
1 6-oz. roll garlic cheese
1 can cream of mushroom soup
½ t. salt
⅛ t. pepper
⅛ t. Tabasco sauce
1 t. Worcestershire sauce

Sauté onion in margarine until soft. Add soup, cheese, and seasonings. Cook on medium heat until cheese melts. Add broccoli and cook 1 min. longer. Serve hot with crackers or chips.

Barbara Moeller
Clark County

HOT PECAN DIP

1 8-oz. pkg. cream cheese
2 T. milk
2½ oz. chipped beef
½ t. garlic
2 T. minced onion
2 T. green onion, chopped fine
1 C. dairy sour cream (or less)
¼ t. pepper
1 C. coarsely chopped pecans
2 T. melted butter
½ t. salt

Combine cream cheese and milk and mix together; add the next 6 ingredients, and mix together. Put mixture into a baking dish. Combine pecans with butter and salt, and sprinkle over the mixture. Bake at 350° for 15–20 min.

Ruth Plumbeck
St. Joseph County

HOT TACO DIP

1 lb. lean ground beef
¼ C. chopped onion
¼ C. catsup
1½ t. chili powder
1 can refried beans
½ t. salt
1 small can diced green chilies
Topping:
½ C. grated cheese
½ C. raw chopped onion
¼ C. green olives, chopped

Brown beef with other ingredients; simmer until onion is tender. Add the topping. Serve hot with corn chips.

Mary K. Hines
Monroe County

HOT TUNA DIP

1 green pepper, chopped
1 medium onion, chopped
1 7-oz. can tuna, well-drained
1 can mushroom soup
5–6 drops Tabasco sauce, or more to taste

Sauté onion and pepper in small amount of

margarine until tender. Mix all ingredients together; heat thoroughly. Serve hot.

Virginia Robbins
Scott County

TACO PLATTER DIP (1)

1 8-oz. pkg. cream cheese	1 T. lemon juice
1 large ripe avocado, mashed	5 tomatoes, diced and drained
1 4-oz. carton dairy sour cream	8 green onions, diced
	10 oz. shredded Cheddar cheese
2 T. mayonnaise	3 T. chili powder
¼ t. salt and pepper	green or ripe olives, diced

Blend first 6 ingredients together; spread on a shallow tray (pizza pan size). Top with tomatoes and onions. Mix together cheese and chili powder; sprinkle over tomato-onion mixture. Serve with taco, nacho, or dorito chips.

Mary K. Hines
Monroe County

TACO PLATTER DIP (2)

3 medium ripe avocados, peeled and mashed	2 cans plain, or jalapeño, bean dip
2 T. lemon juice	1 C. chopped green onions
½ t. salt	3 medium tomatoes, chopped
¼ t. pepper	
1 C. sour cream	4–8 oz. sharp Cheddar cheese, shredded
½ C. mayonnaise	
½ envelope taco seasoning mix	

Mix together avocados, lemon juice, salt, and pepper; set aside. Combine sour cream, mayonnaise, and taco seasoning; set aside. Spread bean dip on large shallow serving platter; cover with avocado mixture. Top with sour cream taco mixture and sprinkle with onions, tomatoes, olives, and cheese. Cover and refrigerate. Serve with tortilla chips.

Eleanor Arnold
Rush County

SPINACH DIP

1 10-oz. pkg. frozen, chopped spinach	1 small onion, minced (optional)
1–2 C. mayonnaise	⅛ t. garlic salt (optional)
1 8-oz. can water chestnuts, drained, chopped (optional)	1 envelope dry vegetable soup mix (use one with no noodle product)

Thaw spinach; squeeze out juice entirely, using a strainer and wooden spoon. Combine spinach with remaining ingredients. Mix well. Cover and refrigerate at least 4 hr.

Julie Wells
Scott County

RAW VEGETABLE DIP (1)

1 C. mayonnaise	½ t. freshly ground black pepper
1 C. sour cream	
2 T. minced onion	½ C. chopped parsley
1 large or 2 small cloves garlic, minced	1 T., or more, prepared mustard
1 t. salt	

Blend all ingredients well and allow to stand covered in the refrigerator 2–3 hr., or overnight.

Ruth Leffler
Tippecanoe County

RAW VEGETABLE DIP
(SOY SAUCE) (2)

2 C. mayonnaise	4 t. minced onion
2 t. vinegar	2 t. water or milk
8 t. soy sauce	2 scant t. ginger

Mix together and refrigerate. Let flavors blend approximately 8 hr. before serving.

Ellen Craig
Randolph County

CRAB MEAT PIZZA SPREAD

11 oz. cream	8 oz. chili sauce
cheese	6½ oz. can crab
2 T. chopped	meat, drained
onion	and flaked
2 t. Worcester-	chopped fresh
shire sauce	parsley

Cream together cream cheese, onion, and Worcestershire sauce. Spread the mixture on 12" plate so it resembles pizza dough. Spread on the chili sauce. Sprinkle on crab meat. Top with parsley. Refrigerate. Serves 20.

Marcia Hicks
Noble County

SHRIMP BUTTER

1½ sticks butter	1 T. minced
8 oz. pkg. cream	onion
cheese	1 4–5 oz. can
2 T. lemon juice	small shrimp
4 T. mayonnaise	

Whip butter and cream cheese together. Blend in lemon juice, onion and mayonnaise until smooth; add shrimp. Chill. Serve with a variety of crackers.

Darle Smith
Marshall County

Beverages

DAIRY PUNCH

12 oz. can frozen	½ gal. lime
lemonade	sherbet
concentrate	2 qt. 7-Up or
6 oz. can frozen	ginger ale
limeade	1 sliced lemon
concentrate	1 sliced orange
1 qt. water	1 qt. sliced
½ gal. vanilla ice	strawberries
cream	(fresh or frozen)
½ gal. milk	

Mix frozen juices in water. Place ice cream and sherbet in punch bowl; break into chunks. Stir in milk. Add fruit juices. Add 7-Up or ginger ale. Stir until sherbet and ice cream are partially melted. Float fruit slices and strawberries on top. Serve immediately. Serves 50.

Mrs. Ken Houin
Marshall County

DANDELION WINE

6 qt. dandelion	3 oranges, sliced
blossoms	thinly, do not
3 gal. water	peel
3 lemons, sliced	10 lb. sugar
thinly, do not	1 cake yeast, dis-
peel	solved in ½ C.
1½ lb. raisins	warm water

Boil blossoms and water ½ hr.; pour into large jar or plastic container. Add fruit and sugar; mix well; let cool. Add yeast; stir. Let stand 3 days (longer in cool weather). Stir well each day. Strain; pour into bottles. Do not tighten caps until wine is no longer working; then tighten caps to prevent evaporation. Wine will be better if allowed to "rest" for 6 mo.

Marge Finley
Madison County

FROZEN PIÑA COLADA
COCKTAIL MIX

1 45-oz. can pineapple-grapefruit juice	1 qt. vodka
	1 12-oz. can frozen lemonade, thawed
2 pt. Piña Colada Mix (Holland House, etc.)	7-Up

Mix first four ingredients together; place in either pint or quart containers and freeze. To serve, spoon 2–3″ of mix into a tall glass and add 7-Up. Makes 4 qt. of mix. When frozen, will keep indefinitely.

Mary Alice Roberts
Starke County

SANGRIA

1 bottle red burgundy (750 ml.)	1 lemon
	1 orange
small can frozen pink lemonade	sugar to taste

Pour wine onto unthawed lemonade; stir until blended. Add a small amount of water and sweeten to taste. Slice unpeeled lemon and orange as thinly as possible; add to wine mixture. Cover and refrigerate 2–4 hr. Pour into glasses filled with crushed ice.

Joan Abbott
Monroe County

Soups

HOT BEAN POT SOUP

1 lb. dry pinto or kidney beans	1 C. chopped onion
1 lb. hot Italian sausage	1 t. marjoram leaves
1 t. basil leaves	1 4-oz. can chopped green chilies
2½ qt. beef broth, or 8 beef-flavored bouillon cubes and 2½ qt. water	shredded Cheddar or Monterey Jack cheese (optional)

Rinse beans; soak overnight and drain. Brown sausage; drain. Add onions; cook and stir until onions are transparent. Add beans; stir in beef broth or bouillon and water, basil, and marjoram. Bring to a boil; lower heat and simmer covered 2 hr., or until beans are tender. Stir in chilies; heat through. Sprinkle each serving with shredded cheese and serve hot.

Hazel Steele
Hancock County

MEATBALL MINESTRONE

2 lb. ground beef	1½ t. thyme leaves
2 C. chopped onion	2 C. chopped cabbage
5 T. instant beef bouillon	1 can garbanzo beans
8 C. water	4 oz. spaghetti
2 16-oz. cans tomatoes	grated Parmesan cheese
¼ t. pepper	

Combine beef with 1 C. onion and 2 T. bouillon; mix well. Shape into small meatballs; brown, and reserve 2 T. drippings. Cook remaining onion in drippings until tender. Add meatballs, water, tomatoes, remaining instant bouillon, thyme, and pepper. Simmer 1 hr. Add cabbage, garbanzo beans, and spaghetti. Cook 15 min. longer, or until spaghetti is tender. Sprinkle cheese over each serving. Makes 4 qt. Freezes well, but omit spaghetti and add when reheating.

Carolyn Robinson
White County

MEATBALL SOUP

Meatball mixture:

2 lb. ground beef	6 C. water
⅛ t. pepper	6 beef bouillon
¼ C. finely	cubes
chopped	3–4 C. sliced
parsley	celery
⅓ C. fine cracker	¼ C. long-grain
crumbs	rice
2 t. seasoned salt	2 t. salt
2 eggs, slightly	6 C. tomato juice
beaten	3 C. sliced carrots
2 T. milk	2–3 C. diced
3 T. flour	potatoes
2 T. oil	1 T. sugar
Vegetable	2 bay leaves
Mixture:	½–1 t. marjoram
4–6 onions, cut	(optional)
in eights	1 12-oz. can mex-
	icorn (optional)

Combine meatball ingredients; mix thoroughly and form into walnut-sized balls. Dip in flour; lightly brown on all sides in oil. Set aside. Mix vegetables (except corn), water, and spices together in large kettle; add meatballs. Bring to boil; lower heat and cook slowly until vegetables are tender. Corn if used, should be added last.

Marge Diener
White County

BEEF BARLEY VEGETABLE SOUP

2 lb. soupbone	2 C. cooked
(½ meat)	tomatoes
2 qt. water	2 T. minced
¼ t. pepper	parsley
1½ T. salt	1 C. cubed
¼ C. barley	carrots
¼ C. chopped	½ C. chopped
onion	celery
1 C. peas	

Place meat, soupbone, water, seasonings, and parsley in soup kettle. Cover and cook slowly 1 hr. Add barley and cook 1 hr. longer. Remove soupbone. Add carrots, onion, peas, celery, and tomatoes. Cook 45 min. Serves 8.

Esther Wallpe
Decatur County

GLORIOUS MESS

4 lb. ground beef	1 T. oregano
1 qt. canned	1 T. thyme
tomatoes	1 t. pepper
1 C. celery and	1–2 T. chili
leaves, chopped	powder
2 medium	1 can cream of
onions,	mushroom
chopped	soup
4 t. salt	2 cans chili beans

Brown meat, drain; add onions and cook until onions are tender. Add tomatoes, celery, and seasonings and cook 30 min. longer. Add soup and chili beans and continue to simmer. Can be simmered all afternoon. To serve, ladle mixture into individual bowls and top with any of the following: corn chips, chopped onions, chopped lettuce, grated longhorn cheese, or chopped tomatoes. Serves 12–16.

Mrs. Robert Dawes
Wabash County

MOCK TURTLE (BEEF) SOUP

1½ lb. lean	1 C. ketchup
ground beef	1–2 lemons, sliced
6 C. water	to taste
1 large onion,	5 t. mixed pick-
chopped	ling spices (tied
1 T. salt	in cloth)
1 C. sliced celery	½ C. flour
1 lb. carrots,	6 hard-cooked
grated	eggs, sliced

Cook beef, water, salt, onion, celery, ketchup, and spices in Dutch oven until meat is done; remove spice bag. Add carrots and sliced lemon; cook until carrots are tender. Brown flour in skillet, lightly; add to soup. Add sliced eggs.

Lorraine Hale
Clark County

CHICKEN SOUP

2 qt. broth
1½ C. cooked chicken, cut up
½ C. sliced water chestnuts
1 3-oz. can sliced mushrooms, undrained
6 green onions (tops, too), minced
1 C. cooked rice
salt, pepper, and soy sauce to taste

Bring broth to a boil; add all remaining ingredients, and heat. Serve with chow mein noodles, if desired.

Faye Ice
LaGrange County

TUNA CHEESE CHOWDER

1 T. minced onion
2 T. butter or margarine
1 can Cheddar cheese soup
1 7-oz. can flaked tuna
½ C. milk
1 1-lb. can tomatoes
1½ t. parsley flakes
½ t. salt
⅛ t. pepper
⅛ t. thyme

Sauté onion in butter; stir in soup. Slowly stir in milk. Chop tomatoes and add to soup; add remaining ingredients. Simmer covered for 10 min.

Betty J. Craig
Grant County

CREAMED ONION SOUP

1½ large onions, thinly sliced and separated into rings (3 C.)
2 T. butter or margarine
1 T. flour
1 qt. milk
1 t. salt
dash pepper
2 beaten egg yolks

Cook onions in butter about 10 min. (tender but not brown). Sprinkle with the flour; cook and stir over low heat until blended. Add milk all at once; cover and simmer 20 min. Add salt and pepper. Stir a small amount of hot mixture into egg yolks; return to soup mixture, stirring until blended. Season to taste. Sprinkle each serving with grated Parmesan cheese. Serves 6.

Mrs. Earl Ballinger
Union County

FRENCH ONION SOUP (1)

12 onions, thinly sliced (5 C.)
4 T. butter
1 T. dark rum (optional)
6 1″ slices French bread
6 slices 50% fat Swiss cheese
6 T. grated Parmesan cheese
¼ t. Tabasco
4 C. beef bouillon
½ t. Worcestershire sauce
½ t. Kitchen Bouquet
salt, freshly ground black pepper (to taste)

Sauté onions in butter 15 min. until golden brown; add bouillon, Worcestershire, Tabasco, Kitchen Bouquet, pepper, salt, and rum. Bring to a boil; reduce heat, cover, and simmer for at least 1 hr. Toast bread, pour soup in soup cup, cover with bread, and both cheeses. Bake at 350–375° until brown on top.

Mary Jane Miller
Whitley County

FRENCH ONION SOUP (2)

2 lb. yellow onions, sliced	2 qt. beef broth
1 T. olive oil	¾ C. vermouth (optional)
3 T. butter or margarine	5 ¾" slices French bread, halved and toasted
1 t. brown sugar	
2 T. molasses	
1 t. salt	2 C. grated Swiss cheese
1 t. pepper	
3 T. flour	

Combine onions and fats and sauté covered for 15 min., stirring occasionally. Stir in sugar, salt, and pepper. Simmer covered 35 min., stirring occasionally. Stir in flour, stirring constantly. Gradually add broth and vermouth. Cook over medium heat until thickened. Reduce heat and simmer 20 min. Divide soup into oven-proof bowls or cups, top with toast and cheese. Broil until cheese melts.

Wavalene Johnson
Allen County

BEV'S HEARTY POTATO SOUP

3 medium potatoes, diced	3 C. milk
1 stalk celery, diced	¾ C. cubed Velveeta
3 green onions, diced	1½ t. salt
water	dash pepper
4 T. flour	crumbled bacon bits

Cook potatoes, celery, and onion in very small amount of water; do not drain. Lower heat to simmer. In shaker, mix flour, salt, pepper, and 1 C. milk; add to hot vegetables and stir well. Add 2 C. milk and simmer until thickened and hot. Add cheese and stir until melted. Garnish with crumbled bacon. Serves 6.

Bev McClure
Union County

EASY VEGETABLE SOUP

1 lb. ground beef	1 C. each: sliced carrots and celery
1 C. chopped onion	
1 clove garlic, minced	2 16-oz. cans stewed tomatoes
1 15-oz. can kidney beans	5 beef bouillon cubes
1 C. frozen green beans	1 T. parsley flakes
¼ C. uncooked rice	1 t. salt
	⅛ t. pepper

Cook beef, onion, and garlic in Dutch oven until beef is browned; drain. Add 3½ C. water and remaining ingredients, except the green beans. Bring to a boil; reduce heat and simmer 40 min. Add green beans; simmer 10 min.

Doris Shuppert
St. Joseph County

Brunches

Brunches—those creative "happenings" at the noon hour—are one of the happiest and easiest ways to entertain. No one expects an elaborate production and yet there is a feeling of specialness in the air. Try any of the easy or make-ahead entrées that follow, mix up a salad (spinach, perhaps), add a light dessert and something to drink and you're home free.

Main Dishes

SUNDAY BRUNCH FOR A BUNCH

Sauce:

4 slices bacon, diced	salt and pepper to taste
½ lb. chipped beef, shredded	Scrambled eggs:
	16 eggs
¼ C. butter or margarine	¼ t. salt
	1 C. evaporated milk
2 4-oz. cans sliced mushrooms, drained	¼ C. butter or margarine, melted
½ C. flour	reserved mushrooms
1 qt. milk	

Sauté bacon. Remove pan from heat; add chipped beef, butter, and ¾ of the mushrooms (reserve remaining for garnish). Mix well. Sprinkle flour, salt, and pepper over the bacon-mushroom mixture. Gradually stir in milk; cook over medium heat until sauce is thickened and smooth, stirring constantly. Set sauce aside. Combine eggs with salt and milk and scramble in butter in a large skillet. In large baking pan (or 2, or more, smaller ones) arrange 4 layers (two of scrambled eggs and two of sauce, ending with the sauce). Garnish with reserved mushrooms. Cover and bake at 275° for 1 hr. Can be prepared the day before and refrigerated. If refrigerated, bake 1½ hrs. Serves 12–16. *Optional: Add 1 C. shredded sharp cheese to sauce.*

Rosemary Kincaid
Monroe County

EGGS MARVELOUS

2 T. butter	⅓ C. half & half
1 T. chopped green onion	¼ t. lemon juice
6 eggs, beaten	1 3-oz. pkg. cream cheese, cubed
½ t. salt	

Melt butter in double boiler. Add onion and cook 5 min. Combine eggs, cream, salt, lemon juice, and cream cheese. Add mixture to double boiler and cook slowly, stirring often until set. Serves 4–5.

Judy Smith
Allen County

OVERNIGHT FRENCH TOAST

1 loaf French bread, sliced 1″ thick	¼ t. salt
	2 t. vanilla
	1½ T. butter, cut into small pieces
6 eggs	
2½ C. milk	
1 T. sugar	

Arrange bread in one layer in a 9x13″ greased baking pan. Beat together eggs, milk, sugar, salt, and vanilla; pour over bread. Cover dish and refrigerate overnight. Uncover; dot with butter and bake 45–50 min. at 375°. Let stand 5 min. Serves 4–5.

Ruth Colbert
Daviess County

BAKED PANCAKES

2 C. pancake mix	½ C. water
	1 C. light corn syrup
Cinnamon Cream Syrup:	1 C. evaporated milk
2 C. sugar	
2 t. cinnamon	

Prepare pancake mix according to pkg. directions; pour into greased jelly roll pan. Bake at 425° for 15–20 min. Combine syrup ingredients in saucepan and simmer 10 min. Serve with pancakes.

Betty Sendmeyer
Putnam County

WAFFLES

3 C. sifted flour	1½ t. vanilla,
5 t. baking	if desired
powder	⅔ C. melted
1 t. salt	butter (or
3 T. sugar	margarine,
4 large eggs	shortening,
2¼ C. milk	or salad oil)

Melt and cool butter. Sift together into large mixer bowl of electric mixer the flour, baking powder, salt, and sugar. Put eggs into small mixer bowl; beat on high speed for 1 min. Add milk and vanilla to eggs; add to dry ingredients. Beat on medium speed for about 1 min., or until blended. Blend in the shortening. Bake in preheated waffle baker. Freeze leftovers. Toast frozen waffles in toaster.

Thelora Shoemaker
Jay County

CHICKEN CASSEROLE (1)

12 slices bread,	1 4-oz. can mush-
without crusts	rooms, drained
3 C. cut-up	1 C. mayonnaise
cooked chicken	4 eggs, beaten
1 C. chopped	1 can mushroom
celery	soup
¼ C. chopped	2 C. shredded
onion	Cheddar cheese
2 C. milk	

Place 6 slices bread in a greased 9x13″ pan. Mix chicken, onion, celery, and mushrooms and spread over bread. Cover with 6 other slices of bread. Combine milk, mayonnaise, and eggs and pour over top of bread. Refrigerate overnight. Before baking, mix cheese and soup and spread over top of casserole. Bake at 350° for 1 hr. Serves 8.

Virginia Hollingsworth
Boone County

CHICKEN CASSEROLE (2)

6 slices of bread,	1 can cream of
cubed	mushroom
½ C. melted	soup
butter	2 cans chicken
½ C. onion,	noodle soup
chopped	¼ C. melted
2 C. cooked,	butter
diced chicken	1 C. crushed corn
2 eggs, beaten	flakes

Layer bread in bottom of greased casserole. Pour over ½ C. butter; sprinkle onion on bread and place chicken on top. Mix eggs with soups and pour over chicken. Top with cornflakes and melted butter before baking. Bake at 350° for 45 min.

Mary Frances Harvey
Grant County

SUE'S HOT CHICKEN SALAD

9 slices white	½ C. mayonnaise
bread, crusts	9 slices process
cut off	sharp cheese
4 C. cooked	4 eggs, well-
chicken,	beaten
chopped	2 C. milk
½ lb. fresh	1 t. salt
mushrooms,	1 can mushroom
sliced	soup
¼ C. margarine	1 can celery soup
1 8-oz. can water	1 2-oz. jar
chestnuts,	pimiento
drained and	2 C. buttered
sliced	bread crumbs

Line large buttered baking dish with bread; top with chicken. Sauté mushrooms in melted margarine for 5 min.; spoon over chicken. Add chestnuts, dot with mayonnaise, and top with cheese. Combine eggs, milk, soups, and pimiento; pour over top of cheese. Cover dish with foil and refrigerate overnight. Bake at 350° for 1½ hr.

Uncover; top with bread crumbs and bake additional 15 min.

Charlotte Klootwyk
Monroe County

serted in the center comes out clean. Let stand 5 min. Makes its own crust.

Loretta Johnson
Benton County

CHICKEN-MACARONI CASSEROLE

2 C. diced cooked chicken	2 C. milk
1 7-oz. pkg. un-cooked maca-roni or small spaghetti	2 cans cream of mushroom soup
½ lb. grated Cheddar cheese, or cubed Velveeta	1 2-oz. jar pimientoes (optional)
	4 hard-cooked eggs, chopped
½ green pepper, diced	1 t. salt
	1 small onion, diced

Combine and mix all ingredients. Refrigerate overnight. Bake in 13x8½" glass casserole. Bake at 350° for 1½ hr. May substitute tuna for chicken. May also cut ingredients in half and bake 1 hr.

Mary Russell   *Ruthanna Chamness*
Posey County   *Kosciusko County*

CRAB QUICHE

Pastry for a 1-crust 9" pie	1 C. shredded Swiss cheese
1 C. flaked crabmeat	2 eggs, well-beaten
¼ C. freshly grated Parme-san cheese	½ t. salt
	1 t. freeze-dried chives
2 C. light cream	pinch cayenne or curry powder

Brush the bottom of the pie crust with egg white to prevent the filling from soaking into the pastry; chill while preparing the filling. Combine crabmeat with the cheeses and blend well; add the remaining ingredients. Pour into chilled pastry shell and bake at 425° for 10 min. Lower heat to 325° and bake 30 min., or until a table knife inserted in the center comes out clean.

Evelyn Harbaugh
St. Joseph County

QUICHE

12 slices bacon, crisply fried and crumbled	2 T. onion, finely chopped
1 C. shredded Swiss cheese (4 oz.)	½ C. buttermilk biscuit mix
	4 eggs
1¾ C. milk	¼ t. salt
	⅛ t. pepper

Lightly grease a 9–10" pie or quiche pan. Sprinkle bacon, cheese, and onion evenly over bottom of pan; place remaining ingredients in blender and blend 1 min. at high speed. Pour into pie plate. Bake 50–55 min. at 350° until golden brown and knife in-

QUICK QUICHE LORRAINE

1 egg, beaten	1 3½-oz. can French fried onion rings
1 C. evaporated milk	9 slices fried bacon, crumbled
½ t. salt	
½ t. Worcester-shire sauce	single crust for 9" pie
1 C. shredded Swiss cheese	

Precook crust at 425° for 3–4 min. Combine egg, milk, salt, and Worcestershire; stir in cheese. Sprinkle half of onion rings over crust. Pour egg mixture over onion rings. Sprinkle with bacon and remaining onion rings. Bake at 325° for 30–40 min.

Brenda Dunbar
Lawrence County

oil until brown and crisp on both sides. Serve with scrambled eggs.

Edna Chambers
Switzerland County

SAUSAGE QUICHE

1 pie shell, unbaked	1½ C. shredded Cheddar cheese
½ lb. sausage, browned and drained	2 T. flour
	2 t. parsley flakes
	2 eggs, beaten
½ C. onion, chopped	⅔ C. milk

Combine sausage, onion, cheese, flour, and parsley flakes; mix well and put into pie shell. Beat eggs and milk together and pour over sausage mixture. Bake 35–40 min. at 375°.

Note: Quiche crusts will be less soggy if partially baked before filling is added.

Lib Force
Clark County

SCRAPPLE

1½ lb. pork shoulder	¼ C. minced onions
¼ lb. pork liver (optional)	1 t. sage
	¼ t. thyme
1 t. salt	1 t. marjoram
1 C. yellow cornmeal	½ t. pepper

Mix meats with 1 qt. water, cover, and cook 1 hr., or until tender; drain and reserve broth. Chop meat fine. Blend cornmeal and salt with 1 C. cold water and 2 C. reserved broth; simmer, stirring constantly until thick. Stir in meats, onions, herbs, and pepper. Cover mixture and cook very slowly for about 1 hr.; stir occasionally. Pour mixture into 9x5x3″ pan; cool. Chill until firm. Cut into slices about ½″ thick. Fry in hot

HAM PUFF

10–12 slices bread, crusts removed and cubed	6 eggs, beaten
	2 C. ham, cubed
	2 T. minced onion (optional)
2 C. Cheddar cheese, shredded	½ t. salt
	½–¾ t. dry mustard
10 oz. frozen chopped broccoli, cooked and drained (optional)	2 T. parsley flakes
	3 C. milk (use 3½ C. with 12 slices of bread)

Beat eggs, milk, and seasonings together; add bread, cheese, broccoli, onion, and ham. Bake in buttered 9x13″ pan at 350° for 60–75 min. Should be firm but not too solid. Can be refrigerated overnight before baking. Serves 8–12.

Mrs. Edwin Dierlam
St. Joseph County

SAUSAGE BAKE

6 medium potatoes, sliced	1 can tomato soup
1 onion, chopped	1 16-oz. can cream-style corn
salt and pepper	
1 lb. sausage links, sliced	

Place potatoes and onion in greased 2 qt. casserole; salt and pepper to taste. Place sausage over potatoes and spread with soup. Top casserole with the corn. Bake at 350° for 45–60 min. Serves 6.

Catherine Deems
Switzerland County

SAUSAGE AU GRATIN

1 12-oz. pkg. sausage links	1 T. minced onion
1 8-oz. jar Cheez Whiz	½ t. salt
1 C. dairy sour cream	6 medium potatoes, pared, cubed, and parboiled
2 t. parsley flakes	

Combine Cheez Whiz and sour cream; mix well until smooth. Add onion, parsley, and salt. Cut sausage into ½" slices; add sausage and potatoes to cheese mixture. Pour into 1½ qt. casserole dish. Bake at 350° for 40 min.

Mrs. Don Conrad
LaPorte County

SAUSAGE AND BROCCOLI CASSEROLE

1 lb. sausage links, cut into small pieces	3 T. minced parsley
1 10-oz. pkg. frozen chopped broccoli, cooked and drained	2 T. flour
	3 hard-cooked eggs, sliced
	1 can cream of mushroom soup, undiluted
¼ C. shredded mild Cheddar cheese	⅓ C. milk
3 T. chopped green pepper	½ C. dry bread crumbs
2 T. grated onion	3 T. butter, melted

Place broccoli in a lightly greased 1½ qt. casserole. Brown sausage; combine with cheese, green pepper, onion, parsley, and flour. Spoon half of sausage mixture over broccoli in casserole. Top sausage mixture with egg slices; spoon remaining sausage mixture over eggs. Combine soup and milk; pour over sausage layer. Combine bread crumbs and butter; sprinkle over top of cas-

serole. Bake at 375° for 30 min. Serve over hot cooked rice. Serves 6.

Marjorie E. Weiss
Marshall County

SAUSAGE CASSEROLE (1)

1 lb. sausage	1 C. raw rice
1 C. chopped onion	2 t. bottled steak sauce
1 C. celery	⅓ C. Parmesan cheese, grated
1 C. sliced mushrooms	¼ C. chopped pimiento
2 C. chicken or beef broth	

Fry sausage; drain. Sauté onion and celery for 5 min.; add rice, sauté 5 min. more. Heat broth to boiling; add to rice mixture. Add sausage, steak sauce, mushrooms, and pimiento; mix well and simmer until rice is tender. Place mixture in ungreased casserole; add cheese to top and bake at 350° for 1 hr. Serves 8.

Marjorie Quick
Delaware County

SAUSAGE CASSEROLE (2)

4 C. Rice Krispies, 1 C. reserved	12 oz. sharp Cheddar cheese, grated
2 lb. bulk sausage, browned and drained	2 C. rice, cooked
	4 eggs, beaten with 2 cans celery soup
1 medium onion, chopped and browned lightly	

Layer in 9x13" baking pan: Rice Krispies, sausage, onion, rice, and cheese; pour the egg-soup mixture over the top layer. Sprinkle with reserved Rice Krispies. Bake at 350° for 45 min. Serves 6–8. Freezes well.

Mrs. John S. Linn
Elkhart County

SAUSAGE BREAD

2 loaves of frozen bread	1½ t. fennel seed
2 lb. sausage	1 t. garlic salt
6 slices of bacon, sliced in small pieces	1 lb. cheese, grated (your favorite kind)
1 egg	¾ C. Parmesan cheese

Allow frozen bread to thaw and rise. Divide into three balls. Roll each out to a 9x12" rectangle. Fry sausage and bacon enough to allow the grease to flow; drain. Add egg, fennel seed, and garlic salt to sausage-bacon; mix thoroughly. Divide meat mixture into 3 parts and spread evenly over each rectangle of dough. Top each rectangle of dough with equal amounts of the cheeses. Roll up jelly-roll fashion. Pinch together ends and edges to seal. Lightly oil each loaf. Bake on cookie sheet at 350° for 50 min., or until lightly browned. Serve warm. Yield: 12 slices per loaf.

Carol Landrigan
Kosciusko County

SAUSAGE-EGG OLÉ

6 eggs, beaten	1 16-oz. can tomatoes, drained and chopped
½ C. dairy sour cream	
½ lb. Velveeta, cubed	1 1-lb. pkg. of smokey link sausages, cut up
½ green pepper, chopped	

Mix all ingredients together. Put in a greased 2 qt. casserole. Bake at 325° for 50 min. Serves 6.

Marjorie Rumple
Monroe County

EGG, SAUSAGE, AND HASH BROWN CASSEROLE

2 lb. frozen hash browns	1 large can evaporated milk
2 lb. sausage	1 t. salt
¼ C. onion	⅛ t. nutmeg
½ lb. Swiss cheese, grated	¼ t. pepper
5 eggs, beaten	1 T. parsley

Grease a 9x13" pan. Press potatoes into pan and brown in a 425° oven. Brown sausage; drain. Sauté onions; set aside. Sprinkle sausage and cheese over potatoes. Combine eggs, milk, and seasonings and pour into onions; pour over potato mixture. Bake at 425° 20 min., or until inserted knife comes out clean. Serves 10–12.

Louise Friermood
Wabash County

WILD RICE AND SAUSAGE CASSEROLE

2 C. wild rice, cooked	2 4-oz. cans mushrooms, drained
2 medium onions, chopped	½ C. cream
1 lb. mild sausage	¼ C., plus 1 T., flour
½ C. almonds, sliced	pinch of thyme, marjoram, or 1 t. salt and 1 t. Accent
2½ C. chicken broth	

Sauté meat and onions; add mushrooms. Make sauce with flour, broth, cream, and seasonings. Stir over medium heat until thickened; combine with meat and onions. Mix in rice. Pour into 9x13" greased casserole and top with almonds. Bake at 350° for 20 min.

Judy Fleck
White County

HOMEMADE POLISH SAUSAGE

whole pork butt (5–7 lb.), or ground pork	2 t. salt
	½ t. pepper
	½ t. marjoram
2½–3 oz. water per lb. pork	1 section fresh garlic, chopped fine
Seasonings per lb. pork:	

Trim and cut pork into sections that can be easily ground by meat grinder (if not using ground pork); use coarse (large) blade for first grinding. Weigh amount of meat ground. For each lb. pork, measure and mix together seasonings and water. Blend the mixture into ground meat. Refrigerate meat mixture for 10–12 hr. Grind meat again, using fine blade. If using casings, fill as sausage leaves grinder; if not, make patties. Use waxed paper between patties. Refrigerate until meat "takes a set" (6–8 hr.). May be frozen in individual packets or in whatever amounts desired.

Note: Be certain the meat is kept well chilled at all times during the preparation process. Since no preservatives are used, handle the finished product as very perishable. Try to use within 1–2 days.

HOMEMADE PORK SAUSAGE

Follow directions given above, but substitute the following seasoning ingredients per lb. pork: 1 medium dry hot red pepper, crushed fine; ½ t. black pepper; 1 t. sage; 2 t. salt. The water amount remains the same.

Jacqueline Helmle
Howard County

TUNA CASSEROLE

Toast and butter 12–14 slices bread. Cover bottom of greased 9x13″ baking dish with one layer of toast. On each slice of toast put one slice of process cheese food. Cover toast-cheese layer with one large can tuna; drained and crumbled. Spread tuna layer with 2 cans mushroom soup, undiluted. Add second layer of toast and another layer of cheese. Beat 6 eggs, 1 13-oz. can evaporated milk, and 1 C. milk together; pour over layered ingredients. Add a small amount of pepper to egg mixture, if desired, but no salt. Refrigerate at least 3 hr., or overnight. Bake at 325°–350° about 1½ hr. Serves 8.

Almeda Mullen
Marion County

Desserts

COFFEE CAKE (1)

Batter:	1 C. vegetable oil
1 pkg. yellow cake mix	1 C. water
	4 eggs
1 small pkg. instant vanilla pudding mix	Topping:
	¾ C. brown sugar
1 small pkg. instant butterscotch pudding mix	1 t. cinnamon
	½ C. chopped nuts (optional)

Mix ingredients together following cake box directions for mixing procedure. Put into greased and floured 9x13″ pan. Combine the topping ingredients, and sprinkle over the cake batter. Bake 20 min. at 350°. Lower heat to 325° and bake 30 min. longer.

Gladys Houser
Jay County

COFFEE CAKE (2)

Batter:
1 box white cake
mix
½ C. sugar
4 eggs
1 C. dairy sour
cream
¾ C. oil
Sugar Mixture:
4 T. brown sugar
¾ C. pecans
(small pieces)
2 t. cinnamon

Mix together sugar, cake mix, oil, and sour cream. Add eggs, 1 egg at a time, and beat well. Pour ½ of batter in greased, floured bundt or angel food cake pan. Sprinkle more than half of sugar mixture on top. Pour rest of batter and sprinkle with remaining sugar mixture. Bake 1 hr. at 325°. Let stand in pan for 10 min. Remove cake from pan and ice with confectioners' sugar icing.

Medra M. Ball
Switzerland County

AMISH COFFEE CAKE

2 C. brown sugar
¾ C. butter or
margarine
2 C. flour
1 egg
2 t. vanilla
1 t. soda dis-
solved in 1 C.
hot coffee

Mix first 3 ingredients with fork, until crumbly; reserve 1 C. of mixture for topping. To the balance, add egg, vanilla, and soda mixture. Mix well. Pour mixture into a greased and floured 9x13" pan and sprinkle on the reserved topping. Bake at 350° for about 30 min. Sprinkle on powdered sugar after cake is removed from oven.

Joyce French
Henry County

CRUNCHY CINNAMON COFFEE CAKE

3–3½ C. flour
2 pkg. dry yeast
⅓ C. sugar
½ t. salt
½ C. milk
½ C. water
¼ C. butter or
margarine
1 egg
Topping:
½ C. sugar
½ C. flour
½ C. nuts
1 t. cinnamon
½ C. butter or
margarine,
softened

Combine 1½ C. flour, yeast, sugar, and salt; mix well. Heat milk, water, and butter until warm 120–130° (butter does not need to melt); add to flour mixture. Add egg. Blend at low speed until moistened; beat 3 min. at medium speed. By hand, gradually stir in enough flour to make a stiff batter. Spread batter evenly in well-greased 9x13" pan. Cover. Let rise in warm oven (turn oven to lowest setting for 1 min., turn off) for 25 min. Combine all topping ingredients. Sprinkle over batter. With back of spoon, press topping into batter to make random indentations. Bake at 375° for 20–25 min.

Catherine Hunn
St. Joseph County

JEWISH COFFEE CAKE

Batter:
1 box white cake
mix
1 3¾-oz. pkg.
instant vanilla
pudding mix
1 C. sour cream
4 eggs
1 jar maraschino
cherries,
chopped, with
juice
½ C. vegetable
oil
½ 16-oz. jar apri-
cot preserves
Sugar-nut
mixture:
1 C. sugar
½ t. cinnamon
1 C. chopped
pecans
1 t. cocoa

Mix batter ingredients together following cake box directions for mixing procedure. Pour part of batter into greased 9x13" pan. In a separate bowl, mix together the sugar-nut mixture. Alternate layers of batter and sugar-nut mixture, ending with layer of mixture. Bake at 350° for 45 min.

Charlotte Klootwyk
Monroe County

STREUSEL COFFEE CAKE

1 pkg. dry yeast	2 T. sugar
1 C. flour	1 can pie filling
1 yellow cake mix	Glaze:
2 eggs	1 C. confection-
⅔ C. warm water	ers' sugar
5 T. butter,	1 T. corn syrup
melted	1 T. water

In large bowl of electric mixer, combine 1½ C. dry cake mix, yeast, flour, water, and eggs. Beat 2 min. at medium speed. Scrape bowl often. Spread dough in greased 9x13" pan; set aside. In saucepan, make streusel topping by combining reserved cake mix with cooled, melted butter; set aside. Spoon pie filling evenly over dough in pan; sprinkle with 2 T. sugar and then streusel topping. Bake at 375° for 30 min. Blend together ingredients for glaze. Drip glaze over warm cake.

Peggy Schultz
Rush County

HOCUS-POCUS CRISPIES

8 oz. can refriger-	2 T. margarine,
ated crescent	softened
rolls	¼ C. brown
¼ C. chopped	sugar
walnuts or	½ t. cinnamon
pecans	4 t. sugar

Unroll crescent dough into 2 long rectangles; place together, overlapping edges, to form 14x8" rectangle. Firmly press perforations and edges to seal. Spread with margarine. Combine brown sugar, nuts, and cinnamon; sprinkle evenly over dough. Starting at shorter side, roll up, sealing long edge; cut into 8 slices. Place slices on ungreased cookie sheets; flatten each with hand to a 4–5" circle. Sprinkle each slice with about ½ t. sugar. Bake at 400° for 10–15 min., or until golden brown.

Martha Mobley
Monroe County

EASY CARAMEL ORANGE RING

1 T. butter,	½ t. cinnamon
softened	2 10-oz. cans
½ C. orange	refrigerated
marmalade	buttermilk
2 T. chopped	biscuits
nuts	½ C. butter,
1 C. brown sugar	melted

Grease 12 C. bundt pan with 1 T. butter. Place teaspoonfuls of marmalade in pan. Sprinkle with nuts. Combine brown sugar and cinnamon; mix well and set aside. Separate biscuits. Dip biscuits in melted butter and then into sugar mixture. Stand biscuits on edge in pan, spacing evenly. Sprinkle with remaining sugar mixture and drizzle with remaining butter. Bake at 350° for 30–40 min. Cool upright in pan for 5 min.; invert onto serving plate.

Mary Ann Schoenemann
Huntington County

Salads

Salads are a familiar and important item on all American menus. Salad bars, which started in colleges, are now seen everywhere; in the finest restaurants as well as those specializing in fast foods. Whether as a main dish, a side dish, or a luscious dessert, use salads imaginatively to add flavor, nutrition, and variety to any dinner or luncheon.

Try freshly ground black pepper in tossed salads; it adds an extra zing.

After using, rinse wooden salad bowls in warm water. Pat dry immediately. Oil rancidity develops in unwashed bowls.

Use ice to get molded salads off to a quick start. Dissolve each package of fruit-flavored gelatin in 1 cup of boiling water; add 8 to 12 ice cubes and stir constantly 3–4 min. until gelatin starts to thicken. Remove unmelted ice. Let gelatin stand 3–5 min.; add remaining recipe ingredients and chill until firm.

To unmold gelatin successfully, rinse platter or place with cold water so mold will slide on it. Loosen gelatin by running tip of knife between it and the mold. Dip mold to rim in warm (never hot) water for a few seconds. Place platter atop mold, hold tightly and invert quickly. Lift off pan. This procedure is a bit scary the first time around, but practice does increase self-confidence.

Main Dish Salads

ORIENTAL CHICKEN SALAD

2 C. diced, cooked chicken	1 C. diced celery
1 C. white seedless grapes	½ C. cashew nuts
1 C. pineapple chunks	¾ C. Chinese noodles
	½ C. mayonnaise

Combine chicken, grapes, pineapple, celery, and mayonnaise; chill. Just before serving, add nuts and Chinese noodles. Serve on lettuce. Serves 6–8.

Alice Porter
St. Joseph County

TACO SALAD

1 head lettuce, broken into small pieces	1 can kidney beans, rinsed and drained
1 small onion, chopped	4 oz. shredded Cheddar cheese
2 tomatoes, cut up	1 8-oz. bottle Catalina dressing
1 lb. hamburger, browned, drained, and cooled	1 small bag taco chips, crushed

Mix first 6 ingredients together. Add dressing and taco chips just before serving. Serves 4.

Dorothy Janes
Clark County

Variations:

(1) Use ½ C. French dressing and a dash of Tabasco instead of Catalina dressing.

Margaret Rund
Perry County

(2) Use 8 oz. oil and vinegar dressing with garlic mix instead of Catalina dressing.

Suburbanites E. H. Club
LaPorte County

(3) Combine Italian with either French or Russian dressing instead of Catalina dressing.

Alfreda Wesner
White County

(4) Add ½ C. stewed tomatoes and ½ envelope powdered taco sauce to browned hamburger. Use pinto beans instead of kidney beans and Western dressing instead of Catalina dressing.

Patricia Ann Wilderson
LaGrange County

TROPICAL PORK SALAD

1½–2 C. cubed cooked pork roast	1 8-oz. can pineapple chunks, drain and reserve 2 T. juice
2 C. cooked rice	½ C. salad dressing
½ C. chopped green pepper	¼ t. ginger
½ C. sliced celery	
½ t. salt	

Combine pork, rice, green pepper, and celery in bowl; add pineapple chunks. Combine salad dressing, pineapple juice, ginger, and salt; mix well. Pour dressing over salad ingredients; toss lightly. Chill well. Garnish with mint or watercress. Serves 4.

Ouida Maloney
Hendricks County

HOT POTATO SALAD WITH FRANKS

½ lb. frankfurters	¼ C. bacon drippings
5–6 potatoes, boiled in jackets, cubed	½ C. chopped green pepper (optional)
½ C. chopped onion	½ C. vinegar
	1 egg, beaten

2 t. sugar   ⅛ t. pepper
1 t. salt   ¼ t. dry mustard

Cook frankfurters in water for 7 min.; slice into bite-sized pieces. Combine potatoes with green pepper and onion; set aside. Heat bacon drippings in skillet and add vinegar,

egg, sugar, and seasonings; stir and heat thoroughly. Add potato mixture and frankfurters. Heat and serve. Serves 6.

Kay Metzger
Kosciusko County

Vegetable Salads

CABBAGE-CARROT SALAD

2 C. shredded   1 T. lemon juice
      carrots   Yogurt dressing:
2 C. shredded   1 C. plain yogurt
      cabbage   ¼ t. salt
½ C. celery,   1 T. honey
      diced   2 t. lemon juice
1 C. raisins

Combine salad ingredients; add dressing and mix well. Serves 10–12.

Vina Williams
Jefferson County

COLESLAW

2 C. shredded   2 t. salad oil
      cabbage   2 t. lemon juice
½ C. thinly sliced   1 t. freshly grated
      red onion   or prepared
¾ C. shredded   horseradish
      carrot   ⅛ t. salt
½ C. plain yogurt   ⅛ t. pepper

In bowl, toss together cabbage, onion, and carrot. Stir together yogurt, oil, lemon juice, and horseradish; add salt and pepper. Toss dressing with cabbage mixture; chill several hr. Serves 4.

Margaret Pinkerton
Grant County

FRED HARVEY COLESLAW

1 medium head   ½ T. salt
  cabbage   ½ t. dry mustard
1 small onion   ½ t. celery seed
½ C. sugar   ½ C. peanut oil
1 t. sugar   ½ C. vinegar

Shred cabbage and onion; cover with ½ C. sugar. Mix remaining ingredients together and bring to a boil. Pour over cabbage; refrigerate 4 hr.

Helen Fox
Delaware County

CAESAR SALAD

1 clove garlic   juice of 1 lemon
½–¾ C. olive oil   ½ t. salt
    (may substitute   pepper to taste
    vegetable oil)   1 egg
2 heads romaine,   1 can anchovies
  washed, dried,   1 C. croutons
  and broken into   ½ C. Parmesan
  2″ lengths   cheese, grated

Cut garlic clove into small pieces and marinate in oil over night. Add oil and lemon juice to crisp romaine and toss. Add salt and pepper. Boil the egg for 1 min., and drop from shell onto salad. Add anchovies; add cheese and croutons. Toss lightly. Serves 6.

Debbie Lemar
Huntington County

ZIPPY CARROT AND GREEN BEAN SALAD

2 C. carrots, slices or strips, cooked and drained	½ small onion, chopped
2 C. green beans, cut or whole, cooked and drained	2 stalks celery with leaves, chopped
Dressing:	2 T. salad oil
4 T. lemon juice	¼ t. basil
	¼ t. oregano
	salt and pepper to taste

Combine the dressing ingredients. Toss the cooked vegetables in dressing; refrigerate in a tightly covered container overnight. Turn container several times before serving. Serve cold. Serves 4–6.

Janet Carlson
Fountain County

MACARONI SALAD

1 7½-oz. box macaroni and cheese, cooked and cooled	½ C. salad dressing
2–3 boiled eggs, chopped	celery, chopped (optional)
3–4 T. sweet pickle relish	onion, chopped (optional)

Combine all ingredients and mix well. Serves 6.

Thelma Hardwick
Rush County

ITALIAN MACARONI SALAD

1¼ C. tiny shell macaroni (4 oz.), cooked and drained	1 C. cream style cottage cheese
¼ C. Italian salad dressing	1 C. dairy sour cream
	½ C. celery, chopped

¼ C. chopped green pepper	2 T. milk
1 hard-cooked egg, chopped	1 T. sliced green onion with tops
	½ t. salt

Toss hot macaroni with Italian dressing; let stand 30 min. Stir in cottage cheese, sour cream, celery, green pepper, egg, milk, onion, and salt. Chill. Serves 6.

Mrs. John Ellert, Jr.
Vanderburgh County

ITALIAN GREEN BEANS

fried bacon, crumbled	½ C. chopped dill pickles
2 10-oz. pkg. frozen green beans, cooked, drained	1 clove garlic
	½ t. salt
	½ C. salad oil
small red onion, sliced and in rings	¼ t. rosemary
	¼ C. vinegar
	½ t. oregano

Combine beans, onion rings, and pickles; set aside. Mash garlic with salt; add remaining ingredients and shake in covered jar. Pour dressing over beans; refrigerate several hours, or overnight. Garnish with bacon. Serves 6–8.

Patricia Marshall
Morgan County

PICKLED NOODLES

1 lb. pkg. ritoni (or similar pasta)	2 cloves garlic, minced
¼ C. vegetable oil	1 t. pepper
2 C. sugar	2 t. prepared mustard
1 T. salt	1½ C. vinegar
1 t. garlic salt	1 onion, finely chopped
1 unpeeled cucumber, finely chopped	pimientos for color

Cook pasta as directed on package, adding vegetable oil to water. Drain well and rinse with cold water; drain again. Heat sugar, pepper, mustard, salt, vinegar, and garlic salt until sugar dissolves; add onion, cucumber, and garlic and pour over pasta. Cover and refrigerate at least 48 hr.

Freda Neeley
Martin County

RICE SALAD (1)

Marinade:	1 C. coarsely
1½ t. salt	chopped celery
⅛ t. pepper	1 C. pared cu-
dash cayenne	cumber,
¼ C. cider	chopped
vinegar	½ C. chopped
½ C. salad oil	green onion
Salad:	½ C. sliced
6 C. cooked rice,	radish
warm	4 hard-cooked
1½ C. mayon-	eggs, peeled
naise or salad	and coarsely
dressing	chopped
1 T. mustard	

Combine ingredients for marinade; mix well. Pour marinade over rice; toss to coat well. Refrigerate covered 2 hr. Before serving, add all remaining ingredients; toss lightly. Serves 8.

Elizabeth Tuttly
Randolph County

RICE SALAD (2)

3 C. cooked rice,	2 C. firmly
hot	packed fresh
½ C. Italian	spinach, cut in
dressing	thin strips
1 T. soy sauce	1 C. sliced
½ t. sugar	radishes

1 medium zuc-	½ C. coarsely
chini, cut in	chopped
thin strips	walnuts
¾ C. sliced celery	

Combine salad dressing, soy sauce, and sugar; stir into rice. Cover and chill at least 2 hr. Before serving, add vegetables and nuts; toss lightly.

Sara E. Riddle
Hancock County

BAKED SAUERKRAUT SALAD

1 qt. jar sauer-	1 pt. can toma-
kraut,	toes, undrained
undrained	½–1 lb. bacon
¾–2 C. sugar	

Cut bacon into small pieces and fry slightly to remove some of the fat. Combine all ingredients and bake at 325° in uncovered 9x13″ dish for 3 hr. If mixture browns too quickly, cover with aluminum foil. The juice should cook down to about ⅓. Serves 10–12.

Almeda Mullen
Marion County

SPINACH SALAD (1)

1 lb. spinach,	½ lb. bacon,
washed, dried,	fried and
and torn into	crumbled
bite-sized	Dressing:
pieces	½ C. salad oil
1 C. water chest-	2 T.–½ C. sugar
nuts, sliced	¼ C. catsup
1 small onion,	2 T. Worcester-
chopped	shire sauce
1–2 hard-cooked	¼ C. red wine
egg(s)	vinegar

Combine all dressing ingredients, and heat but do not boil; cool. Combine spinach, water chestnuts, and onion; pour dressing over and toss. Garnish with bacon and egg.

Mary Margaret Wagoner
Cass County

SPINACH SALAD (2)

1 8–12 oz. pkg. fresh spinach, washed, trimmed, and dried	½ C. mayonnaise
	4 hard-cooked eggs, chopped
	2 green onions, chopped
Dressing:	2 apples, chopped
8 oz. dairy sour cream	2 T. lemon juice

One-half hr. before serving, add dressing to spinach. Serves 8.

Virginia Redinger
Marshall County

SPINACH SALAD (3)

1 8–12 oz. pkg. fresh spinach, torn into bite-sized pieces	3 slices bacon, fried and crumbled
2–3 bananas, sliced	½ C. toasted walnut pieces
	Russian dressing

Toss all ingredients in salad bowl. Serve immediately. Bananas may be sprinkled with lemon juice to retard browning. *Note:* Place walnuts in shallow pan and bake at 350° until lightly browned. Watch carefully; they are easily overtoasted.

Suzee Alexander
Owen County

INDIAN SPINACH SALAD (4)

Dressing:	2 t. sugar
¼–C. white vinegar	½–1 t. dry mustard
¼–½ C. salad oil	1½ t. curry powder (optional)
2 T. chutney, chopped	

Combine dressing ingredients in a screw top jar and chill. Place torn spinach in a large salad bowl. Top with chopped apples, raisins, peanuts, and green onions. Shake dressing; pour over the salad and toss. Serves 6–8.

Alma Fraze   *Catherine Farmer*
Randolph County   *Monroe County*

MARINATED TOMATOES

6 tomatoes, sliced	2 t. sugar
1 C. drained ripe olives, sliced	⅛ t. turmeric
	¾ t. cumin
2 chopped green onions	¼ t. black pepper
¼ C. chopped parsley	5 T. olive oil
Marinade:	4 T. lemon juice
1 t. salt	

Mix tomato slices with olives, onions, and parsley. Combine marinade, and add to tomato mixture. Allow to marinate at least 2 hr.

Karen Stumph
Hancock County

MARINATED VEGETABLES

⅓ C. salad oil	1 small head cauliflower, broken into florets, cooked 4 min.
⅓ C. cider vinegar	
2 T. green pepper, finely chopped	15 oz. can garbanzo beans, heated and drained
1 T. parsley, chopped	
1 t. salt	2 C. cucumber, unpared and sliced
¼ t. paprika	
⅛ t. pepper	1 C. carrots, cut in thin strips

Place oil, vinegar, green pepper, parsley, salt, and spices in a large bowl; mix well. Add vegetables; mix gently. Cover; marinate for several hr., or overnight, in refrigerator. Mix occasionally. For best eating quality, use within a few days.

Victory Extension Homemakers
Grant County

MIXED VEGETABLE SALAD (1)

1 bunch fresh broccoli	2 cucumbers, sliced
1 head fresh cauliflower	1 container cherry tomatoes
1 lb. fresh mushrooms, sliced	1 large bottle Italian dressing
1 large onion, cut into rings	

Cut or tear all vegetables into bite-sized pieces. Pour Italian dressing over everything; toss, and cover. Let stand all night to marinate. Stir occasionally. Serves 8–12.

Sherri Wynn
Hancock County

MIXED VEGETABLE SALAD (2)

½ head cauliflower	1 small jar pimientos
4–5 stalks broccoli	Dressing:
4–5 stalks celery	½ C. sour cream or yogurt
5–6 green onions	½ C. mayonnaise
1 10-oz. pkg. frozen green peas, thawed	1 pkg. dry Italian dressing mix

Cut vegetables into bite-sized pieces and refrigerate. Mix dressing. Several hours before serving, toss dressing with vegetables in large bowl. Serves 10–12.

Connie Mangold
Dearborn County

MIXED VEGETABLE SALAD (3)

1 15-oz. can corn, drained	⅓–1 C. chopped green peppers
1 15-oz. can peas, drained	⅓ C. sweet relish, drained (optional)
1 15-oz. can carrots, drained (optional)	¼–1 C. sugar
	¼–½ C. oil
⅓–1 C. chopped onions	¼–¾ C. vinegar
	salt, pepper, and
⅓–1 C. chopped celery	celery seed to taste

Boil sugar, oil, vinegar, and seasonings together 2–3 min. Pour over vegetables while hot. Serve salad hot or cold. Serves 15–20.

Ruth Heidegger   *Ann Ekstrom*
Jay County   *Fayette County*

ORANGE VEGETABLE SALAD

2 3-oz. pkg. orange gelatin	1 C. shredded carrots
2 C. boiling water	1 C. shredded cabbage
1 C. cold water	⅓ C. raisins
¾ C. mayonnaise	

Dissolve gelatin in boiling water; add cold water. When partially set, add remaining ingredients. Pour into 7x11″ pan; chill.

Do-a-lot E. H. Club
Jay County

VEGETABLE CHEESE MOLD

1 3-oz. pkg. lemon-flavored gelatin	¼ t. salt
	1 C. cabbage, finely chopped
1 C. hot water	½ C. carrot, grated
½ C. cold water	
½ C. mayonnaise	¼ C. green pepper, finely minced
¼ C. blue cheese, crumbled	
1 T. vinegar	

Dissolve gelatin in hot water and add cold water, mayonnaise, cheese, vinegar, and salt; blend well with electric beater at low speed. Pour into freezer tray and freeze until firm at edges but still soft in center. Turn into a well-chilled bowl and beat with electric mixer until fluffy. Fold in vegetables and pour into a 1½ qt. mold. Chill until firm. Serves 6.

Mary Connelley
Grant County

Dessert Salads

APPLE SALAD

1 No. 2 can pineapple, drained, juice reserved	Dressing: 1 C. pineapple juice
6 apples, diced	1 T. lemon or orange juice
1 C. celery, diced	1 egg
	2 heaping T. flour
¾ C. nuts	½ C. sugar

Cook dressing ingredients together until thick; cool. Mix salad ingredients with cooled dressing. Cover and place in refrigerator. Keeps for several days. Can substitute liquid sweetener for sugar.

Frances Haines
Jay County

APRICOT SALAD

1 No. 2 can crushed pineapple and juice	1 8-oz. pkg. cream cheese, softened
½ C. sugar	1 C. ice water
1 3-oz. box apricot gelatin	1 pkg. whipped topping

Mix pineapple and sugar; bring to a boil. Stir in cream cheese and gelatin and keep stirring until cheese is almost dissolved. Add ice water and set aside to thicken. Whip topping following pkg. directions and blend into gelatin mixture; pour into 9x9″ pan. Sprinkle nuts on top; refrigerate.

Kay Johnson
Clark County

BLUEBERRY SALAD (1)

2 pkg. grape gelatin	1 can blueberry pie filling
2 C. boiling water	8 oz. pkg. cream cheese
juice from pineapple	½ C. sugar
1 large can crushed pineapple, drained	1 C. dairy sour cream
	1 t. vanilla
	½ C. pecans

Dissolve gelatin in boiling water; add pineapple juice. When mixture begins to thicken, add pineapple and pie filling. Pour into 9x13″ pan; chill until firm. Beat cream cheese, sugar, sour cream, and vanilla together; frost top of salad and sprinkle with nuts.

Hallie Tyson
Greene County

BLUEBERRY AND SOUR CREAM SALAD (2)

First layer:	Second layer:
2 C. heavy cream or half and half	1 3-oz. pkg. raspberry gelatin
1 C. sugar	1 C. boiling water
1 envelope unflavored gelatin, soaked in ¼ C. cold water	1 15-oz. can blueberries and juice, or 1 can frozen blueberries
2 C. dairy sour cream	
1 t. vanilla	

Heat cream and sugar, stirring until sugar is dissolved. Remove from heat; add softened gelatin. Stir well; add sour cream and vanilla. Pour mixture into a 2 qt. ring mold. Refrigerate 45 min., or until set. To make second layer, dissolve gelatin in boiling water; cool and add blueberries. Pour mixture on top of first layer. Chill until firm. Serves 12.

Katherine Hess
Morgan County

CRANBERRY SALAD

1 lb. cranberries	30 marsh-
4 C. water	mallows, cut up
⅛ t. salt	2 C. diced apples
⅛ t. soda	2 C. chopped
1–2 C. sugar	celery
6 oz. strawberry	1 C. chopped
gelatin	nuts

Cook cranberries, water, and salt together. When mixture begins to boil, add soda; boil for 10 min. Add sugar, gelatin, and marshmallows; cool. Add remainder of ingredients; pour into mold and refrigerate.

Marjorie Mickley
Huntington County

FRUIT SALAD

1 16-oz. can fruit	1 C. miniature
cocktail,	marshmallows
drained	seeded, quartered
1 20-oz. can pine-	grapes to suit
apple chunks,	taste
drained	quartered mara-
1 11-oz. can man-	schino cherries
darin oranges,	to suit taste
drained	1 20-oz. can apri-
2 large or 3 me-	cot or peach pie
dium bananas,	filling
sliced	

Stir together first seven ingredients. Fold in pie filling. Chill. Serves 8–10.

Lois Redman
Marshall County

HOT FRUIT MEDLEY SALAD

1 28-oz. can	1 20-oz. can pine-
sliced peaches,	apple tidbits,
drained	drained
1 28-oz. can	1 can cherry pie
pears, drained	filling
and sliced	⅓ C. brown
½ C. rum	sugar

Mix all ingredients together and heat thoroughly. Serve warm or cold. Mixture turns red as it cooks. Serves 15.

Evelyn Sutherlin
Putnam County

7-UP SALAD

2 pkg. lemon	1 C. pineapple
gelatin	juice
2 C. boiling	2 T. flour
water	2 T. butter
2 C. 7-Up	½ C. sugar
1 C. crushed	1 C. heavy cream,
pineapple, juice	whipped
reserved	1–2 eggs, beaten
2–3 bananas,	½ C. grated
sliced	Cheddar cheese
1–2 C. miniature	(optional)
marshmallows	

Dissolve gelatin in water; add marshmallows and cool. Add 7-Up, pineapple, and bananas; set aside. Combine juice, flour, butter, eggs, and sugar; cook over low heat, stirring constantly until mixture thickens. Cool and blend in whipped cream and cheese; pour over firm gelatin mixture. Refrigerate.

Lola Ward   *Madeline Hensley*
White County   *Wayne County*

ORANGE GELATIN SALAD

1 large pkg. orange gelatin	Topping:
2 C. boiling water	1 3-oz. pkg. instant vanilla pudding
1 small can frozen orange juice concentrate	1½ C. milk
	1 8-oz. container frozen whipped topping, thawed
1 small can mandarin oranges, drained	

Dissolve gelatin in boiling water; add remaining ingredients and pour into 7x11″ pan. Chill until firm. Combine pudding and milk for topping. Blend in whipped topping; spread over gelatin mixture.

Margaret Vincent
Jay County

STRAWBERRY PRETZEL SALAD

First Layer:	1 8-oz. container frozen whipped topping, thawed
2½ C. coarsely crushed pretzels	
3 T. sugar	Third Layer:
¾ C. margarine, melted	1 6-oz. pkg. strawberry gelatin
Second Layer:	
1 8-oz. pkg. cream cheese, softened	2 C. hot water
	2 10-oz. pkg. frozen strawberries
1 C. powdered or granulated sugar	

Mix first layer ingredients together and place in a 9x13″ pan. Bake at 350° for 10 min. Cool. Mix first 2 ingredients of second layer together; fold in the whipped topping. Spread on top of pretzel layer and let set. To make third layer, dissolve gelatin in hot water. Add strawberries. When partially set,

pour on top of cream cheese layer. Refrigerate. Serves 12.

Mildred Weissfuss
St. Joseph County

TANG FRUIT SALAD (1)

1 20-oz. can crushed pineapple, drained	½ C. Tang, dry
	½ C. sugar (optional)
1 11-oz. can mandarin oranges, drained	1 3-oz. box instant vanilla pudding mix
2 apples, diced	½ C. nuts (optional)
3 bananas, sliced	

Mix all together. Very good on a hot day.

Extension Homemakers Discussion Club
Ripley County

TANG FRUIT SALAD (2)

2 cans peach pie filling	2 20-oz. cans pineapple tidbits, drained
6 T. Tang, dry	
1 6⅛-oz. box instant vanilla pudding mix	2 bananas
	1 C. chopped pecans (optional)
1 qt. strawberries	

Mix pie filling, Tang, and pudding mix together and refrigerate at least 8 hr. Before serving, add the fruit and nuts.

Georgia Davis
Monroe County

TAPIOCA GELATIN FRUIT SALAD

5 C. water	1 C. crushed pineapple, drained
¾ t. salt	
½ C., plus 1 T., small pearl tapioca	3 C. bananas, sliced
½–1 C. sugar	1 9-oz. container frozen whipped topping, thawed
1 3-oz. box strawberry gelatin	

Bring water and salt to boil; add tapioca and cook 15 min. Add gelatin and sugar; mix well. Let set overnight. Add pineapple, whipped topping, and bananas just before serving.

Sherry Hendricks
Marshall County

FROZEN FRUIT SALAD (1)

1 20-oz. can crushed pineapple, drained	1 14-oz. can sweetened condensed milk
¼ C. lemon juice (optional)	1 13-oz. container frozen whipped topping, thawed
1 20-oz. can cherry pie filling	½ C. chopped nuts (optional)

Mix pie filling, pineapple, nuts, and milk together. Fold in whipped topping. Pour into greased 9x13″ pan. Top with nuts. Freeze.

Leatha Koontz   *Sandy Paterson*
Randolph County   *St. Joseph County*

FROZEN FRUIT SALAD (2)

1 3-oz. pkg. orange-pineapple gelatin	⅓ C. mayonnaise
dash of salt	1 C. whipping cream, whipped
1 C. boiling water	1 medium banana, diced
1 8¾-oz. can pineapple tidbits, drained and juice reserved	½ C. seedless grapes
	¼ C. diced maraschino cherries
¼ C. lemon juice	¼ C. chopped nuts

Dissolve gelatin and salt in boiling water. Add water to pineapple juice to make ½ C.; stir into gelatin with lemon juice. Blend

in mayonnaise; chill until thickened, but not set. Fold fruits, nuts, and whipped cream into gelatin. Pour into 9x5x3″ loaf pan. Freeze until firm. To serve, cut in slices. Serves 8.

Dorothy Frazier
Clark County

FROZEN FRUIT SALAD (3)

4 T. sugar	1 large jar maraschino cherries, drained
4 T. vinegar	
4 eggs, beaten	
1 small bunch Tokay grapes, halved and seeds removed	1 C. pecans, chopped
	1 small pkg. miniature marshmallows
1 small bunch white seedless grapes	2 C. whipping cream
1 No. 2 can chunk pineapple, drained	2 T. sugar
	1 t. vanilla

Cook 4 T. sugar, vinegar, and eggs over low heat until thickened; cool. Mix fruits, nuts, and marshmallows with the sugar-egg mixture. Whip cream; add 2 T. sugar and vanilla. Fold whipped cream into fruit mixture. Freeze overnight. Remove from freezer 10 min. before serving.

Vivian Thrasher
Monroe County

FROZEN GRAPE SALAD

8 oz. cream cheese, softened	2 T. pineapple juice
2 T. salad dressing	5 oz. miniature marshmallows
1 C. heavy cream	1 No. 2 can pineapple bits, drained and juice reserved
2 C. Tokay grapes, halved and seeded	

Blend cream cheese with salad dressing and cream; beat until smooth. Add pineapple bits, marshmallows, and grapes. Pour into 6x10″ glass baking pan. Freeze. (This keeps well 4–6 weeks in freezer.) Remove from freezer; cut into squares when slightly softened. Serve immediately. Serves 8.

Jean Brechbill
DeKalb County

FROZEN PEACHY SALAD

1 No. 303 can dark sweet pitted cherries, drained	1 No. 2½ can cling peach slices, drained
	½ C. peach juice

1 C. miniature marshmallows	¼ C. sugar
	¼ t. salt
1 8-oz. pkg. cream cheese, softened	1 C. plain yogurt

In small saucepan, combine peach juice with marshmallows; stir over low heat until marshmallows are melted. Cool mixture slightly; set aside. Beat cream cheese until smooth; add sugar and salt, and beat until fluffy. Add marshmallow mixture, then the yogurt; mix until smooth. Add the fruit and turn into 7x11″ pan. Freeze.

Rosie McCay
St. Joseph County

Dressings

BLUE CHEESE DRESSING

1 qt. mayonnaise	1 small onion, minced
1 3–4 oz. pkg. blue cheese	1 T. lemon juice
1 clove garlic, minced (large clove or 4 small)	1 t. salt
	1 t. sugar
	¼ t. Tabasco, or hot sauce
2 T. wine vinegar	

Blend all ingredients together; refrigerate.

Rosella Holzer
Ripley County

CUCUMBER PARSLEY DRESSING

1 C. peeled, seeded and chopped cucumber	½ C. mayonnaise
	1 clove garlic, minced
	½ t. salt
1 C. chopped parsley	⅛ t. pepper
	1 C. plain yogurt

Stir together first 6 ingredients. Stir in yogurt. Chill. Makes 2 C.

Dianna Crouse
Union County

CELERY SEED DRESSING

½ C. mayonnaise	1 t. vinegar
1 t. salt	1 t. Dijon mustard
2 t. sugar	
1½ t. celery seed	¼ t. ground pepper

Combine all ingredients and mix well. If refrigerated overnight, add a little more mayonnaise.

Thelma Hardwick
Rush County

POPPY SEED DRESSING

¼ C. honey	½ C. oil
2 T. cider vinegar	2 t. poppy seed
2 t. dry mustard	1 t. grated onion
½ t. salt	

Beat honey, vinegar, mustard, and salt until well blended. Add oil, poppy seeds, and onion; beat slowly. Makes 1 C.

Lilly Jane Hall
Noble County

TANGY FRENCH DRESSING

1 C. tomato juice
2 envelopes instant chicken broth and seasoning mix
4 T. vinegar
1 t. mustard
1½ t. Worcestershire sauce
2 t. dehydrated onion flakes
1 t. sugar, or equivalent artificial sweetener
dash of garlic powder and cinnamon

Blend well in blender or shake together in a covered jar.

Variation: Follow above, but stir in 2 oz. crumbled or mashed Roquefort cheese and mix well.

Marge Hiday
Jay County

Vegetables

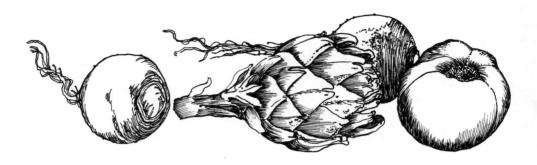

ASPARAGUS OR BROCCOLI CASSEROLE

2 C. asparagus or broccoli, cooked and drained	1 can cream of mushroom soup
2 hard-cooked eggs	¾ C. milk
	1½ C. cracker crumbs

salt and pepper

Sprinkle crumbs to cover the bottom of an 8″ square baking dish. Arrange half of asparagus (or broccoli) over the crumbs. Slice one egg over asparagus. Repeat procedure with crumbs, asparagus, eggs, salt, and pepper. Top with the mushroom soup mixed with the milk. Sprinkle with a few additional cracker crumbs. Bake at 350° for 30 min. Serves 6.

Lillian Quick
Wayne County

EGGPLANT PATTIES

1 medium eggplant	2 T. snipped parsley
1¼ C. cracker crumbs	2 T. sliced green onions
1¼ C. shredded sharp cheese	1 clove garlic, minced
2 eggs, slightly beaten	¼ t. salt
	⅛ t. pepper
2 T. cooking oil	

Pare and cube eggplant. Cook in boiling water in covered saucepan until tender, about 5 min. Drain well and mash. Stir in crumbs, cheese, eggs, parsley, onion, garlic, salt, and pepper. Shape into 8 patties about 3″ in diameter. Cook in skillet in hot oil about 3 min. on each side or until golden brown. Serves 4.

Barbara Moeller
Clark County

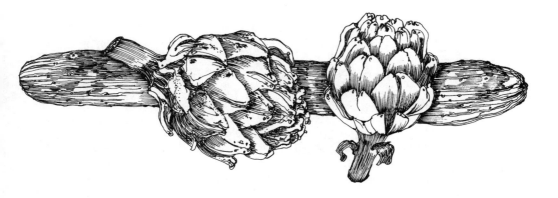

GLAMOUR BEAN CASSEROLE

3 10-oz. pkg.
  frozen French-
  style green
  beans, cooked,
  and drained
butter for
  sautéing
1 large onion,
  chopped
1 small green
  pepper,
  chopped
slivered almonds
1 can cream of
  mushroom
  soup

1 5-oz. can button
  mushrooms
1 8-oz. can water
  chestnuts,
  drained and
  sliced
1 16-oz. can bean
  sprouts,
  drained
½ C. dairy sour
  cream
grated Cheddar
  cheese to taste
herb-flavored dry
  stuffing mix

Sauté onion in butter until tender; remove and set aside. Sauté green pepper until tender; set aside. Brown almond slivers in butter; set aside. Add soup to drained beans; stir in mushrooms, onion, green pepper, water chestnuts, bean sprouts, and sour cream. Put in 3 qt. casserole. Stir together cheese and stuffing mix; sprinkle over vegetables and top with almonds. Bake at 350° for 30 min. Serves 10.

Wilma Linville
Decatur County

SWEET-SOUR BEANS

2 qt. fresh yellow
  beans, cooked
  and drained
1 C. water

½ C. vinegar
½ C. sugar
2 whole cloves
1 stick cinnamon

Combine water, vinegar, sugar, and spices in saucepan and bring to boil. Cook 4–5 min. Pour vinegar mixture over beans; allow to cool. Serve chilled. Serves 6.

Christina Geurs
LaGrange County

BROCCOLI CASSEROLE (1)

2 10-oz. pkg. frozen chopped broccoli, cooked and drained	¼ C. slivered almonds
	1 C. grated Cheddar cheese
1 can mushroom soup	1 C. bread crumbs, buttered
1 C. evaporated milk	

Layer broccoli in shallow baking dish. Mix soup and milk; pour over broccoli. Add almonds. During last half of baking time top with cheese and cover with bread crumbs. Bake at 350° for 20–25 min.

Mary Betty Arburn
Gibson County

BROCCOLI CASSEROLE (2)

2 10-oz. pkg. frozen broccoli, cooked and drained	1 stick margarine, melted
	4 T. margarine
1½ C. party cracker crumbs (Waverly, Ritz, etc.)	3 T. flour
	1½ C. milk
	1 6-oz. jar Old English process cheese spread

Reserve ¼ C. cracker crumbs. Mix remainder of crumbs with 1 stick of margarine and spread in bottom of shallow casserole dish. Arrange broccoli over crumbs. Melt 4 T. of margarine; add flour and mix well. Add milk gradually and cook to boiling point. Add cheese. Pour sauce over broccoli. Sprinkle on reserved crumbs. If desired, sprinkle on ¼ C. sliced almonds. Bake at 350° for 30 min.

Jacksonettes E.H. Club
White County

GOURMET CABBAGE CASSEROLE

1 medium cabbage	½ onion, chopped
4 T. butter	⅔ C. Cheddar cheese, shredded
4 T. flour	
½ t. salt	½ C. mayonnaise
½ t. pepper	3 T. chili sauce
2 C. milk	

Topping:

½ green pepper, chopped

Cut cabbage into small wedges and cook until tender; drain and place in a 9x13" casserole. Melt butter in saucepan; blend in flour, salt and pepper. Cook over low heat stirring until smooth and bubbly. Stir in milk and continue cooking, stirring constantly, until mixture comes to a boil. Continue cooking one additional minute. Spread sauce over cabbage. Bake at 375° for 20 min. Mix green pepper, onion, cheese, mayonnaise, and chili sauce. Spread over top of casserole and bake at 400° an additional 20 min. Serves 8.

Peg Weller
Greene County

FAR EAST CELERY

4 C. celery, sliced diagonally in 1" pieces, cooked crisp-tender; drained	1–2 5-oz. cans water chestnuts, drained and sliced
	1 can cream of chicken soup
2 T. melted butter	½–1 C. soft bread crumbs
¼ C. diced pimientos (optional)	¼–2 C. slivered almonds

Mix water chestnuts and soup with celery. Put in greased casserole dish. Melt butter;

add bread crumbs and almonds. Sprinkle on top of celery. Bake at 350° for 35 min.

Sue Barnett & Gene Riley   *Margie Angermeier*
Randolph County   *Posey County*

ONION PIE

30 saltine crackers, crushed	½ lb. grated cheese
1 stick margarine, melted	1½ C. scalded milk
3 C. onion, sliced thinly	3 eggs, beaten
	1½ t. salt

Mix crackers with melted margarine and use to line the bottom of a shallow casserole dish. Sauté the onions in ¼–½ C. of margarine until golden brown. Place onion on top of crumbs; sprinkle with grated cheese. Mix the milk, eggs, and salt and pour over onion mixture. Bake at 350° for 30 min. or until the custard is set.

Hint: Wipe grater with cooking oil before grating cheese, it cleans easier.

Goldie Jones
Pike County

BARB'S EGGPLANT CASSEROLE

1 medium eggplant, pared, cubed, cooked, and drained	1 can mushroom soup
	½ C. milk
	2 eggs, separated
2 C. coarse bread crumbs	¼ t. salt, or to taste

Heat the soup with milk; add egg yolks and blend well. Add eggplant and blend. Fold in the crumbs. Fold in the stiffly beaten egg whites. Pour into greased casserole. Allow to set 20–30 min. Bake at 375° for 40–45 min. Serve at once. Serves 4–6.

Ruth Tarr
Orange County

CORN-RICE CASSEROLE

1 16-oz. can creamed corn	1 T. sugar
	1 egg, beaten
½ C. instant rice	1 diced onion
¼ C. cream (or half and half)	ground pepper to taste
2 T. butter	bacon

Combine all ingredients, except bacon, in casserole. Top with bacon and bake at 350° for 1–1½ hr. Serves 4–6.

Jane Ford
Wabash County

MUSHROOM CASSEROLE

3–5 T. butter	½ t. salt
1 t. lemon juice	¼ t. nutmeg
1 lb. sliced mushrooms	1/16 t. instant onion powder
3 T. butter or margarine	⅛ t. black pepper
3½ T. flour	4 large eggs yolks, beaten
½ C. chicken broth	1½ C. bread crumbs, mixed with 3 T. butter
1½ C. light cream (or milk)	

Melt 3–5 T. butter in large skillet; add mushrooms and lemon juice. Cook over low heat until mushrooms are tender. Remove from heat and reserve. Melt 3 T. butter in saucepan over low heat; add flour; stir and cook 3–5 min. Add chicken broth, cream, and seasonings and cook until thickened and smooth. Add small amount of hot sauce to egg yolks; stir and combine with sauce in pan. Stir in mushrooms. Turn into shallow greased baking dish. Top with bread crumb mixture. Bake at 400° for 15 min.

Dorothy Avery
Morgan County

POTATO CASSEROLE

8 medium potatoes, boiled, peeled and shredded	1½ C. dairy sour cream
	½ t. salt
1 bay leaf (boil with potatoes)	3 green onions
	1½ C. shredded Cheddar cheese
1 can mushroom soup, undiluted	½ C. crushed cornflakes
2 T. butter	

Warm butter and soup; blend in sour cream, salt, and onions. Blend in 1 C. cheese. Pour mixture over the potatoes and mix well. Put in greased casserole and bake uncovered 30 min. Top with ½ C. cheese and the cornflakes; bake 15 min. longer. Serves 6.

Ruth Brothers
Perry County

POTATOES AND CABBAGE CASSEROLE

4 medium onions, sliced	4 medium cooked potatoes, sliced
¼ C. butter	2 T. butter
1 small head cabbage, sliced thinly	2 C. grated Cheddar cheese
¼ C. flour	1 13-oz. can chicken broth

Melt butter; sauté cabbage and onions. Layer cabbage mixture and potatoes in a 3 qt. casserole. Sprinkle with grated cheese. Melt 2 T. butter; add flour and chicken broth. Mix and heat to thicken; pour over casserole. Bake at 350° for 45–50 min. Serves 6–8.

Mrs. John S. Linn
Elkhart County

MASHED POTATOES FOR A CROWD

5 lb. cooked potatoes, drained and mashed	2 8-oz. pkg. cream cheese
	2 C. cream

Blend cream cheese and cream together; beat into potatoes. Place in 8 qt. casserole. Refrigerate. Before baking, brush with melted margarine and sprinkle with paprika. Bake covered at 350° for 45 min. Serves 20.

Note: Do not use food processor to mash potatoes; it will make them "gummy."

Dorcas Van Duyne
Marshall County

Variation: Substitute dairy sour cream for regular cream and add ¼–½ C. chopped chives.

Jacksonettes E. H. Club
White County

IMPOSSIBLE RATATOUILLE PIE

1 C. chopped zucchini	¼ C. margarine or butter
1 C. pared, chopped eggplant	½ t. basil
	½ t. thyme
½ C. chopped tomato	⅛ t. pepper
	1 C. shredded Monterey Jack cheese
½ C. chopped green pepper	1¼ C. milk
¼ C. chopped onion	¼ C. dairy sour cream
1 medium clove garlic, crushed	¾ C. biscuit mix
	3 eggs
¾ t. salt	

Lightly grease 10x1½" pie plate. Sauté zucchini, eggplant, tomato, green pepper, onion, and garlic in margarine until vegetables are crisp-tender; stir in seasonings. Spread mixture in pie plate; sprinkle with cheese.

Beat remaining ingredients until smooth, 15 sec. in blender on high or 1 min. with hand beater; pour into pie plate. Bake at 400° for 30–35 min. Knife inserted halfway between center and edge should come out clean. Let stand 5 min. Serves 6.

Marilyn Smendzuik
Greene County

COMPANY RICE

2 T. butter	1 can chicken
3 T. minced	rice soup
onion	1 can beef
2 cups celery,	consommé
chopped	1 T. poultry
1 can cream of	seasoning
mushroom	1½ t. salt
soup	¾ C. raw rice

Sauté onion and celery in butter. Mix soups with the consommé and heat; add seasonings, rice, onion, and celery. Pour into buttered casserole; cover and bake 45 min. at 350°. Uncover and stir in ½ C. toasted almonds; bake additional 30 min.

Mrs. Sandy DeMeyer & Ruth Plumbeck
St. Joseph County

GREEN AND YELLOW RICE

3 C. rice, cooked	1 10-oz. pkg. fro-
¼ C. butter	zen chopped
4 eggs, beaten	spinach,
1 C. milk	cooked and
1 lb. grated sharp	drained
Cheddar cheese	½ t. each: mar-
1 T. chopped	joram, thyme,
onion	rosemary, and
1 T. Worcester-	salt
shire sauce	

Melt butter and add to rice. Add milk to eggs, and stir into rice. Add remaining in-

gredients and mix well, but gently. Place in a 2 qt. greased casserole and bake uncovered at 350° for 45 min. Serves 6.

Mary Baxter
Monroe County

SPINACH CASSEROLE (Betty Siefer's)

2–3 10-oz. pkg.	1½–2 C. sour
frozen chopped	cream
spinach	½ C. Cheddar or
1 pkg. dry onion	Parmesan
soup mix or ½	cheese, grated
C. onion, sau-	¼ C. dry bread
téed in	crumbs
margarine	

Cook spinach without salt; drain and combine with soup mix or onion and sour cream. Add salt and pepper to taste. Place in buttered casserole; add cheese and crumbs. Bake at 350° for about 30 min. Serves 8–10.

Recipe also works well as filling for crepes.

Suburbanites E.H. Club
LaPorte County

CHEESY-NUT VEGETABLE PIE

2 C. sliced fresh	1 C. milk
broccoli flower-	1 C. shredded
ets or 1 10-oz.	process Swiss
pkg. frozen cut	cheese (4 oz.)
broccoli	1 C. fresh or
¼ C. sliced green	canned (and
onion	drained) whole
2 T. butter or	kernel corn
margarine	½ C. salted
2 T. flour	peanuts
½ t. dried mar-	2 beaten eggs
joram, crushed	pastry for 2-crust
¼ t. salt	pie

In a saucepan, cook broccoli in small amount of water 5 min.; drain and remove from pan. In the same saucepan, cook onion in butter until tender but not brown; stir in flour, marjoram, and salt. Add milk; cook and stir until mixture is thickened. Cook 1–2 min. more. Stir in Swiss cheese; heat and stir until cheese melts. Remove from heat. Stir in broccoli, corn, and peanuts. Stir in beaten eggs. On lightly floured surface, roll out half of the pastry to a 12″ circle. Fit pastry into a 9″ pie plate (the new clay quiche pans are ideal). Trim edges ½″ beyond rim of plate. Roll out remaining pastry; cut into ½″ strips. Spoon vegetable mixture into pie plate. Weave pastry strips into a lattice atop the vegetables; flute edges of pie. Bake at 350° for 35 min., or until crust is brown. Let stand 5 min. Serves 6.

Try using walnuts, pecans, or cashews in place of the peanuts.

Rosemary Kincaid
Monroe County

EASY GARDEN VEGETABLE PIE

2 C. chopped fresh broccoli or sliced fresh cauliflower, cooked tender-crisp	½ C. chopped green pepper
	1 C. shredded Cheddar cheese
½ C. chopped green onion	1½ C. milk
	¾ C. biscuit mix
	3 eggs
1 t. salt	¼ t. pepper

Lightly grease 10″ pie plate. Mix drained broccoli, onion, green pepper, and cheese in pie plate. Beat remaining ingredients until smooth—15 sec. in blender on high, or 1 min. with hand beater. Pour into pie plate. Bake at 400° for 35–40 min. Knife inserted halfway between center and edge should come out clean. Let stand 5 min. Serves 6.

Lucille Hubeny
Newton County

MIXED VEGETABLE CASSEROLE

20 oz. pkg. California-style frozen vegetables (carrots, broccoli, cauliflower), or same amount of fresh vegetables	2 slightly beaten eggs
	¾ C. cottage cheese
	1 t. Worcestershire sauce
	½ t. salt
	⅛ t. pepper
½ C. shredded Cheddar cheese (2 oz.)	Topping:
	1 T. melted butter
2 T. finely chopped onion	¼ C. fine dry bread crumbs

Cook and drain vegetables. Combine eggs, cheeses, onion, Worcestershire sauce, salt, and pepper. Arrange vegetables in a shallow 1½ qt. baking dish; spoon cheese mixture over top and sprinkle with topping. Bake uncovered at 350° for 15–20 min., or until egg mixture is set. Serve immediately. Serves 6.

Jeannette Wonn
Decatur County

TOMATOES STUFFED WITH ZUCCHINI AL PESTO

6 firm tomatoes	Pesto:
2 medium zucchini	1½ C. fresh basil, chopped
2 T. butter	2 cloves garlic
½ C. chopped onion	⅓ C. olive oil
1 large clove garlic	¾ C. grated Parmesan cheese
grated Parmesan cheese	salt and pepper to taste
salt and pepper as desired	¼ C. pine nuts (optional)

Cut off tops of tomatoes and scoop out insides; sprinkle with salt and turn upside down to drain for 1 hr. Wash and slice zucchini; sprinkle with salt and set aside for 30–40 min. Puree pesto ingredients in blender until smooth. Sauté onion and garlic in butter until golden. Dry zucchini with paper towels and add to onion and garlic: stir-fry for 5–10 min. Add ⅓ C. pesto to zucchini mixture and season to taste. Fill tomatoes with the zucchini mixture. Sprinkle top with grated Parmesan cheese and bake at 350° for 20–30 min.

Doti Pozzatti
Monroe County

TOMATO-ZUCCHINI BAKE

4 C. peeled, chopped tomatoes	¼ t. pepper
	2 t. salt
2 C. chopped zucchini	3 T. oregano leaves
1 C. chopped onion	1½ C. Minute Rice
1 T. parsley	¼ C. grated Romano cheese
⅛ t. garlic powder	½ C. shredded Cheddar cheese

Combine the first 8 ingredients and cook until tender in 4 qt. Dutch oven. Stir in rice. Bake at 350° for 10–15 min. until set. Top with cheeses. Return to oven until cheese is melted.

Sally Swinford
Vermillion County

ZUCCHINI MEDITERRANEAN

¼ C. olive oil	2 T. parsley
8 small zucchini, thinly sliced	1 t. salt
	¼ t. oregano
⅔ C. chopped onion	¼ t. rosemary
1 large clove garlic, minced	4 C. peeled, chopped tomatoes

Heat oil in large skillet; add all ingredients except tomatoes and sauté 20 min. Add tomatoes and continue to cook 5 more min. May be eaten hot or cold. Serves 6–8.

Mary Stenger
Franklin County

Variation: To save on calories, omit the oil; combine zucchini, tomatoes, and onion and bake in 2 qt. casserole for 1 hr. at 350°. Top with grated mozzarella cheese the last 5–10 min. Serve with grated Parmesan cheese.

Janet Stafford
Putnam County

ZUCCHINI SMETANA

3–4 zucchini	¾ C. dairy sour cream
salt and pepper to taste	1 T. fresh dill or dillweed
¼ C. fresh grated Parmesan cheese	Tabasco sauce to taste

Slice zucchini into ¼" slices and place in buttered 1 qt. baking dish. Sprinkle with salt and pepper. Mix sour cream, salt, pepper, dill, and Tabasco together; pour over zucchini and sprinkle with cheese. Cover and bake 30 min. at 375°. Uncover and continue baking until tender; 10–15 min.

Marie Campbell
Warrick County

Breads

While it's true that no man lives by bread alone, it would be difficult to imagine a diet without any.

● Rapid mix bread recipes are recommended for beginning cooks. In these recipes the dry yeast is mixed with other dry ingredients. Liquids for these recipes are heated to very warm (120–130°) before adding to the yeast mixture.

● Note that in bread recipes when the dry yeast is simply dissolved in a warm liquid the liquid is heated to 105–115°.

● Salt in bread recipes helps control the action of the yeast; it needs to be measured carefully.

● To determine whether bread dough has risen double its volume, push two fingers into dough one-half inch. If the dent remains, dough has doubled.

164

Yeast Breads

CORNMEAL YEAST BREAD

5½–6 C. flour (divided)	¾ C. margarine
1 C. yellow cornmeal	½ C. sugar
2 pkg. dry yeast	1½ t. salt
2 C. milk	2 eggs
	melted butter
	sesame seeds

In large electric mixer bowl combine 2 C. flour, cornmeal, and yeast. Combine milk, margarine, sugar, and salt; heat over low heat until very warm (120–130°). Add to flour mixture and mix well. Beat in eggs. Beat ½ min. at low speed, scraping bowl constantly; beat 3 more min. at high speed. Add 1 C. flour and beat 1 min. more. With wooden spoon, stir in enough remaining flour to make a soft dough. Turn out onto lightly floured board; knead about 10 min., or until smooth & satiny. Place in greased bowl, turning once to grease top. Cover; let rise in warm place until doubled in bulk (1 hr.). Grease 2 loaf pans. Punch dough down; divide in half. Roll each into a 9x12″ rectangle. Roll dough from 9″ edge and seal. Seal ends and fold under. Place seam side down in pan. Brush with melted butter; sprinkle with sesame seeds. Cover; let rise until doubled (1 hr.). Bake at 375° 35–40 min.

Dorothy Heaston
Huntington County

MONKEY BREAD

1 C. shortening or lard	1 C. lukewarm water (105–115°)
1 C. boiling water	2 eggs, room temperature
⅔ C. sugar	6 C. flour
1½ t. salt	melted butter or margarine
2 pkg. dry yeast	

Combine shortening, boiling water, sugar, and salt in a bowl and let cool. Dissolve yeast in lukewarm water; beat eggs and add to yeast mixture. Add yeast mixture to shortening. Gradually add flour. Mix thoroughly; cover and let rise 1 hr. Knead dough down. Pinch off chunks and dip into 1 stick of melted butter. Drop chunks in tube pan. (Only use ¾ of dough in tube pan, whole recipe makes pan too full.) If you wish to have a fancy bread, roll chunks in a mixture of cinnamon/sugar before putting into tube pan. Let rise for 1 hr. in a warm place. Bake at 350° for 35–40 min. Cool for about 5 min. and turn out onto a plate. Dribble a glaze of powdered sugar and water over bread.

Jana Adams
Delaware County

SOUR CREAM GARLIC BREAD

½ C. warm water (105–115°)	½ t. fresh garlic, minced
2 pkg. dry yeast	2 eggs, at room temperature
1 C. warm dairy sour cream	4–5 C. flour
6 T. margarine, softened	1 egg white
⅓ C. sugar	1 T. cold water
2 t. salt	grated Parmesan cheese
paprika	

Measure water into large warm bowl. Sprinkle yeast onto water; stir until dissolved. Add sour cream, margarine, sugar, salt, garlic, and eggs. Beat in 3 C. flour until well blended. Stir in flour sufficient to make a soft dough. Cover; let rise until double in bulk. Stir down; turn into greased pie tin. Let rise again until double in bulk. Combine egg white and cold water. Brush loaf with mixture. Sprinkle with cheese and paprika. Bake at 375° for 40 min., or until thump on loaf makes hollow sound. Remove from pan and cool on wire rack.

Lois Ahlhouser
Monroe County

BUNS

½ C. milk	3 C. flour
2 T. sugar	1 egg, beaten
1½ t. salt	1 egg for glaze
¼ C. shortening	2 T. water
1 pkg. yeast	½ t. sesame seeds
½ C. warm water	or poppy seeds
(105–115°)	

Scald milk; pour into bowl over sugar, salt, and shortening. Stir together and cool to lukewarm. Dissolve yeast in warm water. Add yeast, 1½ C. flour, and beaten egg to milk mixture. Beat until smooth; add remaining flour. Let rest 15 min. Divide dough into walnut-sized balls. Beat egg and 2 T. water together; glaze tops of rolls. Sprinkle with seeds. Put on cookie sheet and let rise until double in size. Bake at 400° for 12 min.

These small buns may be made ahead and frozen to be filled later. Some fillings could be frozen in the buns as well.

Carol Sparks
Hancock County

ENGLISH MUFFINS IN A LOAF

2 pkg. dry yeast	2 C. milk
6 C. unsifted	¼ t. soda
flour	½ C. water
1 T. sugar	cornmeal
2 t. salt	

Grease 2 8½x4½″ bread pans and sprinkle with cornmeal. Combine 3 C. flour, yeast, sugar, salt, and soda in mixer bowl. Heat liquids until very warm (120–130°); add to dry mixture and beat well. Stir in rest of flour with wooden spoon (makes a stiff batter). Spoon into prepared pans; sprinkle cornmeal on top of each loaf. Cover with waxed paper and a damp cloth; let rise in a warm place for 45 min. Bake at 400° for 25 min. Remove from pans immediately and cool on racks.

Mrs. Claude H. Brock
Grant County

MAPLE-NUT COFFEE TWIST

1 pkg. hot roll	1 t. cinnamon
mix	⅓ C. chopped
1 egg	nuts
1 t. maple	6 T. margarine or
flavoring	butter, melted
¾ C. warm water	Glaze:
(105–115°)	1½ C. powdered
3 T. sugar	sugar
Filling:	¼ t. maple
½ C. sugar	flavoring
1 t. maple	2–3 T. milk
flavoring	

Dissolve yeast from mix in warm water. Stir in egg, sugar, and maple flavoring. Add hot roll flour mixture; blend well. Knead on floured surface 2–3 min. until smooth and satiny. Place in greased bowl. Cover; let rise in warm place until light and doubled in size, 30–45 min. Combine all filling ingredients, except margarine. Grease 12″ pizza pan. Divide dough equally into 3 balls. On lightly floured surface, roll one ball of dough in 12″ circle. Fit onto bottom of pizza pan. Brush dough with 2 T. melted margarine and sprinkle with about ⅓ C. filling. Continue in same manner, forming 2 more layers and ending with filling. Use a glass to mark a 2″ circle in center of dough (do not cut through dough). Cut from outside edge just to circle, forming 16 pie-shaped wedges. (*Hint:* Use a pizza cutter to cut dough into wedges.) Twist each of the 3-layered wedges 5 times. Let rise in warm place until light and doubled in size, 35–40 min. Bake at 375° for 20 min., or until golden brown. Combine glaze ingredients until smooth. Drizzle over warm coffee cake.

Lucy Schlosser
Marshall County

BUTTER HORNS (Overnight rolls)

1 pkg. dry yeast	3 eggs, beaten
1 C. warm water	½ C. butter,
(105–115°)	melted
½ C. sugar	5 C. flour
1 t. salt	

Dissolve yeast in warm water. Add sugar, salt, eggs, and butter. Mix in flour; refrigerate overnight. In the morning add sufficient flour to handle dough; divide dough in half. Roll each half into a 12″ circle and cut into wedges. Brush each wedge with butter and roll each piece, beginning at wide end. Place on cookie sheet and let rise until double in bulk. Bake 12–15 min. at 425°. Watch carefully because they overbake easily.

Norma Maddux
Decatur County

EASY DROP ROLLS

1½ sticks	1 pkg. dry yeast
margarine	2 C. warm water
¼ C. sugar	(105–115°)
1 egg, slightly	4 C. self-rising
beaten	flour

Melt margarine; add all other ingredients (dough will be soft and sticky). Refrigerate in covered container for several hr. before using. Spoon dough into greased muffin tins, filling ¾ full. Bake at 400° for 20 min.

Helen Fox
Delaware County

FAST SWEET ROLLS

3¼ C. unsifted	2 eggs, beaten
flour	1 pkg. yeast dis-
¼ C. sugar	solved in ¼ C.
1 t. salt	warm water
1 C. margarine	(105–115°)
1 C. milk,	½ C. sugar
scalded and	½ t. cinnamon
cooled	

In one mixing bowl, combine flour, sugar, and salt. Cut in margarine, and add eggs, milk, and yeast. Let set for 2 hr., or refrigerate overnight. Roll out one-half of the dough and sprinkle with half of sugar and half of cinnamon. Roll up and cut. Repeat procedure. Do not let rise. Bake about 12 min. at 400°. Frost with a glaze while hot.

Wanda S. Overmyer
Marshall County

QUICK ROLLS

1 box yellow cake	5 C. flour
mix	2½ C. warm
2 pkg. dry yeast	water (105–
½ t. salt	115°)
2 eggs, beaten	

Dissolve the yeast in a small amount of the warm water. Mix all of the remaining ingredients with the yeast mixture. Let rise 1 hr. in a warm place. Roll out ⅓″ (thin). Spread with soft butter, brown sugar, and cinnamon. Roll up; cut into rolls 1″ thick. Place in buttered pan and let rise until almost double in bulk. Bake at 350° 15 min. These bake very fast.

Mary Oler
Randolph County

SIXTY-MINUTE ROLLS

3 T. sugar	½ C. water
1 t. salt	¼ C. (½ stick)
2 pkg. active dry	margarine
yeast	1 C. milk
3½-4½ C. flour	

In a large bowl thoroughly mix 1½ cup flour, the sugar, salt, and undissolved yeast. Combine milk, water, and margarine in a saucepan and heat over low heat until liquids are very warm (120–130°). Note: margarine does not need to melt. Gradually add liquid mixture to dry ingredients and beat 2 min. at medium speed of electric mixer, scraping bowl occasionally. Add ½ C. flour and beat at high speed 2 min. Stir in enough additional flour to make soft dough. Turn dough out onto lightly floured board; knead until smooth and elastic, about 5–8 minutes. Place in greased bowl, turning dough one time to grease top. Cover and place bowl in pan of water (about 98°). Let rise 15 min. Form into favorite shape. Let rise in warm place (about 90°) 15 min. Bake at 425° about 12 min., or until lightly browned.

Doris Sparks
Monroe County

ELEPHANT EARS

2 C. milk	2 C. warm water
5 T. sugar	(105–115°)
5 T. shortening	6–9 C. flour
2 T. salt	2 qt. vegetable oil
2 pkg. dry yeast	cinnamon sugar

Scald milk; add sugar, shortening, and salt. Cool to lukewarm. Sprinkle yeast onto warm water in a large bowl and stir to dissolve; add milk mixture and 2 C. flour. Beat until smooth. Stir in enough additional flour to make a stiff dough. Turn dough out onto a lightly floured board; knead until smooth and elastic, about 8–10 min. Place in a greased bowl, turning to grease top. Cover and let rise in a warm place, until doubled in size, about 1 hr. Divide dough into 6–8 balls. Roll each out in the form of an elephant's ear. Heat vegetable oil to 375°. Deep-fry "ears" one at a time, for about 3–5 min. on each side, or until golden brown. Serve hot, sprinkled with cinnamon sugar.

Juanita Russell
Lawrence County

Quick Breads

PEPPY APPLE CHEESE BREAD

2 C. flour	1½ C. pared
⅔ C. sugar	cored, shredded
1 t. baking	apples
powder	½ C. shredded
1 t. soda	Cheddar cheese
½ C. shortening	½ C. chopped
2 eggs	nuts

In large bowl combine flour, sugar, baking powder, soda, salt, shortening, and eggs; mix until well-blended. Stir in apple, cheese, and nuts. Mix well. Turn into well-greased 9x5" loaf pan; bake at 350° for 50–60 min.

Marian Schneider
Posey County

BANANA NUT BREAD

3 C. biscuit mix	1 C. mashed
⅔ C. sugar	bananas
2 eggs	¾ C. chopped
½ C. milk	nuts

Beat all ingredients together in large mixer

bowl on low speed for 30 sec.; scrape bowl constantly. Beat on medium speed for 3 min.; scrape bowl occasionally. Pour into greased and floured loaf pan. Bake at 350° for 55–60 min. for large loaf; 30–35 min. for small.

Joy Hall
Rush County

PERSIMMON DATE BREAD

1¼ C. flour	1 C. chopped
1½ t. soda	dates
1½ t. baking	1 C. chopped
powder	nuts, optional
¼–½ t. salt	1 t. vanilla
1 C. sugar	1½ T. melted
½ C. soft bread	butter
crumbs	½ C. milk
1 C. persimmon	
pulp	

Sift together flour, soda, baking powder and salt; add remaining ingredients and mix well. Line a loaf pan with greased brown paper. Pour batter into prepared pan; bake at 350° approx. 1 hr. 15 min.

Clema Perkins
Putnam County

HOLIDAY CARROT BREAD

3 beaten eggs	2 C. shredded
½ C. vegetable	carrot
oil	1 3½ oz. can
½ C. milk	(1⅓ C.) flaked
2½ C. sifted flour	coconut
1 C. sugar	½ C. snipped
1 t. baking	maraschino
powder	cherries
1 t. baking soda	½ C. raisins
1 t. cinnamon	½ C. chopped
½ t. salt	pecans

Combine eggs, oil, and milk. In large bowl sift together dry ingredients. Add egg mix-

ture; mix only until ingredients are thoroughly combined. Stir in carrot, coconut, cherries, raisins, pecans. Turn into 9x5x3" greased, floured loaf pan. Bake at 350° for 45–50 min.

Kathryn Dalton
Monroe County

CUCUMBER BREAD

2 C. diced cu-	½ t. baking
cumber, seeded	powder
1 C. oil	1 t. salt
3 eggs	1 t. cinnamon
3 C. flour	½ C. nut meats
1 t. soda	1 t. vanilla
2 C. sugar	

Mix cucumbers, eggs, and oil in blender until smooth. Sift together dry ingredients; stir in cucumber mixture. Add nuts and vanilla. Bake at 325° for 1 hr. Makes 2 large loaves.

Martha Daggy
Monroe County

BEER BREAD

3 T. sugar	3 C. self-rising
1 12-oz. can	flour
warm beer	

Mix all ingredients together; turn into greased loaf pan. Brush top with shortening or butter. Bake at 375° for 50 min.

Linda Hess
Perry County

BUTTER SWIRL LOAF

½ C. butter or	2 eggs
margarine,	½ C. sugar
melted	¾ C. milk
2 C. flour	Topping:
½ t. salt	⅓ C. sugar
3 t. baking	2 t. cinnamon
powder	melted butter

Sift dry ingredients together. Beat the eggs with an electric mixer until thick and ivory-colored. Gradually add the sugar and ¼ C. melted butter. Add dry ingredients alternately with the milk. Begin and end with dry ingredients. Blend well after each addition. Pour into well-greased 9x5x3" pan. Sprinkle with sugar-cinnamon mixture. Pour remaining ¼ C. butter over batter. Cut through batter several times with a knife to "marble." Bake at 375° for 45–50 min.

Diane Yeager
Porter County

PLUM PRETTY BREAD

1 C. vegetable oil	2 C. flour
2 C. sugar	2¼ t. baking
3 eggs	powder
2 small jars pu-	¼ t. salt
reed plums	½ t. cloves
(baby food)	1 t. cinnamon

Combine vegetable oil and sugar. Add eggs and plums. Sift together dry ingredients and add to first mixture. Pour into 2 greased and floured loaf pans. Bake at 325° for approximately 50 min., or until top cracks. Cool and remove from pans; top with a light glaze, or sprinkle with powdered sugar.

Anna Belle Buskirk
Monroe County

SANDWICH NUT BREAD

3 eggs	3 C. buttermilk
1½ C. brown	1 t. salt
sugar	5 C. sifted flour
¾ C. sugar	1½ C. chopped
2 t. soda	nuts

Beat eggs well; add sugars and beat thoroughly. Mix soda into buttermilk. Stir salt into flour. Add buttermilk and flour alternately to sugar mixture; mix well. Add nuts.

Spoon batter into 2 lightly greased 8x4" loaf pans. Bake at 325° for 45–50 min., or until a wooden pick comes out clean when inserted into the center. Note: This recipe has no shortening.

Georgia Hollingsworth
Marion County

COUNTRY FRESH BISCUITS

½ C. instant non-	6 C. flour
fat dry milk	¼ C. sugar
powder	2 t. salt
¼ C. baking	2 t. cream of
powder (yes,	tartar
the ¼ C. is	2 C. shortening
right)	water

In large bowl, mix well with fork all ingredients except shortening and water. With pastry blender cut shortening into flour mixture until it has the consistency of coarse crumbs; stir in 1½ C. water until moistened. Add more water if mixture is too dry. Turn dough onto floured surface; knead 8–10 times or until smooth. With floured rolling pin, roll dough ⅔" thick. Cut and place 1" apart on cookie sheet. Bake at 400° 20–25 min. or until golden brown. To freeze, prepare biscuits as above but do not bake. Place on cookie sheet; cover and freeze. Place frozen biscuits into plastic freezer bags. Bake the frozen biscuits at 400° about 30–35 min. Will keep frozen for 3 months.

Irene Irons
White County

BACON MUFFINS

2 C. sifted flour	½ C. shortening
2½ t. baking	1 egg, beaten
powder	¾ C. milk
2 T. sugar	½ C. bacon, fried
¾ t. salt	and crumbled

Sift dry ingredients; cut in shortening. Add

crumbled bacon. Combine egg and milk; add to flour mixture. Stir only until dry ingredients are dampened. Turn into greased muffin pans, filling each ⅔ full. Bake at 400° for 25 min. Makes 10 muffins.

Sally Manis
Delaware County

REFRIGERATOR BRAN MUFFINS

15 oz. box raisin bran cereal	1 C. vegetable oil (or melted shortening)
5 C. flour	4 C. buttermilk
3 C. sugar	4 eggs, beaten
5 t. baking soda	
2 t. salt	
1 T. pumpkin pie spice (optional)	

Mix dry ingredients together in a large bowl. Add eggs, shortening, and buttermilk; mix until dry ingredients are moistened. Store in covered container in refrigerator. For muffins, fill greased muffin pans ⅔ full and bake at 400° for 15–20 min. Batter keeps for 6 weeks.

Ivy Daniel   *Doris Dotterweich*
Randolph County   *Delaware County*

CARAMEL CINNAMON MUFFINS

3 T. butter	½ t. salt
⅔ C. brown sugar	1 t. cinnamon
2 C. sifted flour	1 egg
2 t. baking powder	1 C. milk
	2 T. melted shortening

Grease muffin pans and place ½ t. butter and 1 t. brown sugar in each cup. Sift dry ingredients together. Beat egg, add milk, shortening, and remaining ¼ cup brown sugar; add to sifted dry ingredients, stirring only enough to dampen all the flour. Fill muffin pans ⅔ full and bake at 425° for 20 min. Makes 18. If desired, chopped nuts or

raisins may be added to the butter and brown sugar in bottom of the cup.

Jean Myers
Monroe County

HAM-N-CHEESERS

3½ C. flour	1½ C. milk
½ C. sugar	⅔ C. oil
5 t. baking powder	1 C. sharp cheese
1½ t. salt	1 C. chopped ham
2 eggs, beaten	

Stir the dry ingredients together; make a well in the center and add remaining ingredients. Stir only until moistened. Fill well-greased muffin cups ⅔ full. Bake at 400° for 20–25 min.

Sharon Thompson
Jefferson County

FUNNEL CAKES

1 egg	¼ t. salt
⅔ C. milk	¾ t. baking powder
1⅓ C. sifted flour	1 t. soda
2 T. sugar	

Beat egg; add milk. Sift dry ingredients together into mixing bowl; make a well in center and add milk-egg mixture. Beat until smooth; it will make a thin batter. In heavy skillet, or deep fat fryer, heat 1½″ oil, or shortening, to 375°. Take a funnel with a ⅝″ opening, hold a finger over opening, and pour some batter into funnel. Using a swirling, circular motion, drop batter into the hot fat. Use finger to control flow of batter. Make each cake about 6″ in diameter. Fry until golden brown, turning once to brown underside. Drain on paper towels. Serve with confectioners' sugar, or honey. Makes 6–8.

Essie Glaze
Monroe County

Main Dishes and Casseroles

The first item on many grocery lists is meat, poultry, or cheese. The careful shopper is advised to plan meals around grocery store "specials," and to buy extras for freezing when the price is right.

It's important also to remember that a 3 oz. serving of relatively fat broiled sirloin steak will yield 20 grams of protein and a 3 oz. lean hamburger (21 percent fat) also yields 20 grams. Steak's big bonus is psychological, not nutritional.

There are hundreds of recipes for preparing chicken: fried, roasted, grilled, barbecued, stewed—in salads, soups, and casseroles. There are those who believe that no woman can be rich enough, thin enough, or have enough chicken recipes.

For short-term storage of chicken, wrap well in plastic food wrap or bags, or use food-storage containers. Store in coldest part of refrigerator and cook within 2 days.

To freeze whole birds, first remove bag of giblets from body cavity. Wrap bird snugly in moisture/vapor proof freezer wrapping. Wrap and freeze giblets separately. Keep home-frozen chicken 4–6 months at 0°. Cooked frozen chicken keeps well for 2 months.

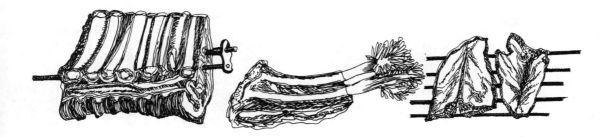

Pasteurized process cheese is a blend of fresh and aged natural cheeses that has been melted, pasteurized, and mixed with an emulsifier. Other ingredients, such as fruits, vegetables, meats, spices, and flavorings may be added. Process cheeses are convenient to use in cooked foods because they melt easily and blend well with other foods.

Pasteurized process cheese *food* is a pasteurized blend of cheeses. It contains less cheese and less fat than process cheese, but has added milk or whey solids. Because it has more moisture it is milder in flavor, softer in texture, spreads more easily, and melts more quickly than regular process cheese. It does not add as much cheese flavor to other foods as natural or process cheese.

Pasteurized process cheese *spread* has even more moisture and less milk fat than process cheese food; otherwise the two are similar. In many recipes the brand name Velveeta is used to indicate the use of process cheese spread. There are a number of other brands that may be successfully substituted for Velveeta.

173

Casseroles

Mastering the art of putting together main-dish casseroles makes it possible for many of us to manage nutritious meals, some measure of gracious dining, and our turn at driving the Little League team to its major game. Most casseroles, or combination dishes, do not require too much last-minute preparation—a bonus in our minimum help kitchens.

For calorie counters, casseroles that are made ahead and chilled provide the opportunity to remove congealed fat easily. When adding herbs to casseroles, exercise restraint; usually ¼ t. of dried herbs per 4 servings. Add herbs to cooked foods the last hour of cooking.

Many critics bemoan the extensive use of canned soups in casseroles. Canned soups, however, because they are made with rice flour, do not separate as easily, or as much, as most home-made sauces. For those who prefer to make their own sauces making up a recipe of White Sauce Mix (see From the Pantry Shelf section in this book) may be a time and energy saver.

Many casseroles freeze well. Plan to cook three times as much of a recipe as usual; eat one portion and freeze two. You will save on both preparation and clean-up time. Cool all combination dishes as quickly as possible before freezing. To hasten cooling, place saucepan of cooked food in a large pan of ice water.

Prepare soups, stews, and casseroles as usual, omitting boiled potatoes. Undercook vegetables to insure against overcooking during the reheating process. Don't completely cook spaghetti, macaroni, or rice; partially cook, or omit entirely, and cook while reheating sauce. Turkey fat becomes rancid more quickly than chicken fat. Use chicken broth for making turkey dishes to freeze.

Don't try freezing potato salad. Since boiled potatoes, mayonnaise, and the whites of hard-cooked eggs are poor choices for the freezer, you are guaranteed a disappointment.

Freezing causes some foods and seasonings to intensify in flavor and others to decrease in strength. Cloves, garlic, black pepper, green peppers, pimiento, and celery increase in flavor, while onions, salt, and chili powder sometimes decrease. Try underseasoning, then adding more herbs and spices, to taste, when heating food.

Use square or rectangular freezer packages, or containers, and you will increase by one-third the amount of food your freezer will hold. Keep freezer space at the proper temperature. Temperatures above 0° drastically reduce storage time, and hasten vitamin and flavor losses. Foods frozen in a 1½ qt. casserole will need about 2 hours to reheat at 375° from the frozen state.

BEEF

ITALIAN RUMP ROAST

Brown an 8 lb. rump roast in hot oven on all sides. Remove from oven and cut long, shallow, across-grain slits into roast. Fill slits with a mixture of grated Romano cheese, salt, and garlic powder. Bake covered at 350° for 3 hr., or until tender. Cool slightly; remove from roaster and slice. Place the slices into the meat juice and hold in very low oven until serving time. May also be served cold. Serves 16.

Mrs. Charles E. Flannagan
Perry County

BRISKET

6 lb. top or bottom round roast beef	4 cloves garlic, minced, or 1 t. garlic powder
Marinade:	1 5-oz. bottle soy sauce
1 15½-oz. can consommé, or 2 beef bouillon cubes in 2 C. water	Sauce:
	4 T. Worcestershire sauce
	1 C. catsup
juice of 1 lemon	4 T. brown sugar

Place beef in marinade made by mixing together soy sauce, consommé, lemon juice, and garlic. Marinade for 12 hr., turning meat occasionally. Pour off marinade; sprinkle meat with paprika and wrap in heavy foil. Bake at 325° until tender, about 4 hr. Cool and refrigerate. Slice cold and arrange vertical slices on strip of aluminum foil. Mix together the 3 sauce ingredients; simmer 10 min. After simmering, add liquid smoke to taste. Drizzle sauce on sliced brisket; separate slices so sauce gets between. Wrap foil tightly around meat and heat at 300° for 1 hr.

Nancy Trott
St. Joseph County

FORGOTTEN RUMP ROAST

5 lb. rump roast (rolled or not)	1 can cream of celery soup
1 pkg. dry onion soup mix	

Place roast on foil; pour celery soup over. Sprinkle on dry soup and wrap tightly. Bake at 325° for 4–5 hr. Test for doneness with fork. When cooked, release juices in foil into pan and thicken for gravy. Add no salt or pepper; it will be well flavored.

Virginia Oard
Vigo County

PEKING ROAST

This recipe makes good use of inexpensive cuts of beef: boiling beef, chuck, brisket, etc. Buy a 3–5 lb. roast and cut slits with a knife completely through the meat. Insert slivers of garlic (optional) and onion into these slits. Put the beef in a bowl and pour 1 C. vinegar over it. Refrigerate for 24–48 hr. When ready to cook, drain off the vinegar, and brown meat in hot oil. Add 2 C. of strong black coffee and 2 C. of water; cover and simmer for 6 hr. on top of stove. About 20 min. before serving, add salt and pepper to taste. *Note:* If more liquid is needed during cooking, add water 1 C. at a time.

Alberta McCormick
White County

SWEDISH FLANK STEAKS

2 lb. flank steak, cut into pieces 3–4" wide and 5" long	½ t. pepper
	1 T. Worcestershire sauce
½ lb. bacon, cut into 4" pieces	1 t. monosodium glutamate (optional)
Stuffing:	Flour mixture:
½ lb. hamburger	½ C. flour
½ lb. sausage	2 t. salt
1 egg, beaten	¼ t. pepper
2 T. chopped parsley	Sauce:
½ small onion, grated	1 C. sliced mushrooms
1 T. light cream	1 12½-oz. can chicken broth
2 T. bread crumbs	3 T. flour
1 t. salt	½ C. milk

Mix together the stuffing ingredients. Spread each steak with stuffing; cross with one strip of bacon. Roll the long way. Tie with string; wrap, label, date, and freeze. Recommended storage time: 6–8 weeks. To serve, defrost flank steaks and coat with mixture of flour, salt, and pepper. Brown in 2–4 T. hot oil; transfer to baking pan. Sauté sliced mushrooms; add chicken broth. Mix flour and milk; blend into broth and cook until thickened. Pour sauce over steaks; cover and bake at 350° for 1–1½ hr. until very tender. Serves 6.

Maxine Harvey
DeKalb County

OVEN-FRIED ROUND STEAK

2 lb. round steak, ½" thick	2 T. milk
1 egg	⅓ C. oil
2 C. finely crushed soda crackers	1 C. water
	1 T. Worcestershire sauce

Cut steak into 8 serving pieces. Beat together the egg and milk. Dip meat into egg mixture; coat with crackers. Brown in hot oil; place in baking dish. Mix water and Worcestershire sauce and pour over meat. Cover and bake at 325° for 1½ hr. Remove cover last 20 min. Serves 8.

Wanda Allen
Wabash County

BARBARA'S BARBECUE

Brown ½ C. of onion, chopped fine, in 1 T. of fat. Brown 2 lb. of hamburger; drain. Mix together the onions and hamburger; add all of the following ingredients and simmer 30–45 min.

½ C. water	½ t. salt
2 T. of vinegar	¼ t. paprika
1 T. Worcestershire sauce	1–2 C. catsup
¼ C. lemon juice	½ T. hot sauce
2 T. brown sugar	1 T. prepared mustard

Serve on hot crusty buns. Serves 10.

Barbara Martin
St. Joseph County

BASIC FROZEN MEATBALLS

2 eggs, beaten	⅓ C. milk
2 C. soft bread crumbs	1½ t. salt
	⅛ t. pepper
⅓ C. finely chopped onion	2 lb. ground beef

Combine all ingredients, except beef. Add beef; mix well and shape into 1" meat balls (makes 48 balls). Place on a baking sheet, cover, and freeze until frozen. Wrap in 2 moisture/vapor proof bags. Seal, label, and freeze. Use in chili, spaghetti, stroganoff meatballs, etc.

Olive Ferguson
Spencer County

SOUR CREAM MEAT LOAF

2 lb. ground beef	⅓ C. milk
1½ C. bread crumbs	1 C. dairy sour cream
2 t. salt	1 C. green onions, sliced
1 t. Worcestershire sauce	4½ oz. jar sliced mushrooms
2 eggs	

In small bowl, combine sour cream, onions, and mushrooms; set aside. In large bowl, combine remaining ingredients; mix well. Shape meat mixture into a loaf on a baking pan; indent 2" "well" in center of loaf. Spoon sour cream mixture into "well." Bake at 350" for 1–1¼ hr. Let stand 10 min. before slicing.

Elizabeth Sadler
Tippecanoe County

ROMA MEAT ROLL

1½ lb. lean ground beef	1 egg
½ C. finely chopped onion	¾ C. cracker crumbs
2 8-oz. cans tomato sauce mixed together with 2 rounded T. grated Parmesan cheese	1 t. salt
	½ t. oregano
	⅛ t. pepper
	2 C. shredded mozzarella cheese

Combine everything but mozzarella cheese, using only ⅓ C. of tomato sauce mixture. Mix well and shape on waxed paper into a flat rectangle about 10x12″. Sprinkle cheese evenly over meat mixture; roll up as for a jelly roll, sealing seams and ends well. Bake at 350° for 1 hr. Drain off excess fat. Pour on remaining tomato sauce mixture; bake an additional 15 min. Serves 6.

Lois Marconnit
Delaware County

POPPIN' FRESH BARBECUPS

¾ lb. ground beef	1 8-oz. can biscuits
½ C. barbecue sauce	¾ C. shredded Cheddar cheese or sliced process cheese food
1 T. instant minced onion	
2 T. brown sugar	

Brown beef; drain. Add barbecue sauce, onion, and brown sugar; set aside. Separate biscuit dough into 12 biscuits. Place 1 biscuit in each of 12 ungreased muffin cups pressing dough up sides to edge of cup. Spoon meat mixture into cups. Sprinkle with cheese. Bake at 400° for 10–12 min., or until golden brown. Recipe ingredients may be prepared, covered with plastic wrap, and refrigerated up to 4 hr. before baking.

Variations: In place of meat mixture, use 1

15-oz. can chili with beans or 1 13-oz. can baked beans and 3 chopped frankfurters.

Lois Janes
Clark County

EASY SLOPPY JOES FOR A CROWD

6 lb. ground beef	1 t. paprika
2 T. vinegar	1 t. chili powder
5 T. Worcestershire sauce	1 16-oz. bottle catsup
1 T. salt	1 16-oz. bottle water
½ t. red pepper (cayenne)	½ t. garlic salt
½ t. pepper	

Brown ground beef. Drain. Place with the other ingedients in a large Dutch oven. Simmer 45 min. Serves 45.

Edna Nolan
Dubois County

GROUND BEEF CASSEROLES

BAKED CHUCK STEAK

1½ lb. ground chuck or hamburger	½ C. flour (optional)
1 can cream of mushroom or onion soup	1 soup can milk
	salt and pepper to taste

Mix together chuck, salt, and pepper. Roll out on floured board (if rolling pin is not used, simply shape into patties on floured board). Cut into squares; brown on both sides in hot fat in skillet. Put in casserole; pour diluted soup over meat. Bake at 350° for 35–40 min. Serves 6.

Rita Robertson	*Cora Brown*
Clay County	*Orange County*

CALICO BEANS

¼ lb. bacon, cut up	1 21-oz. can pork and beans
1 lb. hamburger	½ C. brown sugar
1 medium onion, diced	1–2 T. vinegar
1 16-oz. can kidney beans, drained	½ t. salt
	1 t. dry mustard (optional)
1 16-oz. can lima beans, drained	grated Cheddar cheese
½ C. catsup	(optional)

Brown bacon, hamburger, and onion; drain. Combine meat mixture with beans and turn into a 9x13″ pan. Combine brown sugar, catsup, vinegar, and salt; pour over beans. Bake uncovered at 350° for 45 min. Sprinkle with cheese and bake until cheese melts. Serves 8.

Inez Horn
Randolph County

Helen Wallace
Marion County

BEEF AND NOODLE CASSEROLE

2 lb. ground beef	2 cans tomato soup
1½ C. chopped onion	1 C. water
8 oz. pkg. noodles, cooked and drained	⅓ C. chopped green pepper
	¾ t. salt
2 C. Cheddar cheese, grated	½ C. soft bread crumbs
	3 T. butter

Brown beef and onion; drain. Combine meat and onion with noodles, cheese, soup, water, green pepper, and salt. Put in a 9x13″ baking dish. Combine crumbs and butter and use as a topping. Bake at 350° for 40–45 min.

Olive Ferguson
Spencer County

BEEF AND POTATO SQUARES

1½ lb. ground beef	1 t. salt
1 C. soft bread crumbs	⅛ t. pepper
	3 C. hot mashed potatoes
1 egg, beaten	1 C. grated Cheddar cheese, divided ¾ C. and ¼ C.
½ C. chopped onion	
⅓ C. catsup	

Combine beef, crumbs, egg, onion, catsup, salt, and pepper. Pat mixture into an 8″ square baking dish. Bake at 350° for 30 min. Remove from oven; drain excess fat. Combine potatoes with ¾ C. cheese; spread over meat. Top with ¼ C. cheese and bake 20 min. Cut into squares. Serves 6.
Note: May use sliced process cheese food instead of grated Cheddar.

Betty Foxx
Putnam County

SUNDAY NIGHT CHEDDAR BEEF PIE

1½ lb. ground beef	Topping:
1 egg	½ C. celery slices
⅓ C. chopped onion	2 T. margarine
¾ C. oats	1½ C. sharp Cheddar, shredded
2 T. barbecue sauce	4 oz. can mushrooms, drained
1 t. salt	½ C. buttered crumbs
dash pepper	

Combine the first 7 ingredients and press into bottom and sides of 8″ pie pan. Bake at 350° for 20 min. Drain excess fat; set aside. Sauté celery in margarine. Combine celery, cheese, and mushrooms. Pour into cooled shell and freeze. When reheating, add crumbs and heat in slow oven until piping hot. Serves 6.

Kay Kinnaman
Madison County

CREOLE RICE CASSEROLE

4 slices bacon	1 clove garlic,
1 medium onion,	minced
chopped	1 8-oz. can
½ C. chopped	tomato sauce
green pepper	⅔ C. raisins
1 C. rice,	1 t. salt
uncooked	2 t. chili powder
1–1½ lb. lean	2½ C. shredded
ground beef	Cheddar cheese
1¾ C. water	

Fry bacon until crisp; drain on absorbent paper, crumble, and set aside. In 2 T. of bacon fat, sauté the onion and pepper until tender. Add rice and sauté until golden, stirring constantly. Add ground beef and garlic and cook until meat loses its red color. Add water, tomato sauce, raisins, salt, and chili powder. Heat mixture to a boil, cover skillet, reduce heat, and simmer for 20 min. Put half of rice mixture into a 2 qt. casserole. Sprinkle with half the cheese and half the bacon. Add remainder of rice mixture, bacon, and cheese. Bake at 350° for 15 min.

Sue Childes
Monroe County

HAMBURGER-POTATO CASSEROLE

2 lb. hamburger	½ soup can of
6 potatoes	milk
1 onion	4–5 slices process
1 can cream of	cheese food
mushroom	½ green pepper
soup	salt and pepper

Brown hamburger; drain. Add chopped onion and sauté until tender. Turn into 2 qt. casserole. Peel potatoes and slice over hamburger. Add salt and pepper to taste. Mix soup and milk; pour over potatoes. Cut green pepper into strips and place over casserole; cover and bake at 350° until potatoes are

done—about 50 min. Uncover; remove peppers and place slices of cheese over casserole. Return to oven until cheese melts.

Marian Saalweachter
Posey County

HAMBURGER-ZUCCHINI CASSEROLE

4 C. thinly sliced	½ C. cottage
zucchini,	cheese
cooked tender-	1 C. cooked rice
crisp and	½ C. tomato
drained	sauce
¾ lb. ground	½ t. salt
beef	½ t. dried oreg-
½ C. chopped	ano, crushed
onion	¼ t. pepper
1 clove garlic,	½ C. shredded
minced	Cheddar cheese
1 egg, beaten	

Brown beef, onion, and garlic; drain. Stir rice, tomato sauce, and seasonings into meat mixture. Combine egg and cottage cheese; set aside. Arrange half of zucchini in bottom of 6x10x2" baking dish. Sprinkle with salt (optional). Spoon meat mixture over. Spread cottage cheese over the meat. Top with remaining zucchini. Bake at 350° for 15 min. Sprinkle cheddar cheese around edges of casserole and bake additional 10 min.

Phyllis Ulshafer
Wabash County

LASAGNE

10 oz. lasagne	1 lb. Italian
noodles,	sausage or
cooked,	hamburger
drained, and	1 clove garlic,
rinsed	minced

1 T. basil

1½ t. salt

1 20-oz. can tomatoes

2 6-oz. cans tomato paste

2–3 C. ricotta or cottage cheese

½ C. grated Parmesan or Romano cheese

2 T. parsley flakes

2 beaten eggs

2 t. salt and ½ t. pepper

1 small can mushrooms, drained (optional)

1 lb. mozzarella cheese, sliced very thin

Brown meat; drain. Add next 5 ingredients. Simmer uncovered for 30 min., stirring occasionally. Mix together cottage cheese with remaining ingredients, except mozzarella cheese. Place half of noodles in 13x9x2" pan. Spread with half the cottage cheese mixture and half the meat sauce. Repeat layers. Bake at 375° for about 30 min. Let set before cutting. Serves 12.

Evonne Kuhn
Rush County

NOT QUITE LASAGNE

2 oz. lasagne noodles, cooked and drained

1 lb. ground beef

1 onion, chopped

¼ green pepper, chopped

1 4-oz. can mushrooms, drained

½ t. oregano

½ can tomato soup

6 oz. tomato paste

⅓ C. water

1 T. Worcestershire sauce

4 oz. Cheddar cheese, shredded

Brown beef, onion, and green pepper; drain. Add mushrooms and oregano; set aside. Combine soup, tomato paste, water, and Worcestershire and cook until thick; add to meat mixture. Layer noodles, sauce, and

cheese in baking dish. Bake at 375° for 45 min.

Martha Daniel
Monroe County

CRISPY MACARONI AND CHEESE

3 C. cooked macaroni

1 can celery soup

½ C. milk

½ t. dry mustard

½ lb. ground beef

1½ C. shredded Cheddar cheese

1 can French-fried onions

½ C. Cheddar cheese, shredded

Mix soup, milk, and mustard; set aside. Brown the beef; drain. Mix soup mixture, macaroni, 1½ C. cheese, and ground beef. Bake in a 3 qt. baking dish, at 350° for 20 min. Top with onions and remaining ½ C. cheese; bake 10 min. Serves 6–8.

Mrs. Lewis W. Lafuse
Rush County

MEXICAN CASSEROLE

1 lb. ground beef

1 C. sour cream

⅔ C. mayonnaise

1 C. shredded Cheddar cheese

2 T. chopped onion

2 C. biscuit mix

½ C. cold water

2–3 medium tomatoes, thinly sliced

¾ C. chopped green pepper

Grease 9x13" pan. Brown beef; drain. Mix sour cream, mayonnaise, cheese, and onion together; set aside. Stir biscuit mix and water to form a soft dough. Put dough in pan, pressing dough ½" up sides of pan. Layer beef, tomatoes, and green pepper over dough; spoon sour cream mixture over top. If desired, sprinkle with paprika. Bake at 375° for 25–30 min., or until edges of dough are light brown. Serves 6.

Leona Rhodes
Greene County

TRI-CHEESE MOSTACCIOLI

1 lb. ground beef	8 oz. mostaccioli
½ C. chopped	noodles,
green pepper	cooked,
½ C. chopped	drained
onion	¼ lb. process
16 oz. can	cheese food,
tomatoes	sliced
6 oz. can tomato	2 oz. shredded
paste	Swiss or sharp
¼ C. water	Cheddar cheese
1 bay leaf,	2 oz. shredded
crushed	mozzarella
½ t. salt	cheese
¼ t. pepper	

Brown meat; drain. Add green pepper and onion; cook until tender. Stir in tomatoes, tomato paste, water, and seasonings. Layer half of noodles, meat sauce, ½ cheese slices, and all shredded cheeses in a 9x13" baking dish; repeat layers of noodles and meat sauce. Bake at 350° for 30 min. Top with remaining cheese slices. Continue baking until cheese is melted. Freezes well.

Nancy Wagner
Fountain County

ORIENTAL HAMBURGER CASSEROLE

3 lb. ground beef	⅓ C. water
1 C. chopped	2 7-oz. cans bam-
celery	boo shoots,
1 C. chopped	drained
onion	2 6-oz. pkg.
¾ C. chopped	frozen pea
green pepper	pods, thawed
3 C. water	2 10-oz. pkg.
⅓ C. cornstarch	frozen peas
1 T. sugar	2 3-oz. cans chow
¾ t. ginger	mein noodles
¾ C. soy sauce	

Brown beef, celery, onion, and green pepper; drain. Add the 3 C. water to beef mixture; bring to boiling. Combine cornstarch, sugar, and ginger; blend in soy sauce and the ⅓ C. water. Add to beef mixture; cook and stir until thickened and bubbly. Stir in bamboo shoots and pea pods. Break up frozen peas; add to beef mixture. Turn into 3 1½ qt. casseroles. Cover tightly. Seal, label, and freeze. Bake frozen casseroles covered at 400° for 1½ hr., stirring once or twice during baking. Uncover; top with chow mein noodles and bake 5-10 min. more. (To serve without freezing, simmer until vegetables are tender. Serve over chow mein noodles.)

Betty Sendmeyer
Putnam County

BAKED SPAGHETTI

1½ lb. ground	1 large stalk cel-
beef	ery, chopped
1 32-oz. can	salt and pepper to
tomato juice	taste
1 12-oz. can	grated Parmesan
tomato puree	cheese
2 onions,	1 10-oz. pkg.
chopped	spaghetti,
1 green pepper,	cooked 7 min.
chopped	(not quite done)
2 T. chili powder	

Brown beef; drain. Combine remaining ingredients, except cheese and spaghetti; cook together 30 min. Pour spaghetti into 9x13" greased pan and cover with the cooked ground beef; pour tomato juice mixture over all. Sprinkle generously with cheese. Bake at 375° for 1 hr.

Faye Hill
Monroe County

PIZZAS

PIZZA (FROZEN)

Topping:
1½ lb. ground beef
1½ lb. bulk sausage
1 green pepper, chopped
1 C. mushrooms, sliced (optional)
1 15-oz. can pizza sauce

Brown beef, pepper, and mushrooms; add salt and pepper. Italian spices (oregano, etc.) may be added if desired. Add pizza sauce; set aside to cool.

Crust:
1 pkg. dry yeast
1 C. warm water (105–115°)
1 t. sugar
1 t. salt
2 T. vegetable oil
2½ C. flour
2 C. shredded mozzarella cheese

Mix yeast in warm water; add sugar, salt, and salad oil. Add the flour last; set aside for 5 min. Divide dough in half; roll out and spread in 2 12″ pizza pans. Bake at 425° until half-done, about 8 min. Spread with topping. Sprinkle with cheese. Wrap in foil and freeze. Bake frozen at 450° for 15 min.

Maxine Spenner
LaPorte County

PIZZA BURGERS (1)

1 lb. hamburger
pepperoni, sliced
½ t. salt
dash pepper
½ t. oregano
¾ C. pizza sauce
mozzarella cheese, shredded
English muffins or hamburger rolls

Brown hamburger; drain. Add salt, pepper, and oregano. Mix with pepperoni, cheese, and pizza sauce. Split rolls or muffins in half; spoon mixture on top and broil until cheese melts. Serves 12.

Variation: use ½ lb. sausage and ½ lb. hamburger.

Martha Clabo
Clark County

PIZZA BURGERS (2)

¾ C. lukewarm water (105–115°)
1 pkg. dry yeast
2½ C. biscuit mix
First topping:
1 lb. ground beef, browned and drained
2 C. tomato sauce
¼ C. chopped onions
½ C. green pepper, chopped
salt and pepper to taste
Second topping:
1 t. oregano
2 C. shredded mozzarella cheese

Dissolve yeast in water; add biscuit mix and beat. Turn onto a floured surface and knead until smooth. Let stand 20 min. Divide dough into 6 balls. Roll each ball out to ¼″ and place on greased cookie sheet. Mix first topping ingredients together and spread on top of each pizza. Sprinkle tops with mixture of oregano and mozzarella cheese. Bake at 400° for 20 min., or until crust is brown. Serves 6.

Frances Copes
Franklin County

EASY DEEP-DISH PIZZA

3 C. biscuit mix
¾ C. water
1 lb. ground beef
½ C. chopped onion
½ t. salt
2 cloves garlic, crushed
1 15-oz. can tomato sauce
1 t. Italian seasoning
1 4½-oz. jar mushrooms
½ C. green pepper, chopped
2 C. shredded mozzarella cheese

Lightly grease jelly roll pan or cookie sheet. Mix biscuit mix and water until soft dough forms; shape into a ball and knead 20 times. Pat dough on bottom and up sides of pan with floured hands. Brown beef with onion, salt, and garlic; drain. Layer meat mixture over dough. Mix tomato sauce and Italian seasoning; spread evenly over meat layer. Top with mushrooms, green pepper, and cheese. Bake at 425° until crust is golden brown, abut 20 min. Serves 8.

Betty Zarse
White County

QUICK AND DELICIOUS PIZZA

1 C. warm water	1 15-oz. can pizza
1 pkg. hot roll	sauce
mix	8 oz. grated moz-
2 t. salad oil	zarella cheese

Topping of your choice: sliced mushrooms, chopped green peppers, chopped onions, browned sausage, or hamburger, ham, pepperoni, etc. Prepare hot roll mix, according to pkg. instructions. Knead 3–5 min., cover with bowl, and let rest for 10 min. Divide dough in half; roll each into 12" circle, and spread in pizza pan. Brush with oil, spread with sauce, add toppings, and sprinkle with cheese. Bake at 425° for 20–30 min. Serves 12.

Sherry Dowell
Clay County

CHICKEN AND CHICKEN CASSEROLES

BAKED CHICKEN

1 stick butter or	1 egg, slightly
margarine	beaten

2 T. water	¼ t. garlic pow-
1 2½–3 lb. frying	der, optional
chicken, cut-up	1 t. onion salt,
¼ C. grated Par-	optional
mesan cheese,	½ t. paprika,
optional	optional
1–1¼ C. potato	½ t. salt
flakes	pepper to taste

Melt butter in shallow 9x13" baking pan. In separate bowl, combine egg and water; set aside. Mix potato flakes, seasonings, and cheese together. Dip chicken pieces in egg mixture; roll in potato flake-cheese mixture. Place skin side down in melted butter, turn, and bake skin side up at 400° for 40–60 min.

Eva and Marie Johnson
Delaware County

CHICKEN LOAF NORMANDY

2 C. elbow	2 4-oz. pkg.
macaroni	spiced cheese
3 T. butter	with garlic and
½ C. chopped	herbs, softened
onion	and cubed
3 C. shredded	½ C. heavy or
zucchini (1 lb.)	whipping cream
3 C. minced	1¼ t. salt
cooked chicken	⅛ t. pepper

Cook macaroni according to package directions, but cook only 5–6 min. Grease 9x5" loaf pan; set aside. Sauté onion and zucchini in butter until vegetables are tender. Combine vegetables with remaining ingredients except macaroni; stir until well-mixed. Fold in macaroni; pour into prepared pan. Cover and bake at 375° for 30–35 min., or until hot and bubbly. Cool 10 min.; invert onto serving platter. Cut into slices. Serves 8.

Ruth Libkie
Monroe County

BUTTERMILK CHICKEN

1 frying chicken, cut up	¼ C. butter or margarine
1½ C. buttermilk	1 can cream of
¾ C. flour	mushroom or
1½ t. seasoned	cream of
salt	chicken soup
¼ t. pepper	

Dip chicken in ½ C. buttermilk; roll in mixture of flour, salt, and pepper. Melt butter in a 13x9x2″ pan. Put chicken in pan, skin side down and bake uncovered for 30 min. Turn chicken and bake 15 min. more. Blend remaining 1 C. buttermilk with the soup; pour around chicken. Bake 15 min. more, or until done. Serves 6.

Eva K. Graves
Delaware County

CHICKEN SUPERB

4–5 lb. chicken	1 t. rosemary
1 onion, diced	⅛ t. pepper
1 sprig parsley, chopped	1 C. half and half
½ t. salt	1 16-oz. can peas, drained
5 T. flour	½ C. margarine
1 carrot, diced	1 4-oz. can mush-
1 stalk celery, chopped	rooms, drained

In large pot, simmer chicken with onion, parsley, carrot, celery, rosemary, salt, and pepper until tender. Drain, reserving 1½ C. chicken stock. Skin and bone chicken; set aside. Make sauce by blending flour with ¼ C. stock. Slowly stir in the remaining broth and half and half. Cook over medium heat until thick, stirring constantly. Season with salt and pepper. Place chicken in sauce and freeze. When ready to use, thaw chicken mixture; add peas, mushrooms, and mar-

garine. Cook until flavors have blended well, about 15 min. Serve over rice.

Jill Ellenberger
Wells County

CHICKEN CORDON BLEU

4 whole chicken breasts, split skinned, and boned	2 T. olive oil
	1 clove garlic, split
	1 T. butter
4 slices Swiss cheese	1–1½ C. dry white wine
4 thin slices ham	chopped parsley

Pound breasts until thin. Roll ½ slice cheese in ½ slice ham; place one roll on each chicken piece. Fold chicken in half, lapping edges, and secure with toothpick. Sauté breasts in garlic-seasoned hot oil and butter. When cheese begins to melt from the centers, add wine and simmer until done, about 30 min.

Mary Mulloy
Floyd County

SWISS ENCHILADAS

1 small onion, chopped	2 C. cooked chicken, chopped
1 T. oil	salt to taste
1 garlic clove, crushed	1½ C. half and half
1 C. tomato sauce	6 6″ tortillas
1 canned green chili, chopped	¼ lb. Monterey Jack or Swiss
3 chicken bouil- lon cubes	cheese, grated

Sauté onion in hot oil until tender. Add garlic clove, tomato sauce, chili, chicken, and salt; simmer 10 min. Dissolve bouillon cubes in hot cream. Dip each tortilla in hot cream mix; cover one side generously with chicken filling and roll up. Arrange rolls in baking dish and pour remaining cream mixture over them. Top with grated cheese; bake 350° for 30 min. The cream thickens to become a delicious sauce. The top may be garnished with avocado slices, sliced ripe olives, etc.

Lois Marcounit
Delaware County

CHICKEN CASSEROLE

cooked, cubed chicken (1 whole chicken)	1 egg
	3 slices day-old bread, cut in cubes
1 can mushroom soup with ½ can water	½ stick margarine, melted
1 can chicken noodle soup with ½ can water	cracker crumbs or crushed corn flakes (15 crackers)

Beat egg; blend in soups and water. Add bread cubes and chicken. Don't add any salt. Pour into buttered casserole. Top with cracker crumbs which have been stirred in melted butter. Bake at 350° for 45 min. Serves 6–8.

Virginia Bosstick
Dearborn County

CHINESE CHICKEN CASSEROLE

1 2½-oz. jar whole mushrooms, drained	½ C. milk
1½ C. diced celery	1 8½-oz. can peas, drained
¼ C. sliced green onions	1 C. diced cooked chicken
3 T. butter, melted	½ C. salted cashews
1 can cream of mushroom soup	⅛ t. pepper
	1 3-oz. can chow mein noodles, half reserved for topping

Sauté mushrooms, celery, and onions in butter. Combine all ingredients in a 1½ qt. casserole. Top with reserved noodles. Bake at 375° for 20-25 min. Serves 4.

Lorraine Cooper
LaPorte County

CHICKEN AND CHEESE BAKE

8 oz. lasagne noodles, cooked	⅔ C. milk
½ C. chopped green peppers	4 oz. can mushrooms, drained
½ C. chopped onion	¼ C. pimiento
3 t. butter	3 C. diced cooked chicken
1 can cream of chicken soup	2 C. grated sharp Cheddar
½ t. basil (optional)	½ C. Parmesan cheese

Sauté green pepper and onion in butter; stir in soup, milk, mushrooms, pimiento, and basil. Place half the cooked noodles in a 9x13" baking dish. Top with half of chicken, mushroom mixture, and cheese. Repeat the layer and bake at 350° for 1½ hr. Serves 10.

Loretta Bossung
White County

CHICKEN-BROCCOLI CASSEROLE

1 fryer, cooked and cut into bite-sized pieces	½ rounded C. mayonnaise
1 bunch fresh broccoli	1 t. curry
	1 T. lemon juice
1 can cream of chicken soup	1 8-oz. can water chestnuts, drained and sliced
½ rounded C. dairy sour cream	2–3 oz. sharp Cheddar, grated

Cook broccoli stems 5 min.; add broccoli heads and cook additional 7 min. Rinse with cold water; drain. Place broccoli in bottom of greased 9x13" baking dish; layer chicken on top. Mix together soup, mayonnaise, sour cream, curry, lemon juice, and water chestnuts; spread on top of chicken. Sprinkle on cheese; bake at 350° for 30 min.

Ingelore Welsh
Monroe County

CHICKEN RICE CASSEROLE

2 C. cooked chicken, cut up	1 can cream of celery soup
2 C. cooked rice	2 small onions, diced
½ C. slivered almonds (optional)	1 C. mayonnaise
	2 t. lemon juice
1 can cream of chicken soup	¾ C. diced celery
	1 t. salt

Mix all ingredients together; place in greased 2 qt. casserole. Sprinkle top with potato chips; bake at 375° for 1 hr. Let stand 15 min. Serves 10.

Note: 1 pkg. of frozen peas and 1 can drained mushrooms may be added.

Emma L. Burris
Monroe County

CHICKEN AND RICE CASSEROLE

¾ stick margarine	1 can cream of mushroom soup
10–12 chicken pieces	1½ C. Minute Rice
1 can cream of chicken soup	salt, pepper, garlic salt, and
1 can cream of celery soup	paprika to taste

Melt margarine in 9x13" casserole dish. Mix undiluted soups and rice together; add to margarine and mix. Lay chicken pieces on top. Sprinkle with seasonings. Do not cover. Bake at 250–300° for 2½–3 hr. Serves 5–6.

Barbara Pell
Brown County

CHICKEN STUFFING CASSEROLE (1)

2 large carrots, sliced	¼ C. flour
	1 2-oz. jar chopped pimiento
8 oz. Cheddar cheese, shredded	1 8-oz. pkg. seasoned stuffing mix
1 10¾ oz. can chicken broth	
¼ C. butter	¼ C. butter, melted
4 C. diced cooked chicken	

Cook and drain carrots. Melt ¼ C. butter in saucepan; stir in flour. Add broth; stir until thickened. Add cheese and stir until cheese melts. Stir in chicken, carrots, and pimiento. Spread in shallow 2 qt. casserole. Mix stuffing with melted butter; spread over chicken mixture. Bake at 375° for 30 min. Serves 8.

Janice Sebasty
St. Joseph County

CHICKEN AND STUFFING CASSEROLE (2)

3–4 C. cooked, diced chicken	1 8-oz. pkg. chicken stuffing mix
1 can cream of chicken soup	1 t. celery seed
3 C. broth	¼ C. diced onion

Place chicken in a greased 8x12" casserole. Sprinkle celery seed and onion over chicken. Combine soup with ½ C. of broth and spread over chicken. Combine stuffing mix with remaining broth; spread on top. Cover with foil and bake ½ hr. at 375°. Uncover and bake additional ½ hr.

Hallie Tyson
Greene County

CHICKEN SUPREME

2 cans cream of mushroom soup	1 2-oz. jar chopped pimiento, drained
2 cans cream of chicken soup	2 C. chopped celery
1 small can evaporated milk	3 C. cubed chicken
4 C. Chinese noodles	1 4-oz. can mushrooms, drained
1 green pepper, chopped	¼ C. slivered almonds

Turn contents of cans of soup into large mixing bowl; blend in milk. Add remaining ingredients. Place mixture in buttered 13x9x2″ glass baking dish. Bake uncovered 1 hr. and 15 min. at 350°. Serve over Chinese noodles or rice. Serves 12.

Myra Crosier
Hancock County

CHICKEN TETRAZZINI

6 whole chicken breasts, cut in half	2 cans cream of chicken soup
1½ lb. mushrooms	2 cans cream of celery soup
4 T. butter	1 pint dairy sour cream
1 T. lemon juice	⅔ C. Parmesan cheese, grated
1 grated onion	¾ lb. spaghetti, cooked, drained, and cooled
1 t. garlic salt	
1½ T. Worcestershire sauce	
1 t. oregano	
⅓ C. celery	

Sauté mushrooms in butter for 3–5 min.,

shaking the pan frequently; add to cooled spaghetti. Combine soups and seasonings and heat; remove from heat and stir in sour cream and sherry. Add ½ the sauce to the spaghetti and mushrooms; place the spaghetti in a greased baking dish. Place chicken breasts on top and cover with rest of sauce. Sprinkle top with cheese. Bake at 325° for 1 hr. Serves 12.

Ruth Plumbeck
St. Joseph County

POTATO AND CHICKEN CASSEROLE

4 C. sliced raw potatoes	1 T. flour
1 C. cooked chicken, cut into chunks	1 t. salt
	¼ t. pepper
	2 T. butter
1 can cream of chicken soup	potato chips or bread crumbs for topping
½ C. milk	

Grease 2½ qt. casserole dish; arrange alternate layers of potatoes and chicken. Add salt, pepper, and flour. On low heat, melt butter and add soup and milk; heat until blended. Pour soup mixture over other ingredients. Top with crushed potato chips or bread crumbs. Bake covered for 45 min.; remove cover and bake 15–30 min. longer. Serves 6.

Mary Ham
Daviess County

PORK AND PORK CASSEROLES

SAUSAGE-SAUERKRAUT BALLS

8 oz. bulk sausage	1 14-oz. can kraut, drained and squeezed dry
¼ C. finely chopped onion	

2 T. dry bread crumbs	pinch of garlic salt
1 3-oz. pkg. cream cheese	1/4 C. flour
1/4 t. pepper	2 well-beaten eggs
2 T. parsley (fresh or dried)	1/4 C. milk
1 t. prepared mustard	1 C. bread crumbs

Brown sausage and onion; drain. Add kraut and 2 T. bread crumbs. Combine cream cheese, parsley, mustard, garlic salt, and pepper; stir into sauerkraut mixture; chill. Shape into balls; coat with flour. Add milk to beaten eggs. Dip balls into egg-milk mixture and roll in bread crumbs. Fry in deep fat to brown, about 1 min. Bake at 375° for 15–20 min. Good with horse-radish or mustard sauce.

Note: After deep frying, you can freeze. Bake when ready to serve.

Patsy Kirkendall
Howard County

CASSEROLE SAVOY

1 1/2 lb. lean pork shoulder, cubed	1 8-oz. pkg. medium noodles, cooked and drained
1 onion, chopped	
1 C. celery, diced	
1 small can tomato sauce	1 can mushroom soup
1 C. water	1 10-oz. pkg. frozen peas, cooked
1 t. salt	
1/2–1 t. pepper	
1 t. thyme	

Sauté pork shoulder in hot vegetable oil; add celery, and cook 4 min. Add onion; cook 1 min. Add tomato sauce, salt, pepper, and thyme; cook 45 min. Mix all ingredients together; place in 2 qt. casserole. Bake at 375° for 30 min.

Mary Lambert
LaPorte County

HAM AND BROCCOLI BAKE

1 8-oz. jar Cheez Whiz	2 10-oz. pkg. frozen chopped broccoli
2 cans cream of chicken soup	4 C. diced cooked ham
1/2 C. milk	2 C. instant rice
1/2 C. chopped onion	1/2 t. Worcestershire sauce
4 T. butter	

In large bowl, blend cheese spread, soup, and milk. Sauté onion in butter until tender. Cook broccoli until almost tender; drain. Add onion, broccoli, ham, rice, and Worcestershire to soup-cheese mixture. Turn into 2 1 1/2 qt. casseroles. Cover tightly. Seal, label, and freeze. Bake frozen casserole, covered at 400° for 1 1/2 hr. Uncover and continue cooking for 30 min. Bake unfrozen casserole at 350° for 35–40 min. Each casserole serves 4–5.

Rita Carpenter
Pulaski County

HAM AND POTATO STRATA

2 C. diced cooked ham	1 small onion, chopped and sautéed (optional)
1 1/2 C. diced Velveeta	
1 4-oz. can pimientos, drained	6 medium potatoes
2 T. milk	1 can Cheddar cheese soup

Scrub potatoes and remove bad spots; dice with peelings on. Cook in water until tender; drain. Combine ham, cheese, pimiento, and onion (if used) and spread mixture in buttered 8x12″ baking dish. Cover with cooked potatoes. Pour soup mixed with milk over top. Bake uncovered at 350° for 30 min.

Zada McMillian
Grant County

MAIN DISH ACCOMPANIMENTS

WHIPPED BUTTER

1 lb. margarine	1 t. butter flavor-
1 C. buttermilk	ing (optional)
1 C. vegetable oil	dash of salt

Combine ingredients and beat until mixture looks like whipped cream. Refrigerate.

Hazel Henley   *Lola Thomas*
Brown County   *Clay County*

CHEESABUTTER

1 C. butter,	¼ t. pepper
softened	2 C. Cheddar
1½ t. Italian herb	cheese,
seasoning	shredded
¼ t. garlic	2 t. lemon juice
powder	

In mixer bowl, beat together butter and seasonings with whip or electric mixer at medium speed until fluffy, 3–5 min. Throughly blend cheese and lemon juice into butter mixture. Portion as desired, or shape into a log, using 2 C. of mixture for log approximately 12″ long and 1½″ in diameter. Wrap in plastic wrap; store in refrigerator. To serve, cut in ½″ thick slices. Makes 2 C.

Hot Serving Suggestions: English muffin spread—broiled; instant garlic bread—warm oven; drizzled onto baked potatoes; pour—over sauce for Brussels sprouts, broad beans, broccoli; center of double-patty burger—edges sealed before cooking; dressing for fish sticks; glorified London broil and other "dry" cuts.

Cold Serving Suggestions: on rye rolls—split; pumpernickel open-face sandwiches; melba rye rounds; canapés—filling stretcher;

lunchmeat roll-ups—mixed with bread crumb stuffing.

Barbara Brookshire
Putnam County

SHAKE AND BAKE MIXTURE FOR FRIED CHICKEN

1 C. flour	¼ t. pepper
2 t. salt	¼ t. garlic salt
1 t. paprika	milk

Put dry ingredients in a bag; dip pieces of chicken in milk, then drop in bag; shake well and fry.

Wanneta Cooper
Steuben County

SKINNY DIP COATING FOR CHICKEN, CHOPS, ETC.

1 9-oz. pkg.	1 T. celery salt
bread crumbs	1 T. dried celery
½ C. vegetable	leaves
oil	½–1 T. pepper
1 T. salt	1 T. minced dried
1 T. paprika	onion

Mix all ingredients together. Rinse meat with water and dip in mix. Cook as usual; either fry or bake. Keep unused portion of mix in freezer.

Mrs. Louise P. Walker
Dearborn County

SWEET-SOUR HOT MUSTARD

1 C. dry mustard	8 T. whipping
1 C. vinegar	cream
1 C. sugar	¼ C. white wine
2 eggs, beaten	(medium to dry)
3 T. butter	

Mix mustard and vinegar together; allow to "sit" overnight at room temperature. Add remaining ingredients to mustard mixture. Cook over low heat, stirring constantly, for about 20 min., or until the consistency of custard. After cooking, refrigerate in covered jar.

Joan Abbott
Monroe County

BARBECUE SAUCE

2 T. butter	2 T. vinegar
2 small onions,	1 C. catsup
diced	1 T. dry mustard
2 T. brown sugar	1 T. celery seed

Sauté onions in butter until light brown. Add all other ingredients and bring to a boil; simmer for 15 min.

Nina Holle
Cass County

BARBEQUE SAUCE FOR CHICKEN

1 lb. margarine,	4 T. Worcester-
melted	shire sauce
1 pint vinegar	1 t. garlic powder
2 oz. Accent	1 t. pepper
4 T. salt	

Heat all ingredients thoroughly to dissolve spices. Brush on chicken. Sufficient for 3–4 chickens.

Ethel Green
Steuben County

ROSÉ STEAK SAUCE

2 beef bouillon	1 C. rosé wine
cubes	2 T. catsup
½ C. boiling	¼ t. thyme
water	1 clove garlic
2 T. cornstarch	½ C. thinly sliced
¼ C. melted	green onions
butter	

Dissolve bouillon cubes in boiling water. Blend cornstarch with melted butter and stir in bouillon and wine. Add catsup, thyme, and garlic and cook, stirring constantly until thickened. Reduce heat; cover and continue cooking 10 min. Add onion and continue cooking 5 min. Serve hot. Makes 1 C.

Sheila Whitehead
Clay County

BIG MATCH SPECIAL SAUCE

⅓ C. creamy	1 C. mayonnaise
French dressing	1 T. sugar
¼ C. sweet	¼ T. pepper
pickle relish,	1 t. dry minced
undrained	onion

Blend all ingredients together and keep refrigerated in covered container. Delicious on hamburgers or fish. Makes 2 C.

Kitty A. Garnand
Marshall County

TERIYAKI SAUCE

1 C. soy sauce	2 T. fresh ginger,
5 C. water	grated; or 1 T.
5 T. sugar	powdered
1 T. salt	ginger
2 T. fresh diced	1 T. black pepper
garlic	

Dissolve sugar, salt, and pepper in soy sauce and water; mix all ingredients together and soak 12–13 chops overnight (6–8 hr.) for best results. Grill outdoors, or broil in oven.

Beverly Givens
Madison County

THE SWEET SHOP

Desserts

For many of us something special to eat still means something sweet. In spite of all our best intentions we tend to reward ourselves, and others, with sinfully sweet and rich foods. Do plan your desserts so that they complement a meal. Surely if sweets are not a three times a day occurence we will be forgiven?

When recipes call for sour milk and you don't have any, put 1 T. lemon juice or white vinegar in a measuring cup and add milk to make 1 cup. Stir, and let mixture clabber for about 5 minutes.

LEMON BISQUE

1 13-oz. can evaporated milk	⅓ C. honey
	⅛ t. salt
	3 T. lemon juice
1 3 oz. pkg. lime or lemon gelatin	1 grated lemon rind
	1½ C. vanilla
1 ¼ C. boiling water	wafer crumbs (3 doz.)

Thoroughly chill can of milk. Dissolve gelatin in boiling water; add honey, salt, lemon juice, and rind. Cool until mixture is partially set. Beat milk until it is stiff. Whip gelatin mixture into whipped milk. Spread half of crumbs in 9x13" pan; pour lemon mixture over crumbs. Top with remaining crumbs and refrigerate.

Note: Gelatin flavors may be varied. Various fruits may be added, if desired. Also, evaporated milk whips easier if chilled in freezer tray until ice crystals form around the edge.

Donna Jo Brizendine
Morgan County

CRANBERRY MARSHMALLOW CREAM

1 lb. fresh or frozen cranberries, ground	1 C. sugar
	1 10½-oz. bag miniature marshmallows
1 20-oz. can crushed pineapple, drained	
	2 C. heavy cream, whipped

Mix together cranberries, pineapple, and sugar in large bowl. Fold marshamllows into whipped cream. Fold whipped cream mixture into cranberry mixture; chill until serving time. Makes 20 (½ C.) servings.

Note: If you prepare recipe a day or two ahead, chill cream and cranberry mixtures separately. Fold together before serving.

Gladys Armstrong
Lawrence County

RHUBARB CRUMBLES

1 C. sifted flour	1 t. cinnamon
¾ C. uncooked oatmeal	4 C. rhubarb, diced
1 C. brown sugar, firmly packed	2 T. cornstarch
	1 C. sugar
½ C. melted butter	1 C. water
	1 t. vanilla

Mix together the flour, oatmeal, sugar, butter, and cinnamon. Press ½ the mixture into a 9" square baking pan and cover with rhubarb. Combine cornstarch, sugar, water, and vanilla; cook until thick and clear. Pour over rhubarb. Top with remaining crumbs. Bake at 350° for 1 hr. Cut into squares and serve warm.

Florine Wagoner   *Loretta Mueller*
Rush County   *LaPorte County*

APRICOT AND PINEAPPLE DESSERT

1 8-oz. can crushed pineapple (do not drain)	1 3-oz. pkg. orange gelatin
	1 8-oz. pkg. cream cheese, softened
¼–¾ C. sugar	
2 4¾-oz. jars strained apricot baby food	1 9-oz. carton frozen whipped topping

Heat pineapple and gelatin until gelatin dissolves. Remove from heat; add sugar, baby food, and cream cheese. Mix well, but do not beat. Chill until lightly thickened. Fold in whipped topping and spoon into 8" pan. Sprinkle with pecans and chill until firm. Serves 9.

Mary Jane Reuter
Lawrence County

Variation: Use 6 oz. pkg. apricot gelatin and 20 oz. can crushed pineapple instead of 3 oz. orange gelatin and 8 oz. can pineapple. Chill and whip one large can evaporated milk and substitute for frozen whipped topping.

Myrna Soper
Union County

APPLE DESSERT

1 box yellow cake mix	½ C. brown sugar
⅓ C. butter or margarine, softened	½ C. chopped walnuts
	1 t. cinnamon
2 eggs	1 C. sour cream
1 can apple pie filling	1 t. vanilla

Combine cake mix, butter, and one egg; mix until crumbly. Press mixture into ungreased 9x13″ pan; spread with pie filling. Combine brown sugar, nuts, and cinnamon; sprinkle over apple layer. In small bowl, blend sour cream with remaining egg and vanilla; pour over sugar mixture. Bake at 350° for 40–50 min.

Elizabeth Sadler
Tippecanoe County

CHOCOLATE ECLAIR DESSERT

Filling:	Frosting:
1 lb. pkg. graham crackers	2 T. margarine
2 3-oz. pkg. instant French vanilla pudding mix	2 oz. chocolate, melted
	2 T. white corn syrup
3 C. milk	2 T. milk
1 9-oz. carton frozen whipped topping, thawed	1 t. vanilla extract
	1½ C. powdered sugar
sliced bananas (optional)	

Grease a 9x13x2″ baking dish; line the bottom of dish with whole graham crackers. Combine pudding mix and milk in a large bowl; beat until thickened. Fold whipped topping into pudding mixture. Pour ½ pudding mixture over graham cracker layer in pan. Top with another layer of graham crackers. Pour remaining pudding mixture over crackers; top with another layer of graham crackers. Refrigerate. Combine all frosting ingredients in a large mixing bowl; beat well until of spreading consistency. Spread over top of last graham cracker layer; chill at least 24 hr. Serves 16.

Virginia Seitz   *Kay Peas*
LaPorte County   *Wabash County*

PINEAPPLE TAPIOCA DESSERT

¼ C. minute tapioca	1½ T. lemon juice
¾ C. sugar	⅓ C. diced orange sections
⅛ t. salt	
½ C. pineapple syrup	1 C. drained, crushed pineapple
1 C. water	
½ C. orange juice	

Combine tapioca, sugar, salt, pineapple syrup, and water in saucepan. Heat to boiling, stirring constantly. Cook until tapioca is clear. Remove from heat and add orange and lemon juice; stir well. Add fruit and chill. Serves 6.

Mable Heidegger
Jay County

BLUEBERRY OR CHERRY SURPRISE

Pan lining:	Filling:
18–20 graham crackers	1 3-oz. pkg. lemon gelatin
¼ lb. margarine, melted	1 C. hot water
	4 T. lemon juice

1 8-oz. pkg.
   cream cheese,
   softened
1 C. sugar
1 t. vanilla
1 13-oz. can
   evaporated
   milk

Topping:
1 small pkg.
   lemon gelatin
1 C. hot water
1 can blueberry
   or cherry pie
   filling

Roll graham crackers into crumbs and add margarine. Line a 9x13" pan; chill. Dissolve gelatin in hot water; add lemon juice and cool until partially set. Mix cream cheese, sugar, and vanilla together; combine with gelatin. Thoroughly chill milk. Whip until very stiff. Fold into gelatin mixture. Pour into prepared pan and refrigerate for 1 hr. To prepare topping, dissolve gelatin in hot water. Refrigerate until syrupy, but not too thick. Add blueberry or cherry pie filling. Spread over filling and refrigerate.

Gail Dailey
LaPorte County

HIMMEL FRITTER

2 eggs
1 C. sugar
2 heaping T. flour
2 t. baking
   powder
½ lb. dates,
   chopped

½ lb. nuts,
   chopped
5–6 oranges
4–5 bananas
1 C. whipped
   cream

Beat eggs; add sugar, flour, baking powder, dates, and nuts. Bake 30 min. at 400°. When cool, crumble into oblong pan. Place orange slices (sweetened to taste) and bananas over date mixture. Top with whipped cream. Serves 12.

Note: Date mixture can be made 2 or 3 days ahead and stored in an airtight container.

Jeanette Shaw
Randolph County

FRUIT PIZZA

1 pkg. "slice and
   bake" sugar
   cookies
½–1 C. pow-
   dered sugar
9 oz. frozen
   whipped top-
   ping, thawed
1 8-oz. pkg.
   cream cheese

your choice of
   fruit (straw-
   berries, ba-
   nanas, drained
   crushed pine-
   apple, man-
   darin oranges)

Slice cookies, press into a pizza pan; bake 10–12 min. and cool. Blend sugar and cream cheese; mix and spread on first layer. Make a layer of fruit and finish with a layer of whipped topping.

Lisa King   *Doris Hellems*
Henry County   *Madison County*

Variations:

(1) With srawberries, use 1 pkg. strawberry glaze over strawberries before adding whipped topping.

Patty Breeden
Monroe County

(2) In place of whipped topping, spread fruit with orange marmalade.

Doris Spaulding
Washington County

ANGEL PUDDING

1 C. sugar
2 eggs
4 rounded T.
   flour
1 t. baking
   powder
1 C. nuts,
   chopped

1 C. chopped
   dates
1 13-oz. carton
   frozen whipped
   topping
1 C. miniature
   marshmallows

Mix first 6 ingredients together; spread in a thin layer on a cookie sheet. Bake at 325°

for 20 min. Cool; crumble into pieces. Fold into whipped topping; fold in marshmallows.

Dorothy McGill
Howard County

OZARK PUDDING

1 egg	1 t. vanilla
¾ C. sugar	½ C. chopped
3 T. flour	nuts
1¼ t. baking	½ C. pared and
powder	chopped apples
⅛ t. salt	whipped cream

Beat egg; add sugar gradually, beating until smooth. Stir together flour, baking powder, and salt; blend with egg mixture. Stir in vanilla. Add nuts and apple; mix well. Pour into a buttered 9″ shallow pie plate and bake at 350° for 20–25 min. Serve with whipped cream or ice cream. Serves 4–5.

Wilma M. Linville
Decatur County

WALNUT PUDDING

1 C. brown sugar	1 C. brown sugar
1 C. sugar	1 C. milk
2½ C. water	2 C. flour
2 T. butter	2 t. baking
Cake mixture:	powder
2 T. butter	1 C. walnuts

Bring first 4 ingredients to a boil; pour into ungreased 9x13″ cake pan. Mix cake mixture ingredients together and spoon onto the liquid in pan. Bake at 350° for 35–40 min.

Vera Biery
Greene County

STRAWBERRY-RHUBARB PUFF

1 16-oz. pkg. fro-	1 10-oz. pkg. fro-
zen rhubarb,	zen strawber-
thawed	ries, thawed
½ C. sugar	⅓ C. vegetable
2 C. flour	oil
2 T. sugar	⅔ C. milk
3 t. baking	butter
powder	2 T. sugar
1 t. salt	1 t. cinnamon

Mix rhubarb, strawberries, and ½ C. sugar in an ungreased 9x9x2″ pan. Place in the oven at 350°. Measure flour, 2 T. sugar, baking powder, and salt into bowl. Pour oil and milk into measuring cup (do not stir together). Pour all at once into flour mixture. Stir until mixture cleans side of bowl and forms a ball. Drop dough by 9 spoonfuls onto hot fruit. Make an indentation in each biscuit; dot with butter. Mix 2 T. sugar and the cinnamon; sprinkle on biscuits. Bake at 350° for 20–25 min. Serve warm. Serves 9.

EH Club
Delaware County

APPLE STRUDEL WITH WHITE ICING

2 C. flour	2 T. butter
½ t. salt	⅛ t. cinnamon
2 T. sugar	2½ C. peeled,
4 t. baking	cored, sliced
powder	apples
6 T. shortening	White Icing:
⅔ C. milk	2 T. hot water
Filling:	1½ C. confec-
¼ C. brown	tioners' sugar
sugar	½ t. vanilla

Sift flour, salt, sugar, and baking powder; cut in shortening and add milk to make a soft dough. Turn out on floured board and knead dough gently. Roll out into a rectangle ¼″ thick. For the filling: Spread the butter on the dough; mix remaining ingredients together and spread over butter. Roll jelly roll fashion; curve into a semicircle. Bake at 400° for 30 min. For the icing: Add hot water to sugar and beat until well-blended; add vanilla. Spread on warm, not hot, strudel.

Theresa Holbert
Ripley County

"GREEN STUFF"

1 large can fruit cocktail, drained	1 large can crushed pine-apple, not drained
2 C. miniature marshmallows	¾ C. (more or less) chopped pecans
2 3½-oz. pkg. pistachio instant pudding (do not add milk)	1 12-oz. carton frozen whipped topping

Mix dry pudding with all other ingredients; chill.

Leila Mae Smith
Hancock County

BLITZ TORTE

1 C. sifted flour	1¼ C. sugar
1 t. baking powder	4 eggs, separated
½ t. salt	1 t. vanilla
½ C. shortening	3 T. milk

Sift together flour, baking powder, and salt; set aside. Cream shortening with ½ C. of the sugar; add beaten egg yolks, vanilla, milk, and sifted dry ingredients. Spread this mixture in 2 greased 8″ cake pans. Beat egg whites until stiff, but not dry. Add the remaining sugar (¾ C.) gradually and beat until egg whites hold shape. Spread over mixture in pans. Bake 25 min. at 350°, or until light brown. When cool spread with custard or strawberries and whipped cream.

Helen Ewing
Putnam County

PINEAPPLE REFRIGERATOR TORTE

12 graham crackers, finely crushed	30 large marshmallows
1 C. crushed pineapple, drained	1 C. whipped cream
	½ C. nut meats
½ C. hot water	½ t. vanilla

Reserve ¼ C. of cracker crumbs; press remainder onto the bottom of an 8x8″ pan. Combine marshmallows with the hot water and stir over low heat until melted; cool and add whipped cream, nuts, pineapple, and vanilla. Pour over crumbs in pan and sprinkle reserved crumbs on top. Chill several hours. Serves 9.

Betty Foxx
Putnam County

CHEESECAKE TARTS

3 8-oz. pkg. cream cheese, softened	1½ t. vanilla
	Topping:
	1 C. sour cream
1 C. sugar	¼ t. vanilla
5 eggs, beaten	¼ C. sugar

Beat cream cheese; add sugar and beat until light and fluffy. Add eggs and vanilla; beat again. Pour mixture into foil paper cups until almost full. Bake at 300° for 30 min. Mix topping ingredients together slightly. Cool tarts 5 min., until there is an indentation. Put 1 T. topping on tart. Leave plain or spoon 1 t. jam or jelly onto each tart. Bake again at 300° for 5 min.

Jacqueline Foley
Cass County

COTTAGE CHEESE TARTS

½ C. cottage cheese	1 C. flour
½ C. margarine	jelly

Mix the first three ingredients together and chill overnight. Roll out (not quite as thin as pie crust). Cut into 3–4″ squares. Place jelly in center of each square. Fold and seal. Bake at 450° for 12 min.

Marjory Foster
Fountain County

FREEZER DESSERTS

BANANA SPLIT DESSERT

½ C. brown sugar	1 C. chocolate chips
1 C. flour	1½ C. evaporated milk
2 C. chopped nuts	2 C. powdered sugar
3 ripe bananas	1 T. vanilla
½ gal. ice cream	
½ C. butter	

Mix brown sugar, flour, and 1 C. nuts; spread on cookie sheet and bake at 375° for 15 min., stirring every 5 min., until golden brown. Place crumbs in 9x13″ pan. Place sliced bananas over crust; spread evenly. Slice ice cream into ½″ slices and layer over bananas. Sprinkle 1 C. nuts over ice cream and freeze. Melt butter and chocolate chips; add evaporated milk and powdered sugar and cook until thick and smooth. Add vanilla. When cool, pour over ice cream and replace in freezer. Serves 18.

Mary Ann Schoenemann
Huntington County

CHOCOLATE SUNDAE DESSERT

20 Oreo cookies, crushed	1 C. chocolate chips
¼ C. melted butter	½ C. margarine
½ gal. ice cream	2 C. powdered sugar

1½ C. evaporated milk	9 oz. frozen whipped topping, thawed
1 t. vanilla	

Combine cookie crumbs and ¼ C. melted butter. Reserve 1 C. crumbs; press remainder of crumbs into bottom of 9x13″ pan. Freeze. Slice ice cream in ½″ slices; place on crumbs and freeze until firm. Melt chocolate chips and ½ C. margarine. Add powdered sugar and milk. Cook until thick and creamy, stirring constantly. Add vanilla; cool and spread over ice cream. Freeze until firm. Spread whipped topping over chocolate layer and sprinkle with chopped nuts and reserved crumbs. Store in freezer. Remove from freezer 10 min. before serving.

Alternate crust recipe: 1¼ C. graham cracker crumbs, ¼ C. brown sugar and ¼ C. melted butter.

Doris Stevenson
White County

Variation: Make crust of 2 C. vanilla wafer crumbs and use chocolate chip mint ice cream.

Pat McGuffey
Hancock County

ICE CREAM DESSERT

2–4 C. rolled oats	½–1 C. chopped nuts
1–2 sticks margarine	2 qt. vanilla ice cream
½–1 C. brown sugar	1 jar butterscotch topping
½–1 C. coconut	

Melt butter on cookie sheet (one with sides); mix in oats, sugar, nuts, and coconut. Spread out on pan and toast at 350° about 20 min., stirring occasionally. Remove from oven and cool. Pat half of this mixture into a 9x13″ dish and top with slightly softened ice cream.

Sprinkle on remaining oats mixture and drizzle butterscotch topping over. Freeze.

Mable Houser
Huntington County

CINDER "CAKE"

1 large pkg. chocolate cream cookies, crushed	½ C. chopped nuts
½ gal. vanilla ice cream	8 oz. frozen whipped topping, thawed chocolate syrup

Spread ice cream in a 9x13" pan; sprinkle with crushed cookies. Pour chocolate syrup evenly over top of cookies. Spread whipped topping over syrup and sprinkle with nuts. Freeze; remove from freezer 5 min. before serving.

Jean Wrightsman
Monroe County

FROZEN PEANUT BUTTER DELIGHT

Peanut Butter Crust:	¼ C. peanut butter
½ C. brown sugar	1 t. vanilla
¼ C. margarine	½ C. sugar
½ C. smooth peanut butter	2 eggs
1 C. flour	2 C. frozen dessert topping (4½ oz.), thawed
Filling:	
1 8-oz. pkg. softened cream cheese	1 C. chocolate chips (8 oz.)

Cream brown sugar, margarine, and peanut butter. Add flour and blend until mixture is crumbly. Sprinkle into a 9x13" pan and bake at 350° for 20 min., stirring occasionally. Reserve ⅓ of mixture for top and press remainder into bottom of pan. Combine first four filling ingredients and beat until

smooth. Add eggs, one at a time. Fold in dessert topping. Pour mixture over crust. Melt chocolate chips, and drizzle over filling. Marble with knife blade. Sprinkle with reserved crumbs and freeze. Will keep 1–2 weeks in freezer. Remove from freezer 15–20 min. before serving. Serves 12–15.

Gloria Huey
Greene County

STRAWBERRY AND CREAM CHEESE FREEZE

Basic Crust:	2 10-oz. pkg. frozen strawberries, thawed and drained, ½ C. juice reserved
1 C. flour	
1 3½-oz. pkg. lemon pudding mix	
¼ t. salt	
½ C. shortening	2 8-oz. pkg. cream cheese, softened
2 T. butter	
1 egg	
Filling:	½ C. sugar
2 pkg. whipped topping, whipped	

To make crust, mix all crust ingredients together. Blend 30 sec. at low speed in electric mixer; blend 1 min. at medium speed. Spread in 9x13" pan; bake at 350° for 12–15min. In large bowl of electric mixer, combine cream cheese and sugar at low speed. Beat at high speed for 3 min. until smooth and creamy. Add reserved strawberry juice and beat 1 min. at medium speed. Fold in strawberries and whipped topping; pour over cooled crust. Freeze covered with foil overnight. Serves 16.

Linda Trips
Boone County

EASY LEMON FREEZE

2 T. butter, melted	1 15-oz. can sweetened condensed milk
1 C. graham cracker crumbs	1½ C. whipped topping
1 21-oz. can lemon pie filling	lemon slices (optional)
½ C. lemon juice	

Combine butter and crumbs, and reserve 1 T. for topping. Pat remainder into bottom of buttered 8x8″ baking dish. Combine pie filling, milk, and lemon juice; mix until smooth. Spread mixture into prepared pan, top with whipped topping and reserved crumbs. Freeze 3 hr. Garnish with lemon slices.

Junetta Sims
Monroe County

CHOCOLATE FREEZER PIE

¾ C. flour	6 oz. pkg. chocolate chips
¼ C., plus 2 T., margarine, softened	⅓ C. sugar
⅓ C. finely chopped walnuts	2 T. milk
	⅛ t. salt
3 T. brown sugar	1 envelope dessert topping mix
3 oz. pkg. cream cheese, softened	2 T. margarine
	¼ C. chocolate chips

Combine flour, ¼ C. margarine, walnuts, and brown sugar; mix with hands (fork) until crumbly. Press mixture firmly on sides and bottom of 9″ pie pan. Place an 8″ pie pan firmly inside. Bake 15 min. at 350°; remove top pie pan and cool. Melt the 6 oz. chocolate chips over hot water; cool. Blend chocolate, cream cheese, ⅓ C. sugar, milk, and salt at highest speed on electric mixer until smooth. Prepare topping mix as directed on pkg. Fold chocolate mixture into whipped topping; pour into baked crust. Melt 2 T. margarine and ¼ C. chocolate chips over low heat. Drizzle over top; marble top by drawing spatula back and forth across top of pie. Freeze until firm. Remove from freezer 15 min. before serving. Serves 8.

Martha Mobley
Monroe County

MINT ICE CREAM PIES

12 oz. pkg. chocolate chips	6 T. butter
4 C. Rice Krispies	mint ice cream, softened

Heat chocolate chips and butter in double boiler until melted. Add Rice Krispies; mix well. Pat into 2 pie pans to form crusts. Spoon in ice cream. Freeze. Decorate with chocolate shavings or crushed peppermint sticks.

Lois Jones
St. Joseph County

FROSTY PUDDING FREEZE POPS

1 3-oz. pkg. any flavor instant pudding mix	2 C. frozen whipped topping, thawed
1½ C. milk	

Prepare pudding as directed, using only 1½ C. milk. Blend in whipped topping. Pour into plastic holders or small dixie cups (use plastic spoons as handles). Freeze until firm: 4 hr. or overnight.

Barbara Patten
Vanderburgh County

PUDDING WICHES

1½ C. milk	½ C. peanut
1 small pkg. in-	butter
stant pudding	graham crackers
mix	

Blend milk and peanut butter. Add pudding mix and beat well; let stand 5 min. Spread filling ½" thick on graham cracker squares; top each with another cracker. Freeze until firm. Makes 12.

Nancy Sinders
Clay County

CHOCOLATE ICE CREAM ROLL

¾ C. sifted cake	1 T. lemon juice
flour	5 eggs, separated
¼ t. salt	1 C. sugar
4 T. cocoa	

Sift flour, salt, and cocoa together 4 times; set aside. Beat egg yolks; add lemon juice to yolks and beat with mixer until thick enough to hold soft peak. Beat egg whites until stiff but not dry. Fold sugar into whites in small amounts; fold in egg yolks. Fold in flour mixture in small amounts. Pour batter into jelly roll pan lined with paper and bake 12–15 min. at 350°. Turn out onto towel, roll, and cool. Unroll and spread with any flavor ice cream (softened enough to spread); roll and place on tray, cover with wrap. Store in freezer.

Patricia Marshall
Morgan County

BUTTERMILK SHERBET

2 C. buttermilk	⅔ C. sugar
1 egg white	1 t. vanilla
1 C. crushed	pinch of salt
pineapple	

Mix buttermilk, salt, pineapple, vanilla, and all but 2 T. of sugar; freeze to mush. Beat

egg whites stiff; add 2 T. sugar. Transfer frozen mixture to cold mixing bowl and beat until fluffy; add egg white and return to freezing tray.

Wilma Runyan
Dubois County

RASPBERRY SWIRL

1½ C. graham	¼ t. salt
cracker crumbs	2 C. frozen
6 T. melted	whipped top-
butter	ping, thawed
4 T. sugar	2 10-oz. pkg.
6 eggs, separated	frozen red
2 8-oz. pkg.	raspberries,
cream cheese,	partially
softened	thawed
2 C. sugar	

Combine crumbs, melted butter, and 4 T. sugar. Lightly press mixture into well-greased 9x13" pan. Bake at 375° for 8 min.; cool thoroughly. Beat egg yolks until thick; add cream cheese, sugar, and salt and beat until smooth. Beat egg whites until stiff peaks form. Add egg whites and dessert topping to cheese mixture; gently swirl raspberries into mixture and spread into crust. Freeze; cover and store in freezer. Serves 12.

Jolene E. Barwick
Elkhart County

ICE CREAM TORTE

60 Ritz crackers,	1¾ C. milk
rolled into fine	1 qt. orange-
crumbs	pineapple ice
1 stick marga-	cream, softened
rine, melted	1 large container
2 pkg. instant	frozen whipped
coconut cream	topping,
pudding mix	thawed

Mix cracker crumbs and margarine together; pat into a 9x12" loaf pan. Beat together the pudding, milk, and ice cream; spread on crust; freeze. Top with a layer of whipped topping.

Orpha L. Hasty
Grant County

Variations:

(1) Use instant French vanilla pudding with vanilla ice cream.

Helen Rushton
Hancock County

(2) Use instant lemon pudding and vanilla ice cream.

Blanche Cripe
Elkhart County

FROZEN PIÑA COLADA TORTE

1 3½-oz. can flaked coconut, toasted (1⅓ C.)
1 14-oz. can sweetened condensed milk
½ C. cream of coconut
¼ C. light rum
1 8-oz. can crushed pineapple, well-drained
2 C. whipping cream, whipped

Combine milk, cream of coconut, and rum; stir in pineapple. Fold in whipped cream. Pour ⅓ cream mixture into aluminum foil-lined 9x5" loaf pan. Sprinkle with half the coconut. Repeat layering with ⅓ cream mixture, remaining coconut, and remaining ⅓ cream mixture; cover. Freeze 6 hr.,

or until firm. To serve, remove from pan; peel off foil and slice.

Mary Alice Roberts
Starke County

MOCK WHIPPED CREAM

2 T. flour
½ C. milk
¼ C. butter
¼ C. shortening
½ C. sugar
1 t. vanilla

Cook flour and milk over low heat stirring until thick. Pour into dish and cool; set aside. Cream butter and shortening for 4 min. Add sugar slowly, beating another 4 min. Add flour paste; beat 4 min. Add vanilla. May be used as whipped cream or as frosting.

Evelyn Ryden
Delaware County

HEAVENLY HOT FUDGE SAUCE

½ C. butter or margarine
4 sq. unsweetened chocolate
3 C. sugar
¼ t. salt
1⅔ C. evaporated milk (1 can)
1 t. vanilla

Melt butter and chocolate in the top of double boiler. Stir in sugar gradually, about ¼ C. at a time, being sure the sugar is completely blended before making another addition. Mixture will become very thick and dry. Add salt; slowly stir in milk, a little at a time. Continue to cook 7–8 min. to blend flavors and dissolve the sugar. Remove from heat and add vanilla. Serve hot or cold. Great on ice cream. Makes 1 qt.

Cheri Birky
Porter County

Cakes

Many homemakers prefer to bake their cakes from scratch, not only because they have developed the necessary skill to produce an enviable end product, but also because they believe they have better control over the freshness and quality of the ingredients used. On the other side of the coin, many of us would never bake a cake at all if we didn't have access to a boxed cake mix. Cake mixes are time and energy efficient, and are an inexpensive alternative to making cakes from scratch. Whichever method you choose, the suggestions that follow may help you achieve a quality product.

- Grease cake pans with shortening. Do not use oil, butter, or margarine.
- Use all-purpose flour unless the recipe states cake flour.
- Begin and end with dry ingredients when adding dry and liquid ingredients.
- Push batter to sides of cake pans; gently tap pans on counter tops to remove air bubbles.
- Cool cake in pans 10 min. before removing, unless recipe states otherwise.
- Cut cakes into halves, quarters, or slices before freezing.

STRAWBERRY ANGEL FOOD CAKE DESSERT

One large baked angel food cake, broken into small pieces. Put half of cake into a sheet cake pan; set aside. Soften 2 pkg. unflavored gelatin in 4 T. cool water; add 1 C. boiling water and stir until dissolved. Add 1 C. sugar and stir to dissolve. Add 2 C. cut strawberries; refrigerate until partially set (like unbeaten egg whites). Whip 2 pkg. whipped topping according to pkg. instructions. Fold topping into gelatin. Put ½ of mixture over first layer of cake. Make a second layer of cake and top with gelatin mixture. Refrigerate.

Martha Tischendorf
Clark County

EASY APPLESAUCE-CINNAMON CAKE

¼ C. sugar	2 t. cinnamon
1 pkg. yellow cake with pudding mix	15 oz. jar applesauce (1⅔ C.)
	3 eggs

Combine sugar and cinnamon; set aside. Blend cake mix, applesauce, and eggs in large mixer bowl until moistened. Beat 2 min. at highest speed. Pour ½ batter into greased and floured bundt or tube pan. Sprinkle with sugar mixture. Cover with remainder of batter. Bake at 350° for 35–45 min. Cool in pan 25 min. Turn onto serving plate. Cool completely and dust with confectioners' sugar.

Karen Nichols
Union County

14 CARAT CAKE

2 C. sifted flour	2 t. cinnamon
2 t. baking powder	2 C. sugar
1½ t. salt	1½ C. vegetable oil
1½ t. soda	4 eggs
2 C. finely grated raw carrots	½ C. chopped nuts
1 8½-oz. crushed pineapple, well drained	1 3½-oz. flaked coconut (optional)

In large bowl, sift together flour, baking powder, soda, salt, and cinnamon. Add sugar, vegetable oil, and eggs; mix well. Add carrots, pineapple, nuts, and coconut; blend thoroughly. Pour into greased and floured layer cake pans or a 9x13″ pan. Bake at 350° 35–40 min. for layers, longer for 9x13″ pan. Cool and frost with cream cheese frosting.

Carolyn Taylor
Whitley County

$100 CAKE

2 C. sifted cake flour	1½ C. milk
2 t. baking powder	1 C. nut meats
½ t. salt	Icing:
½ C. butter, softened	½ lb. butter, softened
2 C. sugar	2 sq. unsweetened chocolate, melted
2 eggs	1 box confectioners' sugar
4 oz. unsweetened chocolate, melted	1 egg
	1 t. lemon juice
2 t. vanilla	1 C. nut meats

Sift dry ingredients together. Cream butter and sugar; add eggs and beat well. Add chocolate. Add vanilla. Add sifted dry ingredients and milk alternately. Stir in nuts. Bake at 350° in 2 9″ layer pans for 30–35 min. Beat together the first 5 icing ingredients; stir in nuts. Frost cool cake.

This recipe came from the Waldorf-Astoria several years ago. It is very rich.

Cheri Birky
Porter County

HOLIDAY CAKE

1 baked 10" tube chiffon cake
1 3-oz. pkg. vanilla pudding
¼ lb. candied cherries, cut up
1 C. chopped pecans
¼ lb. candied pineapple, cut up
½ C. flaked coconut
2 C. heavy cream, whipped
¼ C. sugar

Prepare vanilla pudding, according to pkg. directions; cool and stir in fruit, nuts, and coconut. Fold sugar into whipped cream; set aside. Split cake into three layers. Spread pudding between the layers. Frost top and sides of cake with whipped cream. Garnish with candied fruit. Refrigerate. Serves 12.

Laura Gaerte
Noble County

CHOCOLATE CHIP CAKE

1 box devil's food cake with pudding mix
¼ C. oil
2 eggs
1¼ C. water
1 3-oz. pkg. instant chocolate pudding
1 C. chocolate chips
Chocolate Frosting:
1 box confectioners' sugar
7 T. milk or cream
2 sq. unsweetened chocolate, melted
2 T. butter
1 t. vanilla
pinch of salt

Beat cake mix, oil, eggs, water, and pudding on medium speed of electric mixer for 2 min. Fold in chocolate chips. Pour into a greased and floured 13x9x2" pan. Bake at 350° for 35–45 min. Cool. Beat frosting ingredients together until creamy. Frost cooled cake.

Amzel Hubbard
Crawford County

CHOCOLATE CHERRY CAKE

1 box chocolate cake mix
20 oz. can cherry pie filling
2 eggs, well beaten
½ t. almond extract

Mix all ingredients well with spoon. Grease 9x13" baking pan. Bake at 350° for 35–45 min. Top with favorite frosting. Serves 12.

Lois Scott
Kosciusko County

CHOCOLATE-DATE, SELF-ICED CAKE

1 C. chopped dates
1 C. boiling water
1 t. soda
½ C. shortening
1 C. sugar
2 eggs
2 t. cocoa
1 t. vanilla
1¾ C. flour
½ t. salt
½ t. cream of tartar
1 6-oz. pkg. chocolate chips
¾ C. nuts

Combine dates, water, and soda; let stand until cool. Cream shortening and sugar; add eggs and beat well. Add cocoa and vanilla; blend well. Sift together flour, salt, and cream of tartar; add to creamed mixture and stir until well-blended. Fold into date mixture. Pour into a greased 13x9x2" pan. Sprinkle chocolate chips and nuts over the top and bake at 350° for 30 min.

Evelyn Brunson
White County

CINNAMON CAKE

½ C. shortening
⅔ C. sugar
1 egg
1 t. vanilla
1½ C. flour
1 t. soda
¼ t. salt
2 T. cinnamon
1 t. baking powder
1 C. buttermilk

Cream shortening and sugar; add egg and

vanilla and beat well. Sift dry ingredients together and add alternately with butter-milk. (*Note:* Batter will be stiff.) Pour into a greased and floured 8″ square pan. Bake at 350° for 25–30 min. Serve warm with whipped cream.

Kay Hart
Clay County

COCONUT CAKE (1)

1 box yellow cake mix	1 t. vanilla
1 6-oz. pkg. coconut	1 C. water
1 small can evap-orated milk	1 8-oz. carton frozen whipped topping, thawed
½ C. sugar	6 oz. coconut

Mix cake following pkg. directions; add 6 oz. pkg. coconut. Bake in greased and floured 9x13″ pan. Cool cake for 10 min.; poke all over with a fork. Mix milk, sugar, vanilla, and water; stir and pour over warm cake. Cool in refrigerator. Combine 6 oz. coconut with whipped topping and frost cake.

Margie Jean Angermeier
Posey County

COCONUT CAKE (2)

Frosting:	1 C. sugar
18 oz.-frozen coconut	Cake:
8 oz. dairy sour cream	1 box white cake mix, plus 2 T. sugar

Mix all frosting ingredients together and refrigerate for 24 hr. Prepare white cake mix, plus sugar, as directed on the box. Bake in layers. Cool and frost. Cover and refrigerate for 7 days.

Doris Hughes
Spencer County

CRANBERRY SPICE CAKE

½ C. shortening	½ t. cloves
1 C. sugar	¼ t. salt
1 egg	Cranberry Cream Cheese Frosting:
1 C. raisins	
1¾ C. sifted flour	1 3-oz. pkg. cream cheese
1¾ C. canned whole cran-berry sauce	½ t. salt
1 t. baking powder	¼ C. canned whole cran-berry sauce
1 t. soda	
1 t. cinnamon	powdered sugar

Cream shortening and sugar. Add egg; stir in raisins. Sift dry ingredients together; stir into creamed mixture. Stir in cranberry sauce. Spoon into 2 greased 8″ cake pans, or 1 9x13″ pan. Bake at 350° for 30–40 min. Combine cream cheese, cranberry sauce, and salt; beat until well-blended. Gradually add sugar until frosting is of right consist-ency to spread.

Elizabeth H. Franklin
Owen County

BRANDIED-FRUIT STARTER FOR FRIENDSHIP CAKE

1 20-oz. can sliced peaches, chopped with juice	2½ C. sugar
	1 pkg. dry yeast

In a 1 gal. glass or crockery jar with loose-fitting lid, combine sugar, peaches, and yeast; stir daily for 10 days. Do not refrigerate. On 10th day add:

1 15-oz. can chunk pine-apple, with juice (cut chunks in half)	2½ C. sugar
	1 15-oz. can fruit cocktail with juice

Stir daily for 10 days. On 20th day add 2

9-oz. jars chopped, drained maraschino cherries. Stir daily until the 30th day. Drain juice from fruit. Reserve fruit to be used for cakes. Store fruit and juice in glass jars in refrigerator until ready to use. Keeps well. In remaking starter, use 1½ C. of drained juice in the first step of the brandying process with 2½ C. sugar and 20 oz. can peaches. Do not use yeast. The yeast is used only to start peaches and sugar fermenting the first time.

FRIENDSHIP CAKE

3 eggs	1 t. baking soda
2½ C. sugar	1 t. cinnamon
1 t. vanilla	½ t. salt
1 t. orange flavoring	1 C. flaked coconut
1 t. black walnut or butternut flavoring	1 C. chopped dates
1 C. oil	1½ C. brandied fruit from starter
3½ C. flour	

Beat together eggs, sugar, vanilla, orange and butternut flavorings, and oil. Stir together flour, baking soda, cinnamon, and salt. Add ¼ C. flour mixture to the coconut mixture and reserved fruit from fruit starter and mix well. The batter will be stiff; if it is too stiff to work, add more fruit or juice from starter. Put into a greased and floured large tube or bundt pan. Bake at 325° for 1 hr. and 15 min. Let cool in pan 15 min. before removing.

Ruth Higbie
Jefferson County

FRIENDSHIP CAKE, MIX STYLE (1)

1 3-oz. box instant vanilla pudding	⅔ C. oil
	4 eggs
	1 box yellow cake mix

1½ C. brandied fruit, drained well	½–1 C. chopped pecans
	1 C. raisins

Combine pudding, oil, eggs, and cake mix. Beat 3 min. in electric mixer at medium speed. With spoon, blend fruit, floured nuts, and raisins into batter. Pour or spoon into greased and floured bundt pan. Bake at 350° for 40–60 min.

Katherine Hess
Morgan County

FRIENDSHIP CAKE, MIX STYLE (2)

1½ C. brandied fruit	⅔ C. oil
1 box butter-pecan cake mix	4 eggs
	1 3-oz. box instant butter-pecan pudding
1 C. pecans	

Combine ingredients and pour or spoon into greased bundt pan. Bake at 325° for 50–55 min. Let cool before removing from pan.

Ruth Higbie
Jefferson County

CHRISTMAS FRUIT CAKE

2 eggs, beaten	2 C. candied cherries (12–13 oz.)
2 C. water	
2 pkgs. date, apricot, nut, or cranberry quick bread mix	2 C. candied pineapple, chopped, or 2 lb. candied fruit mixture
2 C. pecans, chopped	
2 C. raisins	

Grease and flour bottom and sides of 12" fluted tube pan, or 10" tube pan. Combine eggs and water; add remaining ingredients. Stir mixture by hand, until all ingredients are combined. Pour into prepared pan. Bake at 250° for 75–80 min., or until toothpick inserted comes out clean. Wrap in foil or plastic wrap, and store in refrigerator. Glaze with warm corn syrup and decorate with candied fruit and nuts.

Lorena Russell
Hamilton County

STAINED GLASS WINDOW FRUIT CAKE

1½ lb. pitted dates	2 t. baking powder
1 lb. candied pineapple chunks	½ t. salt
	4 eggs, beaten
1 lb. candied cherries	½ C. dark or light corn syrup
2 lb. walnuts or pecans	¼ C. brown sugar
2 C. flour	¼ C. oil

Grease 10" tube cake pan; line with greased paper. Mix fruit and nuts together; set aside. Sift dry ingredients; set aside. Beat eggs and brown sugar together. Add oil and syrup. Add dry ingredients in 3 equal amounts, beating well after each addition. Pour batter over fruit mixture; mix and pack firmly into pan. Bake at 275° about 2 hr. and 15 min., or until top appears dry. Cool in pan. Can be baked in 2 9x5x3" loaf pans.

Viola Macy
Whitley County

GRAHAM CRACKER CRUMB CAKE

½ C. flour	⅔ C. sugar
1 t. baking powder	⅔ C. light brown sugar
½ t. soda	3 eggs
½ t. salt	1 t. vanilla
1½ C. graham cracker crumbs	1 C. buttermilk
½ C. butter or margarine, softened	1 C. chopped walnuts

Stir together flour, baking powder, soda, and salt; mix with crumbs and set aside. Cream butter and sugars together. Beat in eggs one at a time; add vanilla and beat well until fluffy. Add flour mixture to egg mixture alternately with buttermilk, beating just to blend. Stir in walnuts. Spread in greased 9" square baking pan. Bake at 350° for 40 min. Serves 10.

Dorothy Niehaus
Posey County

ORANGE-PINEAPPLE DELIGHT CAKE

1 box butter cake mix	1 20-oz. can crushed pineapple (not drained)
4 eggs	
1 11-oz. can mandarin oranges (not drained)	9 oz. frozen whipped topping, thawed
½ C. oil	

Pineapple whipped topping:

3 oz. box instant vanilla pudding

Mix cake ingredients together and beat 3–4 min. Bake at 350° for 30–40 min. Bake in either a 9x13" pan or in layers. Cool. Whip dry pudding mix and pineapple together; fold in whipped topping. Frost cooled cake.

<table>
<tr><td>Rosemary Berry
Whitley County</td><td>Mary C. Brown
Gibson County</td></tr>
</table>

SAD CAKE

1 lb. brown sugar	1 C. nuts
4 eggs	1 C. coconut
½ C. butter, softened	2 C. biscuit mix

Beat first 3 ingredients by hand, until fluffy. Then add last 3 ingredients. Stir together.

Bake in a 9x13" greased pan at 350° for 35 min. Sprinkle with powdered sugar.

Emma Daggs
Dubois County

PEACH CAKE

¾ C. flour	1 20-oz. can
1 t. baking	peaches,
powder	drained, reserv-
½ t. salt	ing 3 T. liquid
1 egg	8 oz. cream
½ C. milk	cheese,
3 T. margarine	softened
1 3-oz. box in-	½ C. sugar
stant vanilla	1 T. sugar
pudding	½ t. cinnamon

Mix the first 7 ingredients; pour into a greased 8x8" pan. Place drained fruit on batter. Mix cream cheese, sugar, and reserved liquid; spread over batter and fruit. Combine sugar and cinnamon; sprinkle over cream cheese mixture. Bake at 350° for 30–35 min.

Karen Hollabaugh
Marshall County

CHIPS OF CHOCOLATE PEANUT BUTTER CAKE

Crumb mixture:	½ t. soda
2¼ C. flour	1 C. milk
2 C. brown sugar	1 t. vanilla
1 C. peanut	3 eggs
butter	Topping:
½ C. margarine,	6–8 oz. chocolate
softened	chips
Filling:	6–8 oz. peanut
1 t. baking	butter bits
powder	

Combine ingredients for crumb mixture and blend at low speed in large mixing bowl until crumbly. Reserve 1 C. crumbs. To re-maining crumb mixture in large bowl, add filling ingredients. Blend at low speed until moistened; beat 3 min. at medium speed. Pour batter into greased and floured 9x13" pan, and sprinkle with the 1 C. reserved crumbs. Next sprinkle chips and bits over crumbs. Bake at 350° for 35 min., or until toothpick comes out clean. Serves 15.

Frieda Masters
Fayette County

PIÑA COLADA CAKE

1 pkg. white cake	1 8-oz. can
mix	crushed pine-
1⅓ C. water,	apple in juice,
minus 2 t.	minus 2 t.
3 eggs	1 small pkg. co-
¾ C. flaked	conut cream in-
coconut	stant pudding
2 t. rum flavoring	mix
⅓ C. oil	9 oz. frozen
Piña Colada	whipped top-
Frosting:	ping, thawed
2 t. rum flavoring	

Combine cake mix, water, eggs, flavoring, and oil. Beat 2 min. in electric mixer at medium speed; fold in coconut and pour into 2 greased and floured 9" cake pans. Bake at 350° for 30–35 min. Beat pine-apple, pudding, and flavoring until well-blended; fold in whipped topping. Fill and frost cake. Refrigerate.

Thelma Esche
Posey County

CREAM CHEESE POUND CAKE

1 stick butter or	2 C. sifted cake
margarine	flour
8 oz. cream	1 t. baking
cheese	powder

½ t. salt   1½ t. vanilla
1½ C. sugar   grated rind of 1
2 eggs   lemon
¼ C. milk

Bring butter and cream cheese to room temperature. Cream in sugar; beat until very smooth. Sift all dry ingredients together. Add eggs, one at a time, to creamed mixture; beat well. Add dry ingredients, milk and vanilla alternately. Beat 2–3 min. Beat in lemon rind. Put in greased and floured 9x5x3" loaf pan. Bake at 350° for 1 hr.

Mary P. Vollat
Switzerland County

PUMPKIN WITH CAKE
1 large can evap-   ½ t. salt
  orated milk   1 C. sugar
1 large can   1 t. nutmeg
  pumpkin mix   ½ t. cinnamon
  (Libby's)   ½ t. ginger
3 eggs   ¼ t. cloves

Mix all ingredients together; pour into 9x13" pan. Sprinkle 1 box yellow cake mix over mixture. Sprinkle on 1 C. chopped nuts. Dribble 1½ sticks of melted margarine over top. Bake at 350° for 1 hr. Serves 12.

Mrs. Robert Wetnight
Monroe County

RHUBARB CAKE (1)
2 C. chopped   1 egg
  rhubarb   1 t. soda
1½ C. sugar   1 t. salt
½ C. shortening   2 C. flour
1 t. vanilla   Glaze:
  (optional)   ½ C. sugar
1 C. buttermilk   1 t. cinnamon
  (or sour milk)   8 T. butter

Mix sugar and shortening. Add egg, buttermilk, soda, salt, rhubarb, and flour. Pour into greased 9x13" cake pan and bake 30 min. at 350°. Five minutes before removing from oven, mix sugar, cinnamon, and butter for glaze. Pour over top of cake. *Note:* Topping or icing may be added before baking. Also, biscuit mix may replace the flour.

Country Cousins E.H. Club
Spencer County

Variation: Use brown sugar instead of white. Sprinkle top before baking with ½ C. sugar and 1 t. cinnamon.

Jean Buschmann
Marion County

RHUBARB CAKE (2)
In a 13x15" baking pan, spread 1 qt. raw chopped rhubarb (may be frozen). Sprinkle with 1 C. of sugar. Then sprinkle with 1 small box of strawberry gelatin. Finally, mix a two-layer lemon cake mix according to directions on the box and spread over rhubarb-gelatin mixture. Bake at 325° until done. Serves 12–16.

Ida Flick
Orange County

7-UP CAKE
1 box lemon cake   Icing:
  mix   1½ C. sugar
¾ C. oil   1 stick margarine
4 eggs   1 T. flour
1 bottle (12 oz.)   1 C. drained
  7-Up   crushed
1 3¾-oz. pkg. in-   pineapple
  stant lemon   2 eggs
  pudding   1½–2 C. coconut

Mix all ingredients together in electric mixer 2 min. Bake in 9x13" greased pan for 30–35 min. at 350°. Mix all icing ingredients together in a saucepan and cook over medium heat until thick; add coconut. Cool. Spread on cake.

Susan Goldman
Spencer County

Variation: For icing: use 3 T. flour, no eggs, 1½ C. pineapple; remaining ingredients are the same.

Marjorie Quick
Delaware County

VANILLA SHEET CAKE

2⅔ C. flour	2 eggs
2 C. sugar	2 t. vanilla
½ C. margarine	1 t. cinnamon
½ C. oil	1½ t. soda
1 C. water	⅔ C. buttermilk

Mix flour and sugar together. Bring margarine, oil, and water to a boil and pour over flour mixture; beat thoroughly. Beat in eggs, vanilla, cinnamon, soda, and buttermilk. Pour into a greased 11x17" pan. Bake at 350° for 20 min. Frost with cream cheese frosting and sprinkle with chopped nuts or toasted coconut.

Alice McCoy   *Marlene Stone*
Ripley County   *Parke County*

SWEDISH SPICE CAKE

2¼ C. flour	1½ C. sugar
1½ t. soda	¾ C. butter or
1 t. salt	margarine,
3 t. cinnamon	softened
1 t. ginger	5 eggs
¼ t. cloves	2 t. vanilla
½ C. finely	1½ C. sour cream
chopped	confectioners'
filberts	sugar (optional)

Stir together flour, soda, salt, and spices; set aside. Grease 9 C. fluted pan or 10" plain tube pan. Sprinkle bottom of pan with filberts, to coat; shake out excess and reserve for other use. In large bowl, cream butter and sugar. Beat in eggs one at a time; beat until light and fluffy. Beat in vanilla. Stir in flour mixture alternately with sour cream until well mixed. Spoon into prepared pan; spread smooth. Bake at 325° for 1 hr. Cool in pan on rack 10 min. Better when stored few days. Before serving, sprinkle lightly with confectioners' sugar.

Mrs. Leonard Rhoades
Kosciusko County

STRAWBERRY SHORTCUT CAKE

1 C. tiny	1½ C. sugar
marshmallows	½ C. shortening
2 C. frozen	3 t. baking
strawberries,	powder
thawed in juice	½ t. salt
1 3-oz. pkg.	1 C. milk
strawberry	1 t. vanilla
gelatin	3 eggs
2¼ C. flour	

Grease bottom of 9x13" pan. Spread marshmallows evenly on bottom. Combine strawberries and gelatin; set aside. Combine remaining ingredients; beat 3 min. Pour batter over marshmallows. Spoon strawberry mixture evenly over batter. Bake 35–40 min. at 375°.

Towne & Country E.H. Club
Grant County

TWINKIE CAKE

1 box yellow cake	1 C. sugar
mix	½ t. salt
Filling:	½ C. shortening
1 C. milk	½ C. margarine
5 T. flour	1 t. vanilla

Prepare cake mix per pkg. directions, using 2 9" round cake pans. Place cake in freezer to cool; it will be easier to split later. Mix milk and flour for filling; bring to boil, then cool. Beat until fluffy. Add rest of ingredients, one at a time, beating well after each addition. Remove cake from freezer and using a piece of string split each cake in half. Spread filling on top of each layer. Serves 10.

Janey Goad   *Norma Gates*
LaPorte County   *Hendricks County*

WINE CAKE

1 pkg. butter brickle cake mix	1 3-oz. pkg. instant vanilla pudding mix
4 eggs	¾ C. sherry
¾ C. oil	

Mix all ingredients well and beat 5 min. Pour into a greased and floured bundt pan. Bake 1 hr. at 350°. Mix 1 C. powdered sugar and enough wine to make a glaze; drizzle over the baked cake.

America Welch
Posey County

ZUCCHINI AND CARROT CAKE

2 eggs	1 C. carrots, grated
1 C. sugar	
⅔ C. oil	1 C. zucchini, grated and drained
1¼ C. flour	
1 t. baking powder	½ C. chopped nuts
1 t. soda	
1 t. cinnamon	

Beat eggs and sugar in electric mixer until foamy; gradually beat in oil. Add dry ingredients and beat on high for 4 min. Stir in zucchini, carrots, and nuts. Grease a 9x9x2" pan. Bake at 350° for 35 min.

Alma Michel
Whitley County

ZUCCHINI-ORANGE CAKE

1 C. butter or margarine, softened	2 C. light brown sugar
	3 C. sifted flour
1 T. grated orange rind	3 t. baking powder
1 t. cinnamon, ½ t. nutmeg, and ¼ t. cloves	⅓ C. orange juice
	1 C. shredded unpared zucchini
4 eggs	

Cream butter, orange rind, cinnamon, nutmeg, cloves, and brown sugar together until light and fluffy; beat in eggs, one at a time. Sift together flour, baking powder, and salt; blend into creamed mixture alternately with orange juice. Stir in zucchini. Turn into a greased 10" tube pan. Bake at 350° for 55–65 min. Cool 10 min.; remove from pan and cool completely. Spread top with white glaze.

Elizabeth Tuttle
Randolph County

BLACK BOTTOM CUPCAKES

Cream cheese mixture:	1 C. sugar
	¼ C. cocoa
1 8-oz. pkg. cream cheese, softened	1 t. soda
	½ t. salt
	1 C. water
1 egg	⅓ C. oil
⅓ C. sugar	1 T. vinegar
⅛ t. salt	1 t. vanilla
1 12-oz. pkg. chocolate chips	chopped nuts (optional)
Chocolate Mixture:	
1½ C. flour	

Beat together cheese, egg, salt, and sugar. Stir in chocolate chips; set aside. Sift dry ingredients together. Add water, oil, vinegar, and vanilla. Beat until well-mixed. Fill paper or aluminum foil baking cups ⅓ full with chocolate batter. Drop 1 heaping t. of cream cheese mixture into chocolate batter. Sprinkle with nuts and sugar, if desired. Bake at 350° for 30–35 min. Makes 20 cupcakes.

May Richter
Ripley County

COCONUT FROSTING

1 small can evap-orated milk	1 C. pecans
	1 C. flaked
1½ C. sugar	coconut
1 stick margarine	1 t. vanilla

Combine milk, sugar, and margarine. Bring to a boil and cook for 4 min. Remove from heat and add pecans, coconut, and vanilla. Pour over a very warm cake. Frosts a 9x13" cake.

Peg West
Delaware County

Pies

• Use pie pans that are not shiny, such as glass or dull aluminum. Shiny pans reflect heat away from the pie during baking and may produce a soggy crust. For the same reason do not place pie pan on aluminum foil or a shiny baking sheet.

• Since we are a nation of pie eaters and since most dessert pies are high in calories, fat, and sugar, weight watchers may cut down on calories in several ways: make a habit of cutting pies into 8 serving pieces instead of the traditional 6; make one-crust pies; reduce the amount of sugar in the filling; and skip all ice cream and whipped cream toppings.

BLUSH APPLE PIE

5 large apples, sliced
1 small can pineapple tidbits, drained
1 t. lemon juice
½ C. sugar (a little more if apples are sour)
2 T. flour
¼ C. cinnamon red-hots
⅛ t. salt
2 T. butter

Mix ingredients together; place in 9″ pastry-lined pie pan. Top with second crust; vent. Bake 30–40 min. at 350°.

Helen Ewing
Putnam County

FRENCH APPLE PIE

6 baking apples	1 T. lemon juice
½ C. white wine	1 t. vanilla
½ C. water	½ t. salt
1 C. sugar	pastry for 2-crust
2 T. tapioca	9″ pie

Peel, core, and cut each apple into 8 wedges. Combine wine, water, sugar, tapioca, lemon juice, vanilla, and salt in saucepan. Cook 5 min.; add apples and cook until tender. Bake pastry shell at 450° for 12–15 min. until lightly browned. Place apples and syrup in baked pie shell. Make lattice top with other crust and put over apples. Bake at 350° for 15 min., or until top is browned. Serves 6–8.

Shirley J. Campbell
Brown County

BANANA-COCONUT CHIFFON PIE

1 pie shell, baked	1½ C. milk
1 C. flaked coco-nut, browned in 325° oven for 5–8 min.	½ t. vanilla
	¼ t. almond extract
	3 egg whites
1 envelope unfla-vored gelatin	½ C. whipping cream
⅔ C. sugar, divided	2 bananas, sliced crosswise

Mix gelatin, ⅓ C. sugar, milk, and a dash of salt in saucepan. Heat slowly, stirring constantly, until gelatin dissolves; remove from heat and stir in vanilla and almond. Pour mixture into a large bowl; put bowl in pan of ice water. Chill 15 min., or until syrupy, stirring several times. Beat egg whites until foamy; beat in remaining ⅓ C. sugar, 1 T. at a time. Continue beating until meringue stands in soft peaks. Beat whipping cream until stiff. Fold meringue, then whipped cream and ½ of the coconut into the milk mixture. Cover bottom of pie shell with one layer of banana slices; top with ½ coconut mixture. Make a second layer of bananas and top with remaining mixture. Sprinkle with coconut. Chill.

Ellen Hummel
Marshall County

BISHOP PIE

1 small pkg. in-stant vanilla pudding	2 C. milk
	2 C. vanilla ice cream, softened
1 small pkg. in-stant chocolate pudding	1 8″ baked pie crust or graham cracker shell

Prepare pudding with 1 C. milk per pkg. of pudding. Add the vanilla ice cream and mix thoroughly. Pour into pie shell. Chill. Serves 8.

Ruby Porter
St. Joseph County

BOB ANDY PIE

1 9″ unbaked pie shell	4 T. flour
	1 t. cinnamon
1 scant C. brown sugar	⅛ t. cloves
	¼ t. salt
¼ C. butter	2 C. milk,
2 eggs, separated	warmed

Mix sugar, flour, and spices together; add egg yolks and beat. Add milk and butter. Fold in egg whites which have been beaten until stiff. Bake in shell at 325° for 40–45 min. Serves 4–6.

Dorothea L. Foust
Wells County

CHERRY "CHEESE CAKE" PIE

1 small container of frozen whipped top-ping, thawed	1 small can fro-zen lemonade
	1 can of cherry pie filling

1 15-oz. can sweetened condensed milk

2 9″ graham cracker shells

Blend together whipped topping, lemonade and milk; pour into pie shells. Top with pie filling.

Lois Stephens
Monroe County

FRENCH SILK CHOCOLATE PIE

1 pie shell, baked
½ C. margarine
¾ C. sugar
1 4-oz. bar sweet German chocolate, melted

1 t. vanilla
2 eggs
1 12-oz. container frozen whipped topping, thawed

Cream margarine; gradually add sugar, creaming until light and fluffy. Blend in melted chocolate and vanilla. Add eggs, one at a time, beating 5 min. after each egg. Fold ½ of dessert topping into chocolate mixture. Turn into pie shell. Chill 1–2 hr. Before serving, add remaining whipped topping. Sprinkle with shaved chocolate or chopped pecans (optional).

Jean Beuoy
Grant County

NO-CRUST GERMAN CHOCOLATE PIE

2 oz. sweet German chocolate
½ C. butter or margarine
1 t. vanilla

3 beaten eggs
1 C. sugar
3 T. flour
1 C. chopped walnuts

Melt chocolate and butter over low heat. Stir in vanilla; cool. Combine eggs, sugar, and flour and beat until well-blended (do not overbeat); fold in cooled chocolate mixture and nuts. Pour mixture into lightly greased and floured 9″ pie plate. Bake at 350° for 1 hr., or until knife inserted in

center comes out clean. Best refrigerated overnight before serving. Garnish with scoops of whipped or ice cream.

Rosalie McGuire
Monroe County

CRANBERRY MERINGUE PIE

1 deep dish pie shell, baked
1¾ C. sugar
½ C. water
4 C. cranberries
2 T. flour

4 eggs, separated
¼ t. salt
2 T. butter
1 t. vanilla extract
4 T. powdered sugar

Cook sugar and water until sugar dissolves; add cranberries. Cook until berries stop popping; cool slightly. Mix flour, salt, and egg yolks until smooth; stir in 3 T. of hot cranberry juice. Add egg mixture to berries; simmer for 3 min. Stir in butter and vanilla; set aside to cool slightly. Turn warm filling into baked pie crust. Cover with meringue made from stiffly beaten egg whites and powdered sugar. Bake at 425° for 4½ min.

Mrs. David Wright, Sr.
Vanderburgh County

CREAM CHEESE PIE (1)

Crust:
1¼ C. graham cracker crumbs
¼ C. melted butter
Filling:
1 8-oz. pkg. cream cheese
½ C. sugar

1 T. lemon juice
½ t. vanilla
dash of salt
2 eggs
Topping:
1 C. dairy sour cream
2 T. sugar
½ t. vanilla

Combine crumbs and butter. Mix thoroughly and press onto bottom and sides of 8″ pie plate. Blend sugar, lemon juice, vanilla, and salt into cream cheese. Add eggs one at a time, beating well after each addition. Pour into crust. Bake at 325° for 25–30 min. Remove from oven and cool 5 min. Combine ingredients for topping and spread on baked pie. Chill several hr. Serve topped with fresh sliced sweetened strawberries. Serves 6.

Darle Smith
Marshall County

CREAM CHEESE PIE (2)

1 8-oz. pkg. cream cheese, softened	1 8-oz. container frozen whipped topping, thawed
⅓ C. sugar	
1 C. dairy sour cream	1 baked 9″ graham cracker crumb crust
2 t. vanilla	

Beat cheese until smooth; gradually beat in sugar. Blend in sour cream and vanilla. Fold in whipped topping, blending well. Spoon into crust. Chill until set, at least 4 hr. Serve topped with sweetened fresh fruit, if desired, or garnish with sliced strawberries.

Nancy Sinders
Clay County

DERBY PIE

1 C. sugar	2 eggs, slightly beaten
½ C. self-rising flour	1 C. chocolate chips
1 stick margarine, melted and cooled	1 C. pecans, chopped
1 t. vanilla	

Mix all ingredients together and pour into unbaked pie shell. Bake at 325° for 50 min.–1hr.

Helen Cadle
Orange County

DIVINITY PIE

3 egg whites	1 C. sugar
23 Ritz crackers, crushed fine	1 pkg. whipped topping
½–1 C. pecans, chopped fine	2½ T. instant cocoa (optional)

Beat the egg whites until stiff; add sugar gradually. Add vanilla; fold in cracker crumbs and nuts. Put mixture into a buttered pie plate. Bake 25–30 min. at 350°. Cool. Whip topping according to package directions; add cocoa. Spoon topping into shell; refrigerate for at least 3 hr. Freezes well.

Maurine Bassett
DeKalb County

GRASSHOPPER PIE

1 C. chocolate chips	¼ t. salt
1 T. shortening	3 T. green crème de menthe
1½ C. finely chopped nuts	1 T. crème de cacao
½ lb. large marshmallows (35)	1½ C. heavy cream, whipped
⅓ C. milk	

Line a 9″ pie pan with aluminum foil. Combine chocolate chips and shortening over hot (not boiling) water; stir until melted and smooth. Add chopped nuts; mix well and spread mixture evenly on bottom and up sides (not rim) of foil-lined pan. Chill in refrigerator until firm, about 1 hr. Lift chocolate shell out of pan; peel off foil and place shell on serving plate. Chill in refrigerator until ready to use. Combine over hot (not boiling) water marshmallows, milk, and salt; heat until marshmallows melt. Remove from heat; add liqueurs and stir until blended. Chill mixture in refrigerator until slightly thickened, about 1 hr.; gently fold in whipped cream. Pour filling into shell and chill until firm, about 1 hr.

Helen Fischer
Vigo County

LEMON CHESS PIE

1 9″ unbaked pie shell	¼ C. milk
1 C. sugar	¼ C. lemon juice
1 T. cornmeal	1 T. lemon rind, grated
1 T. flour	¼ C. melted
4 eggs, beaten	butter

Mix flour, sugar, and meal with fork. Mix in other ingredients. Pour into pie shell and bake at 350° for 35–40 min.

Dona Nash
Posey County

LEMON AND RAISIN PIE

1 C. raisins	1 C. water
juice of one lemon	1 T. cornstarch
1 C. sugar	

Combine all ingredients and boil 10 min. Bake in double crusts at 350° about 45 min. until top crust is brown.

Leila Mae Smith
Hancock County

MAGIC LEMON MERINGUE PIE

Filling:	1 t. grated lemon rind
1 8″ pie shell, baked	Meringue:
1 15-oz. can sweetened condensed milk	¼ t. cream of tartar
½ C. lemon juice	2 egg whites
2 egg yolks	4 T. sugar

Stir milk, lemon juice, rind, and egg yolks together until thickened; pour into pie shell. Beat egg whites until frothy; add cream of tartar and continue beating until whites are

stiff but not dry. Beat sugar in 1 T. at a time. Pile meringue lightly on pie filling. Bake at 425° until lightly browned.

Mattie Alexander
Monroe County

SLY LEMON PIE

1 9″ pie shell, baked	1 6-oz. can frozen lemonade concentrate, defrosted
1 qt. vanilla ice cream	

Blend ice cream and lemonade in blender or food processor, or mix by hand with egg beater. Pour into pie shell and freeze for at least 2 hr. Remove from freezer 10 min. before serving. Serve with chocolate sauce. Serves six.

Maggy Cobb
Hendricks County

MOCK MINCE PIE

pastry for 2-crust pie	spices to taste: mace, allspice,
1 C. chopped raisins	cinnamon, nutmeg, and/or
juice of ½ lemon	cloves
1 egg, beaten	1 C. sugar
2 T. butter	

Mix all ingredients together; place in pastry-lined pie pan and sprinkle lightly with flour. Cover with pastry and bake at 350° for 40 min. *Note:* Make slits in top crust before baking.

Wilma Runyan
Dubois County

PEACH CRUMB PIE

4 C. sliced peaches	¼ C. butter, melted
3 drops almond extract	½ C. sugar
	2 T. flour

¼ t. salt
Topping:
½ C. flour
½ t. cinnamon

⅓ C. brown
sugar
⅓ C. butter

Combine almond extract and butter. Blend in sugar, flour, and salt. Add peaches. Pour into unbaked pie shell. Combine and sprinkle topping ingredients over fruit mixture. Bake at 450° for 10 min.; then at 350° 35–40 min.

Carol Huelsenbeck
Noble County

PEANUT BUTTER PIE

1 3-oz. pkg.
cream cheese,
softened
1 C. powdered
sugar
½ C. peanut
butter

1 9-oz. carton
frozen dessert
topping,
thawed
1 graham cracker
pie crust

Mix peanut butter and cream cheese together. Beat in sugar gradually; fold in dessert topping. Pour into crust. Refrigerate at least 4 hr., or overnight.

Leota Wood
Clark County

PECAN PIE

1 3¾-oz. pkg.
vanilla pudding
mix
1 C. corn syrup
¾ C. evaporated
milk

1 egg, slightly
beaten
1 C. chopped
pecans
1 8" unbaked pie
shell

Blend pudding with corn syrup. Gradually add evaporated milk and egg, stirring to blend. Add pecans. Pour into pie shell. Bake at 375° for 40 min.

Gloria Huey
Greene County

CITRUS PECAN PIE

1 C. sugar
1 t. salt
1 T. flour
3 eggs
1 C. dark corn
syrup
⅓ C. orange juice

1 T. grated
orange rind
1½ C. chopped
pecans
1 unbaked 9" pie
shell

Combine sugar, salt, and flour. Beat eggs until foamy. Blend eggs, syrup, orange juice, rind, and pecans into dry ingredients. Pour into pastry shell. Bake at 400° for 10 min. Reduce heat to 350° and bake 40 min. longer, or until filling sets and pastry is brown.

Mary L. Wynn
Wayne County

PINEAPPLE PIE

2 graham cracker
pie crusts
Mix:
1 20-oz. can
crushed pine-
apple, drained
½ C. flaked
coconut

1 8-oz. carton
frozen whipped
topping,
thawed
1 15-oz. can
sweetened con-
densed milk
2 T. lemon juice

Pour into crusts. Sprinkle with chopped pecans. Freeze. Can be frozen until served.

Homebuddies E.H. Club
Hancock County

RASPBERRY CUSTARD PIE

In a 9" unbaked pie shell, put 1 heaping C. of fresh raspberries. Mix the following ingredients together and pour over the raspberries:

3 C. milk
3 eggs, beaten

¾–1 C. sugar
½ t. vanilla

Bake at 350° for 40 min., or until just set.

Joan Ford
Jay County

POP IN PAN FROZEN STRAWBERRY PIE

4 qt. strawberries	¾ C. minute
5 C. sugar	tapioca
1 t. salt	¼ C. lemon juice

Mix all ingredients together. Line aluminum pie pans with aluminum foil and fill with the mixture. Freeze before covering filling with foil. When ready to bake, take filling from freezer and pop into dough-lined pie pan. Fit top crust over filling; bake at 425° until juice bubbles up and crust is brown. Makes 5 small or 4 large pies.

Marilyn Detraz
Ripley County

BERRIED TREASURE PIE

graham cracker crust	2 T. milk
1 8-oz. pkg. cream cheese, softened	1 small carton frozen whipped topping, thawed
2 T. sugar	1 pkg. instant lemon pie filling
1 C. or more halved strawberries	1 C. milk

Beat cream cheese, sugar, and 2 T. milk together; spread evenly in bottom of crust. Arrange berries on cheese mixture. Prepare pudding mix with 1 C. milk; fold in whipped topping. Spoon pudding mixture into pie crust and chill until set, about 2 hr. Garnish with berries and frozen whipped topping.

Wilma Whitton
Jefferson County

GREEN TOMATO PIE

pastry for 2-crust pie	1 t. salt
5 C. green tomato slices	1 t. nutmeg or cinnamon
2 T. lemon juice	½ C. cracker or cereal crumbs
1 t. grated lemon rind	1 T. butter
1 C. sugar	1 egg, beaten with 1 T. water
½ C. flour	

Line 9" pie plate with pastry; chill. Sprinkle tomato slices with lemon juice and rind; toss with sugar, flour, and seasonings. Sprinkle crumbs into pie shell; fill with tomato slices and dot with butter. Cover with top crust; puncture. Brush on egg glaze. Bake at 425° for 35–45 min., or until golden.

Madelyn Garnard
Whitley County

WINE PIE

2 9" graham cracker pie shells	2½ C. milk
1 lb. seedless raisins	4 small pkg. instant vanilla pudding mix
½ C. water	1 C. sweet vermouth
½ C. sweet vermouth	2 C. whipping cream, whipped
2½ oz. chopped pecans	

Soak raisins, water, and ½ C. vermouth overnight; drain. Combine pudding mix, milk, and 1 C. vermouth; stir until thickened. Stir raisins and pecans into pudding mixture; fold in whipped cream. Pour mixture into prepared pie shells. Freeze pies until firm. Remove from freezer at least ½ hr. before serving. Serve with additional whipped cream, if desired.

Kate Kroll
Monroe County

Cookies and Candy

Cookies

Bar cookies eliminate rolling, cutting, dropping or shaping, making them less time consuming. Cut bar cookies into diamond, rectangular, or square shapes for serving as snacks. Cut into larger portions and serve as a dessert, with ice cream or whipped cream.

Store crisp, thin cookies in a container with a loose cover. Store soft cookies in a container with a tight-fitting cover. Baked cookies and cookie dough may be stored frozen up to 9 months.

GOLDEN APPLE BARS

Cookie layer:
½ C. margarine
¼ C. shortening
¾ C. confection-
 ers' sugar
1½ C. flour
Apple layer:
2 C. chopped
 Golden Deli-
 cious apples
¾ C. brown
 sugar
1 beaten egg

1¾ C. flour
½ t. salt
¼ C. margarine
1 t. grated lemon
 peel
1 t. vanilla
1 t. baking
 powder
Cinnamon Glaze:
1½ C. confec-
 tioners' sugar
2–3 T. milk
¼ t. cinnamon

Mix cookie layer ingredients together and pat into 10x15″ jelly roll pan. Bake at 350° for 10–15 min. For the apple layer, melt the ¼ C. margarine in saucepan; blend in remaining ingredients. Spread mixture evenly over cookie crust and bake at 350° for 25 min. Cool slightly. Blend glaze ingredients together and drizzle over warm bars. Makes 48 bars.

Lee Aftowski
LaPorte County

BETTY BROWNS

1 C. flour
1 t. cinnamon
½ t. baking soda
½ t. baking
 powder
½ C. melted
 butter or
 margarine

¼ t. salt
1 C. sugar
1 egg
2 apples,
 chopped
½ C. chopped
 nuts

Sift flour, cinnamon, soda, and baking powder together; add butter, sugar, and egg, and mix well. Fold in apples; add nuts. Bake at 350° for 25–30 min. in 8″ pan; cut into bars.

Lorene Sallee
Lawrence County

BUTTER PECAN COOKY BARS

Crust:
2 C. flour
1 C. brown sugar
½ C. soft butter
1 C. chopped
 pecans

Caramel layer:
⅔ C. butter
½ C. brown
 sugar
Topping:
1 C. chocolate
 chips

Combine first 3 ingredients and mix until like fine crumbs. Press mixture evenly into an ungreased 9x13″ pan. Sprinkle with pecans. Combine ⅔ C. butter and ½ C. brown sugar in a saucepan and cook until mixture reaches a full boil; boil 1 min., stirring constantly. Remove from heat and pour over unbaked crust. Bake 18–22 min. at 350°. Remove from oven and sprinkle with chocolate chips. Let stand 2–3 min.; swirl melted chocolate. Cool and cut into bars.

Rosalie McGuire
Monroe County

CARAMEL LAYER CHOCO-SQUARES

about 50 light car-
 amels (14 oz.
 pkg.)
⅓ C. evaporated
 milk
1 pkg. German
 chocolate cake
 mix

¾ C. butter,
 melted
⅓ C. evaporated
 milk
1 C. chopped
 nuts
1 C. chocolate
 chips

In heavy saucepan, combine caramels and ⅓ C. evaporated milk; cook stirring constantly, until caramels are melted. Set mixture aside. Grease and flour 9x13″ baking pan. In large mixing bowl, combine cake mix, butter, ⅓ C. evaporated milk, and nuts; stir by hand until dough holds together. Press ½ of dough into prepared pan. Bake at 350° for 6 min. Sprinkle chocolate chips over baked crust. Spread caramel mixture over chocolate chips. Crumble reserved dough over caramel mixture. Return to oven and bake for 15–18 min. Cool slightly; refrigerate about 30 min. to set caramel layer. Cut into 36 bars.

Beulah Lindley　　　　*Brenda Chapman*
Tipton County　　　　　*Henry County*

CHINESE CHEWS

¾ C. flour
1 C. sugar
1 t. baking
　powder
¼ t. salt
3 well-beaten
　eggs
1 C. chopped
　dates
1 C. chopped
　walnuts or
　pecans

Mix together the first 4 ingredients; add the remaining ingredients. Spread evenly over a 10x14″ greased pan and bake at 350° for 25 min. Cut while still warm. Serve warm with whipped cream or ice cream or cool and serve like a cookie. Serves 12–14.

Joy Jennings
Marshall County

CHOCOLATE CHIP BARS

2 C. brown sugar
2 C. flour
½ C. margarine
1 egg
1 t. salt
1 t. baking soda
1 C. milk
1 t. vanilla
1 C. chocolate
　chips, plus ad-
　ditional for
　topping
chopped nuts

Cream together brown sugar, flour, and margarine; reserve 1 C. for topping. To cookie mixture, add the remaining ingredients. Mix well and pour into 9x13″ greased pan. Sprinkle top with 1 C. reserved crumbs. Top with additional chocolate chips and the nuts. Bake at 350° for 30–35 min.

Lori Kernel
Henry County

CHOCOLATE PECAN BARS

1 C. flour
½ t. soda
¼ t. salt
½ C. brown
　sugar
¼ C. butter
Topping:
1 C. chocolate
　chips
2 eggs
¼ C. brown
　sugar
1 t. vanilla
¼ t. salt
½ C. chopped
　pecans, divided

Sift together the first 3 ingredients; add sugar and mix well. Cut in butter. Press mixture into greased 9x13″ pan. Bake at 350° for 10 min. Melt chips in double boiler. Beat well (2 min. on high speed) eggs, sugar, vanilla, and salt. Spoon in melted chocolate and continue beating until well-blended. Add ¼ C. pecans; stir to mix. Pour chocolate mixture over the partially baked cookie base. Sprinkle with ¼ C. pecans. Bake at 350° for 15 min. Cool; cut into squares.

Frieda Masters
Fayette County

VIENNA CHOCOLATE BARS

2 sticks butter or
　margarine
1½ C. sugar
2 egg yolks
2½ C. flour
2 C. finely
　chopped nuts
1 C. chocolate
　chips
¼ t. salt
4 egg whites
1 10-oz. jar jelly,
　jam, or
　preserves

Cream butter first with ½ C. sugar and then egg yolks. Add flour and knead with fingers. Pat batter out onto a greased 13½ x8¾x1¾ cooky sheet about ⅛″ thick. Bake 15–20 min. at 350°, or until lightly browned. Remove from oven; cool slightly. Spread jelly on top and sprinkle with chocolate bits. Beat egg whites with salt until stiff. Fold in remaining 1 C. sugar and nuts. Gently spread on top of jelly and chocolate. Bake 25 min. at 350°. Cut into bars.

Shirley J. Campbell
Brown County

COOKIE BARS

1 box pound cake mix	2 eggs
2 eggs	1 lb. powdered sugar
1 stick butter, melted	1 8-oz. pkg. cream cheese
chopped nuts	

Mix cake mix, 2 eggs, and butter together; spread in 9x13" pan. Mix together cream cheese, 2 eggs, and powdered sugar; spread over cake mixture. Top with chopped nuts. Bake at 350° for 40 min. When done, sprinkle with powdered sugar (optional).

Lois Beard
Clark County

CINNAMON SLEDGES

1 C. margarine	2 C. flour
½ C. brown sugar	1 T. cinnamon
½ C. sugar	⅛ t. salt
1 egg, separated	1½ C. chopped nuts

Cream together margarine, sugars and egg yolk with an electric mixer. Stir together flour, cinnamon and salt; add to creamed mixture and mix well. Spread batter into a well-greased 10x15" pan. Beat egg white until foamy. With pastry brush spread over top of batter. Sprinkle top with nuts. Bake at 300° for 35–40 min. Cut into squares while hot. Makes 5–6 dozen.

Georgia Hollingsworth
Marion County

CUP COOKIES

1 C. shortening	1 C. cold coffee
1 C. white sugar	1 t. vanilla
1 C. brown sugar	1 C. chocolate chips
2 C. flour	
1 t. soda	

Cream together shortening and sugars. Sift flour and soda together. Add sifted ingredients alternately with coffee to creamed mixture. Mix well. Add vanilla. Fold in chips. Bake in 9x13" pan at 350° for 30 min. Sprinkle with powdered sugar while still warm. Cool. Cut into bars.

Mrs. Earl Ballinger
Union County

DATE AND NUT KISSES

4 egg whites	1 C. dates, cut up
pinch salt	1 C. nuts, chopped
scant 1½ C. sugar	
1 t. vanilla	

Beat egg whites with salt until nearly stiff; add a small amount of sugar at a time. Beat until like marshmallow. Add vanilla. Fold in dates and nuts. Drop by spoonfuls onto well-greased cookie sheet. Bake 30–35 min. at 300°.

Martha Tischendorf
Clark County

DAVIE CROCKETTS

1 C. margarine (2 sticks)	1 t. baking soda
1 C. white sugar	1 t. baking powder
1 C. brown sugar	1 C. chocolate chips
1 t. vanilla	2 C. quick oats
3 eggs	1 C. nuts, chopped
2 C. flour	
1 t. salt	

Cream together first 5 ingredients; add the remaining ingredients. Mix together until well-blended (batter will be stiff and thick). Spread into a greased and floured 15½x10½″ pan. Bake 25–30 min. at 350°.

Carole Lamb
Clay County

FUDGE NUT BARS

1 C. butter or	3 C. quick oats
margarine	1 C. sweetened
2 C. brown sugar	condensed milk
2 eggs	2 T. butter or
2 t. vanilla	margarine
2½ C. flour	½ t. salt
1 t. soda	1 C. nuts,
1 t. salt	chopped
1 12-oz. pkg.	2 t. vanilla
chocolate chips	

Cream 1 C. butter and sugar together; mix in eggs and 2 t. vanilla. Sift together flour, soda, and 1 t. salt; stir in oats. Add dry ingredients to creamed mixture; set aside. In double boiler combine chocolate chips, milk, 2 T. butter and ½ t. salt; heat until mixture is smooth. Stir nuts and 2 t. vanilla into chocolate mixture. Spread about ⅔ of oatmeal mixture into greased 10x15″ jelly roll pan; cover with the chocolate mixture and drop bits of remaining oatmeal mixture over chocolate filling. Bake at 350° for 25–30 min., or until lightly browned. Cut into bars.

Rosalyn Kuhn
Steuben County

EASY TIME HOLIDAY SQUARES

1½ C. sugar	1 T. lemon exract
1 C. butter	1 1-lb. can cherry
4 eggs	pie filling
2 C. flour	

Gradually add sugar to butter in large mixer bowl, creaming at medium speed of mixer until light and fluffy. At medium speed, add eggs, one at a time, beating well after each. At low speed, add flour and lemon extract. Pour batter into well-greased jelly roll pan. Mark off in 20 squares. Place 1 heaping T. pie filling in center of each square. Bake at 350° for 45 min.

Mrs. Joseph Ault
LaPorte County

JAMAICAN FRUIT COOKIE BARS

½ C. shortening,	1 t. salt
softened	1 C. mashed
1 C. sugar	bananas
1 egg, beaten	¾ C. raisins
1 T. lemon	¾ C. nuts,
flavoring	chopped
2 C. flour	(optional)
1 t. cinnamon	grated rind from
1 t. pumpkin pie	1 medium or-
spice	ange (optional)
1 t. soda	

Cream shortening and sugar. Add egg and lemon flavoring; mix well. Add bananas and blend. Sift dry ingredients together into creamed mixture. Add raisins, nuts, and orange rind and mix thoroughly. Spread dough onto a greased jelly roll pan. Bake at 350° for 20 min. Frost if desired.

Judy Kendall
Randolph County

HOLLAND DUTCH COOKIES

1 C. soft	1 C. sugar
margarine	2 C. flour
1 egg, separated	sliced almonds
½ t. cinnamon	

Mix everything together but egg white. Knead. Pat lightly on greased cookie sheet. Brush with unbeaten egg white mixed with water. Sprinkle with almonds. Bake at 300°

for 30 min. Cut while warm and remove from pan.

Variation: Roll out and cut into diamonds. Brush with egg white-water mixture. Sprinkle with chopped walnuts.

Betty Craig
Grant County

INDIANS

1½ sticks butter	2 t. vanilla
2 eggs, beaten	1⅓ C. chopped
1 lb. brown sugar	pecans
1 C. flour	

Melt butter; add sugar and stir until smooth. Cool slightly. Add eggs. Add flour, vanilla, and nuts. Pour into 9x13″ greased and floured pan. Bake at 350° for 30 min. Cut in bars and roll in powdered sugar.

Madeline Howell
Vanderburgh County

HOOSIER HOTSHOT PEANUT BARS

2 C. sifted flour	2 egg yolks
2 t. baking	1 t. vanilla
powder	3 T. cold water
½ t. salt	1 6–7 oz. pkg.
½ C. shortening	chocolate chips
½ C. brown	2 egg whites
sugar	¾ C. chopped
1 C. brown sugar	salted peanuts

Sift flour, baking powder, and salt together; set aside. Cream shortening and add the ½ C. brown sugar; mix well. Blend in egg yolks and vanilla. Add the cold water alternately with sifted dry ingredients to short-ening-sugar mixture (dough will be very stiff). Press dough into two greased and floured 8x8x2″ pans. Sprinkle chocolate chips over dough and press in gently. Beat egg whites until foamy; gradually add the 1 C. brown sugar and beat until stiff. Spread over

chocolate bits. Top with peanuts. Bake at 325° for 30–35 min. Cut into squares while warm.

Claudia Slater
Porter County

QUICK LEMON CRISPIES

2 C. sifted flour	2 small pkg. in-
¾ t. baking soda	stant lemon
a few grains of	pudding mix
salt	3 eggs, slightly
¾ C. shortening	beaten
1 C. sugar	

Sift flour with salt and soda; set aside. Cream shortening and add eggs, sugar, and pudding mix; cream until light and fluffy. Add flour mixture and beat until blended. Drop from teaspoon onto greased baking sheet, about 2½″ apart. Bake at 375° for 8–10 min. Makes 4 dozen.

Jean Carmichael
Delaware County

MOUND BARS

1½ C. graham	1 14-oz. can
cracker crumbs	sweetened con-
⅓ C. sugar	densed milk
⅓ C. butter,	1 C. chocolate
melted	chips
2 C. coconut	2 T. peanut
	butter

Combine crumbs, sugar, and butter; press into bottom of 10x11″ pan. Blend together the coconut and milk; spread over crumb crust. Bake at 375° for 15 min. Melt chocolate chips; stir in peanut butter and spread over warm baked mixture. Cool and cut into bars.

Carolyn Enochs
Sullivan County

PEANUTTY SQUARES

Crust:	½ C. light corn
1 C. flour	syrup
⅓ C. sugar	¼ C. peanut
½ C. butter,	butter
softened	2 eggs
¼ C. salted pea-	½ t. vanilla
nuts, chopped	¼ t. salt
Filling:	1 C. salted
½ C. sugar	peanuts

To make the crust: In 1 qt. mixing bowl of electric mixer, stir together flour and sugar. Add butter; beat at low speed, scraping sides of bowl often, until mixture resembles small peas. Stir in nuts. Press mixture evenly onto sides and bottom of 9x9″ baking pan. Bake at 350° for 12–17 min., or until edges are lightly browned. To make the filling: In same 1 qt. bowl, beat together sugar, syrup, peanut butter, eggs, vanilla, and salt until mixture is light. Stir in peanuts; pour over baked crust. Return to oven; bake 25–30 min., or until filling is lightly browned and set. Cool and cut into bars.

May Richter
Ripley County

PECAN PIE COOKIES

Crust:	1½ C. dark corn
1 pkg. yellow	syrup
cake mix	½ C. brown
½ C. butter,	sugar
melted	3 eggs
1 egg	1 t. vanilla
Filling:	1 C. pecans,
⅔ C. reserved	chopped
cake mix	

To make the crust: Reserve ⅔ C. cake mix. Combine the rest of the cake mix, butter, and egg. Mix well. Press into a greased sheet cake pan. Bake 15–20 min. at 350°, or until light golden brown. To make the

filling: Combine all ingredients, except pecans, and beat for 2 min. at medium speed of electric mixer. Pour over partially baked crust. Sprinkle with pecans. Bake at 350° until filling is set, 15–20 min. Cool and cut into squares.

Jenny Campbell   *Betty Wise*
Posey County   *Randolph County*

PUMPKIN BARS

4 eggs	Cream Cheese
1⅔ C. sugar	Icing:
1 C. vegetable oil	1 3-oz. pkg.
1 16-oz. can	cream cheese,
pumpkin	softened
2 C. flour	½ C. butter or
2 t. baking	margarine,
powder	softened
2 t. cinnamon	1 t. vanilla
1 t. salt	2 C. sifted pow-
1 t. soda	dered sugar

In electric mixer bowl, beat together eggs, sugar, oil, and pumpkin until light and fluffy. Stir dry ingredients together; add to pumpkin mixture and mix thoroughly. Spread batter in ungreased 15x10x1″ baking pan. Bake at 350° for 25–30 min. Cool and frost with Cream Cheese Icing. Cream together cream cheese and butter for the icing. Stir in vanilla. Add powdered sugar, a little at a time, beating well, until mixture is smooth. Makes 2 dozen bars.

Mary & Barbara Curtis
Lawrence County

PAWTUCKET COOKIES

2 squares	⅛ t. salt
chocolate	1 C. sugar
½ C. butter	3 eggs, beaten
¾ C. flour	

Melt chocolate and butter together. Add

flour, salt, and sugar; beat. Beat in eggs. Bake in a greased and floured 8″ square pan at 350° for 25–30 min. *Note:* No leavening.

Ardelle Johnson
LaGrange County

RAISIN BARS

½ C. shortening	1 t. baking
1 C. sugar	powder
1 egg	1 t. cinnamon
2 C. flour	½ t. salt
1 t. nutmeg	1 C. raisins
½ t. soda	1 C. chopped
½ t. pumpkin pie	nuts (optional)
spice	

Grease and flour a 10x15x1″ jelly roll pan. Cover raisins with water and cook until tender. Drain, reserving ¾ C. of the liquid. Cream shortening, sugar, and egg together until fluffy. Sift together dry ingredients; add alternately with raisin liquid to the cream mixture. Stir in raisins and nuts. Spread in prepared pan. Bake at 350° for 20 min. While warm, spread with a thin layer of confectioners' sugar icing. Cut into 30 bars.

Mrs. Don Bacon
Rush County

SEVEN-LAYER BARS

½ stick butter or	1 C. butterscotch
margarine	chips
1 C. graham	1 C. chopped
cracker crumbs	walnuts
1 C. chocolate	1 C. sweetened
chips	condensed milk
1 C. coconut	

Melt butter in a 9x13″ pan. Layer ingredients in pan in order given. Bake for 20–25 min at 350°.

Pauline Degler
Vigo County

SUGAR CREAM SQUARES

1 box yellow cake	8 oz. pkg. cream
mix	cheese
1 egg	2 eggs
1 stick margar-	2 t. vanilla
ine, softened	
1 box powdered	
sugar	

Mix together cake mix, 1 egg, and margarine; pat into a greased and floured 9x13″ pan. Blend together sugar, cream cheese, 2 eggs, and vanilla; spread over cake mixture. Bake at 350° for 35–40 min. Cool and cut into squares.

Naomi Current
Delaware County

TOLL HOUSE PAN COOKIES

2¼ C. flour	¾ C. sugar
1 t. soda	1 t. vanilla
1 t. salt	2 eggs
1 C. butter,	2 C. chocolate
softened	chips (12 oz.)
¾ C. brown	1 C. chopped
sugar	nuts

Combine flour, soda, and salt; set aside. Combine butter, sugar, brown sugar, and vanilla; beat until creamy. Beat in eggs. Gradually add flour mixture; mix well. Stir in chocolate chips and nuts. Spread into greased 11x15x1″ baking pan. Bake at 375° for 20 min. Cool; cut into 2″ squares.

Jeanette Becker
Marshall County

HONEY COOKIES

⅓ C. shortening	2¾ C. flour
⅓ C. brown	1 t. salt
sugar	1½ t. soda
1 egg	2 t. vanilla
⅔ C. honey	

Cream together shortening and sugar. Add egg and honey; mix thoroughly. Stir together flour, salt, and soda and add gradually to creamed mixture; mix well. Stir in vanilla. Chill dough. Roll out to ¼". Flour board (if necessary) to prevent dough from sticking. Cut with cookie cutters. Bake at 350° for 8–10 min. Store in airtight container to soften. May be frosted.

Laura Lienhart
LaPorte County

CHOCOLATE SURPRISES

½ C. shortening	large
1 C. sugar	marshmallows
1 egg	Icing:
1 t. vanilla	2½ C. powdered
½ C. milk	sugar
½ t. salt	dash salt
½ t. soda	5 T. milk
½ C. cocoa	3 T. margarine
1¼ C. flour	5 T. cocoa

Mix together shortening, sugar, egg, vanilla, and milk. Sift together salt, soda, cocoa, and flour; add to first mixture. Mix thoroughly and drop by heaping teaspoonfuls onto greased cookie sheet. Bake 8 min. at 350°. Place half of a large marshmallow in the center of each cookie. Bake 2 min. longer. Ice when cool. Mix together ingredients for icing. Add more milk if necessary.

Mildred Duke
Wayne County

ZUCCHINI DROP COOKIES

1 C. grated	2 C. flour
zucchini	1 t. cinnamon
1 t. soda	½ t. cloves
1 C. sugar	½ t. salt
½ C. shortening	1 C. nuts
or butter	1 C. raisins
1 egg, beaten	

Mix together zucchini, soda, sugar, butter, and beaten egg. Sift in flour, cinnamon, cloves, and salt; stir to blend. Stir in raisins and nuts and drop batter by teaspoonfuls onto greased cookie sheet. Bake 12–15 min. at 375°. Makes 3 dozen.

Margaret Duckworth
Posey County

TRIPLE TREATS

1 C. shortening	2½ C. sifted flour
1 C. light brown	1 t. salt
sugar	1 t. soda
⅔ C. sugar	1 C. chocolate
2 eggs	bits
1 t. vanilla	1 C. cut up dates
½ t. instant	(optional)
coffee	1 C. chopped
2 t. hot water	nuts (optional)

Cream together shortening, sugars, eggs, vanilla, and coffee dissolved in hot water. Sift dry ingredients together and add to creamed mixture. Stir in chocolate bits, dates, and nuts. Drop by teaspoonfuls onto greased baking sheet. Bake at 350° for 15 min. Makes 5–6 dozen.

Lovella Neukam
Dubois County

CARAMEL NUT SLICES

1 C. soft shorten-	½ t. salt
ing (part butter)	1 t. soda
2 C. brown sugar	1 C. chopped
2 eggs	nuts
3½ C. flour	

Cream together shortening, sugar, and eggs. Sift together dry ingredients and stir into creamed mixture; add nuts and mix. Form into rolls 1½–2" in diameter. Wrap in waxed paper and refrigerate overnight. Cut into ⅛" slices and place on ungreased cookie sheet. Bake at 400° for 8–10 min. Makes 12 dozen.

Mattie Wise
Randolph County

LEMON REFRIGERATOR COOKIES

1 C. shortening, softened	½ t. salt
2 t. lemon extract	2 t. baking powder
2 C. sugar	1 C. finely
2 eggs, beaten	chopped nuts
3½ C. sifted flour	

Cream together the shortening, extract, and sugar; beat in eggs. Sift dry ingredients together and add, mixing well. Form in long rolls about 2″ in diameter. Wrap in waxed paper and refrigerate. Slice into desired thickness and bake at 375° for 10 min., or until lightly browned.

Rosella Holzer
Ripley County

DATE WHIRLIGIG COOKIES

2 C. dates, chopped	½ C. water
½ C. sugar	1 C. nuts, finely chopped
1 C. shortening, softened	1½ t. salt
1½ t. grated orange rind	2 C. brown sugar
	2 eggs
¼ t. grated lemon rind	3½ C. sifted flour
	1½ t. soda
	2 T. milk

Combine dates, sugar, and water; cook over low heat stirring constantly until thickened, about 5 min. Add nuts; mix well. Cool and set aside. Combine shortening, fruit rinds, salt, sugar, and eggs. Sift flour and soda together. Add half of flour mixture to shortening mixture and mix well. Add milk and blend. Add remainder of flour and mix well. Divide dough in half; roll each half into a rectangular shape about ½″ thick. Spread a thin layer of date mixture on dough; roll up and wrap in plastic or waxed paper; refrigerate. Cut in ¼″ slices and place on greased cookie sheet. Bake at 375° for 10–12 min.

Clara Isenhart
Jay County

GOLDEN NUGGETS

1 C. dried apricots, coarsely cut up	½ t. almond flavoring
½ C. water	1¾ C. flour
1 C. shortening (part butter)	2 t. baking powder
½ C. sugar	½ t. salt
½ C. brown sugar	1½ C. flaked coconut
1 egg	toasted whole almonds
1 t. vanilla	

Cook apricots in water over low heat 5–10 min. (water should be absorbed); cool. Mix shortening and sugars until fluffy. Add egg, flavorings, and apricots. Stir together flour, baking powder, and salt; mix into sugar-apricot mixture. Chill dough several hr. Drop heaping teaspoonfuls of dough into coconut to coat. Place 2″ apart on lightly greased baking sheet. Top with an almond. Bake 10–12 min. at 350°.

Isabelle Oplinger
Noble County

RITZ DATE COOKIES

8 oz. pkg. chopped dates	1 box Ritz crackers
1 14-oz. can sweetened condensed milk	confectioners' sugar frosting
1 C. chopped nuts	

Simmer milk and dates in heavy pan until thick, stirring constantly; add nuts. Spread 1 t. date mixture on top of each cracker. Bake at 300° for 7 min. on ungreased cookie sheet. When cool, spread frosting on top. Makes about 100 cookies.

Ruth Walters
DeKalb County

chocolate and butterscotch chips together over hot (but not boiling) water, stirring until well blended. Remove from heat; spread evenly over Rice Krispies mixture. Cool until firm. Cut into bars.

Judy Smith
Allen County

NO-BAKE CARAMEL OATMEAL COOKIES

2 C. sugar	1 small pkg. in-
¾ C. margarine,	stant butter-
softened	scotch pudding
1 6-oz. can evap-	mix
orated milk	2½ C. quick oats

Combine sugar, margarine, and milk in saucepan; bring to a boil. Add pudding and oats and remove from heat. Stir to mix. Drop by spoonfuls onto waxed paper. Let cool 15 min.

Barbara Gray
Boone County

KRUNCHIES

3 C. sugar	3 C. peanut
1–½ C. dark corn	butter
syrup	15 C. corn flakes

Combine sugar and syrup; bring to a boil, stirring constantly. Remove from heat immediately. Add peanut butter and corn-flakes; mix well. Spread mixture onto greased cookie sheet. Cut into squares.

Charlene Logan
Putnam County

"CHOCOLATE SCOTCHDROPS"

1 C. light corn	1 C. sugar
syrup	1 C. chocolate
1 C. peanut	chips
butter	1 C. butterscotch
6 C. Rice	chips
Krispies	

Combine sugar and syrup in 3 qt. saucepan. Cook over moderate heat, stirring frequently, until mixture boils; remove from heat. Stir in peanut butter; mix well. Add Rice Krispies; stir until well blended. Press mixture into buttered 9x13" pan. Melt

SAUCEPAN COOKIES

1 C. sugar	pinch salt
2 eggs	½ C. nuts
1½ C. chopped	(optional)
dates	2 C. flaked
2½ C. Rice	coconut
Krispies	

In heavy saucepan combine sugar, eggs, dates, and salt. Cook on medium heat until soft and mixture holds together, about 6–10 min. Remove from stove and cool 2 min. Pour mixture over the Rice Krispies. Mix together lightly; add nuts. Drop by teaspoon into coconut and roll each into a ball. Makes 4 doz.

Edna Stetzel
Huntington County

Candy

BUTTERMILK CANDY

2 C. sugar	1 t. vanilla
½ C. buttermilk	2 T. butter

Combine sugar and buttermilk; cook to soft-ball stage (234°). Add butter; cool to luke-warm (110°). Add vanilla; beat until mixture thickens. Quickly drop by teaspoonfuls onto waxed paper.

For *Variations,* add one of the following: ¼ C. peanut butter in place of butter; ½ C. chopped pecans after beating; ½ C. chopped candied cherries after beating; ½ C. shredded coconut after beating; 1 square unsweetened chocolate to sugar and buttermilk before cooking.

Ruth Tarr
Orange County

TIME-SAVING CARAMELS

2 sticks margarine	⅛ t. salt
1 lb. brown sugar (2¼ C.)	1 15-oz. can sweetened condensed milk
1 C. light corn syrup	1 t. vanilla

Melt margarine in saucepan; add sugar and salt and stir until combined. Add corn syrup; mix well. Add milk; continue cooking and stirring until candy thermometer reaches 245°. Remove from heat and add vanilla. Pour into a buttered 9″ square pan. When cold, cut into squares and wrap.

Aileen Hilgeman
Dubois County

CANDY ROLLS

2½ C. sugar	2 C. marshmallow cream
½ C. corn syrup	
½ C. water	⅓ C. shortening

Place sugar, syrup, and water into a kettle, cook to 256° (or 254°, for a softer piece). Set kettle off heat and add marshmallow cream. Do not stir, but let the marshmallow cream set above the syrup for 10 min. After 10 min., stir together and beat. Add flavoring and coloring as desired. Beat short. (When batch is sufficiently beaten, the batch will break short when paddle is lifted.) Stir in shortening. Pour batch on slab sprinkled with powdered sugar. When cool enough to handle, form into balls or rolls. These may be set aside and dipped in chocolate or caramel later. *Note:* If using nuts and/or fruit, add at the very last of the beating process.

Aileen Hilgeman
Dubois County

COCKYPOP

(like the commercial "Poppycock")

¼ lb. popcorn	1 C. brown sugar
½ lb. pecans	1 C. water
½ lb. almonds	1 stick butter or margarine
2 C. sugar	
¾ C. white corn syrup	½ t. salt

Pop the popcorn (at least 14 C. of popped corn), and add to the pecans and almonds in a large bowl; set aside. Place sugars, syrup, and water in heavy saucepan; cook stirring occasionally, until candy thermometer reaches 300°. Turn heat low and add butter, stirring vigorously. Remove from stove and add salt. Pour cooked mixture over corn and nuts; stir well. Pour onto flat sheet pans to cool. When cool, break into pieces and store in airtight containers.

Mary Alice Roberts
Starke County

CASHEW BRITTLE

2 C. sugar	1 C. flaked
1 C. light corn	coconut
syrup	1 T. butter
½ C. water	1 t. vanilla
1 C. broken	1½ t. soda
cashews	

In heavy saucepan combine sugar, corn syrup, and water; heat and cook over medium high heat until thermometer reaches 250°. Add cashews, coconut, and butter and continue cooking until thermometer reaches 300°. Stir mixture constantly. Remove from heat and add vanilla and soda; stir. Pour into buttered pan; pull out as mixture cools if you like it thin. When cool, break into pieces.

Joan Ford
Jay County

SPICY CEREAL CRUNCH

½ C. margarine	3 C. puffed oat
1⅓ C. brown	cereal
sugar	2 C. Rice Chex
¼ C. light corn	2 C. Corn Chex
syrup	2 C. Wheat Chex
1 t. cinnamon	1 C. raisins
½ t. salt	1 C. nuts

Combine first 5 ingredients in heavy skillet. Stir constantly over medium heat until boiling; boil 3 min. In large buttered bowl, toss cereals, raisins, and nuts. Pour hot syrup over mixture; stir to coat. Spread on cookie sheet or jelly roll pan. When firm, break in pieces.

Ruby Massey
Putnam County

MOM'S NO-COOK CANDY

13 oz. cream	1 box powdered
cheese	sugar (2⅔ C.)
1 T. cream	

Mix ingredients together. Roll out jelly roll style and spread with peanut butter. Roll up. Chill and slice.

Myrna Soper
Union County

FRENCH CHOCOLATES

12 oz. pkg. choc-	¾ C. sweetened
olate chips	condensed milk
1 C. walnuts,	⅛ t. salt
chopped	1 C. chocolate
1 t. vanilla	sprinkles

In top of double boiler, over hot, not boiling, water, melt chocolate chips. Stir in nuts, vanilla, milk, and salt. Cool mixture about 5 min., or until easy to shape. With buttered hands, shape mixture into 1″ balls. Roll each ball in chocolate sprinkles. Makes 1½ lb.

Alice Senseman
Vigo County

NO-COOK FUDGE

1 C. chunky pea-	1¼ C. nonfat dry
nut butter	milk
1 C. white corn	1¼ C. powdered
syrup	sugar
½ C. cocoa	

Combine all ingredients; knead and shape into walnut-sized balls. Stor in airtight container. Can be frozen.

Fannie Hatch
Posey County

QUICK CHOCOLATE FUDGE

¼ C. butter	⅓ C. milk
1 3-oz. pkg.	1¾ C. sifted
chocolate pud-	powdered sugar
ding (not	½ C. chopped
instant)	nuts

Melt butter; add pudding and stir until well-blended. Add milk and bring to a bubbling boil, stirring constantly; boil 1 min. Remove from stove and add sugar. Stir until smooth and well-blended. Add vanilla and nuts. Pour quickly into buttered pan. Cool. Cut into squares.

Aileen Hilgeman
Dubois County

CRISP SUGARED NUTS

2½ C. pecans or	1 t. cinnamon
walnuts	1 scant t. salt
1 C. sugar	½ t. vanilla
½ C. water	

Place pecans or walnuts in shallow pan and heat in oven at 350–375° about 15 min., stirring frequently. Remove from oven. Put sugar, water, cinnamon, and salt in saucepan; cook to soft-ball stage (236°). Remove from heat; add vanilla and nuts. Stir gently until nuts are well coated and mixture becomes creamy. Turn out on buttered platter; separate nuts as they cool.

Alta Williamson
Jay County

SUGAR PECANS

1 lb. pecans	1 C. sugar
1 egg white	1 t. salt
1 T. water	1 t. cinnamon

Beat egg white and water until frothy; pour in pecans and stir until coated. In separate bowl, mix sugar, salt, and cinnamon. Pour sugar mixture over coated pecans and stir; spread on cookie sheet and bake at 300° for 45 min. Stir about every 5 min.

Pam Kerkhof
Hancock County

STRAWBERRY CANDY

1 large pkg.	½ C. flake
cream cheese	coconut
(8 oz.)	½ C. finely
3 small boxes	chopped pecan
strawberry	meats
gelatin	

Mix all ingredients together and chill overnight. Shape into strawberry and roll in red sugar.

Aileen Hilgeman
Dubois County

ENGLISH TOFFEE

2 C. sugar	2 C. butter
1 C. ground nuts	9 oz. milk choco-
(preferably	late candy bars
walnuts)	

Combine sugar and butter in heavy pan; bring to a rapid boil. Stir constantly. When mixture begins to turn light tan, put in candy thermometer and cook to 300°. Remove from stove and stir in nuts; pour into 10x15″ jelly roll pan (do not butter). While still warm, place chocolate on top and let melt. Spread out chocolate smoothly. Place in refrigerator; when cold, break into pieces.

Marcia Ford
Jay County

Index